Microsoft®
Outlook
2016

Denise Seguin

PARADIGM
EDUCATION SOLUTIONS

St. Paul

Senior Vice President: Linda Hein
Editor in Chief: Christine Hurney
Managing Editor: Cheryl Drivdahl
Developmental Editors: Eric Braem, Tamborah Moore
Director of Production: Timothy W. Larson
Production Editors: Shannon Kottke, Carrie Rogers
Cover and Text Designer and Senior Design and Production Specialist: Valerie King
Copy Editor: Joanna Grote
Indexer: Beverlee Day
Testers: Traci Post, Mamie Clark
Vice President Information Technology: Chuck Bratton
Digital Projects Manager: Tom Modl
Vice President Sales and Marketing: Scott Burns
Director of Marketing: Lara Weber McLellan

Care has been taken to verify the accuracy of information presented in this book. However, the author, editors, and publisher cannot accept responsibility for Web, email, newsgroup, or chat room subject matter or content, or for consequences from the application of the information in this book, and make no warranty, expressed or implied, with respect to its content.

Acknowledgments: The author, editors, and publisher would like to thank Janet S. Blum, BA, CAP, Professor, Fanshawe College, for preparing the PowerPoint presentations and Jonathan Van Den Boogaart, Professor, Fanshawe College, for assistance with installing and configuring Exchange Server 2016 and Outlook on the web.

Trademarks: Microsoft is a trademark or registered trademark of Microsoft Corporation in the United States and/or other countries. Some of the product names and company names included in this book have been used for identification purposes only and may be trademarks or registered trade names of their respective manufacturers and sellers. The author, editors, and publisher disclaim any affiliation, association, or connection with, or sponsorship or endorsement by, such owners.

Photo Credits: Cover © fotohunter/Shutterstock.com; pages 8, 9, 134, 135, 136, 138, 145, 146, 153, and 154 © Shutterstock.com

We have made every effort to trace the ownership of all copyrighted material and to secure permission from copyright holders. In the event of any question arising as to the use of any material, we will be pleased to make the necessary corrections in future printings. Thanks are due to the aforementioned authors, publishers, and agents for permission to use the materials indicated.

Paradigm Publishing is independent from Microsoft Corporation, and not affiliated with Microsoft in any manner. While this publication may be used in assisting individuals to prepare for a Microsoft Office Specialist certification exam, Microsoft, its designated program administrator, and Paradigm Publishing do not warrant that use of this publication will ensure passing a Microsoft Office Specialist certification exam.

ISBN 978-0-76387-249-6 (print)
ISBN 978-0-76387-250-2 (digital)

© 2017 by Paradigm Publishing, Inc.
875 Montreal Way
St. Paul, MN 55102
Email: educate@emcp.com
Website: ParadigmEducation.com

Printed in the United States of America

25 24 23 22 21 20 19 18 17 16   1 2 3 4 5 6 7 8 9 10

Contents

Microsoft® Outlook 2016 is a personal information management application that provides tools to send, receive, and manage email; organize schedules and events; keep track of contacts; and maintain to-do lists and other collections of notes. Organizing and managing information related to your personal and professional activities is an essential skill in today's fast-paced world. Often, you can be juggling messages, appointments, contacts, and tasks related to home, work, and volunteer projects throughout the day, seven days a week!

After successfully completing a course using this textbook, you will be able to do the following:

- Compose, send, and respond to email messages, including attachments
- Find, arrange, organize, manage, and archive email messages
- Schedule appointments, events, and meetings and maintain calendars
- Manage contact information and coordinate the data with email and scheduling functions
- Maintain to-do lists and assign tasks to others
- Keep track of activities, short reminders, and ideas
- Customize the Outlook environment and integrate data among the Outlook components and with Microsoft Word to meet individual information needs

Chapter Features

This book, *Microsoft® Outlook 2016*, is designed to teach through a read-and-do approach and provides figures that show what the computer screen will look like at key steps in the execution of a feature. Throughout every chapter, Outlook tools and commands are presented in a clear, straightforward way.

- Each short section of reading is followed by a detailed exercise that provides immediate practice using the new feature.
- Interactive tutorials (accessed through the links menu in the ebook) offer additional hands-on practice with key features.
- Quick Steps boxes in the margins provide easy-to-read summaries of the steps to follow in performing given skills.
- Exchange Server notes, Tips, Outlook on the web boxes, and Outlook.com boxes deliver additional information on special features and topics.

Gradually, these elements help you build information management skills along with confidence in using the software. At the end of each chapter, review, reinforcement, and assessment activities provide checkpoints to ensure mastery of the chapter topics.

Textbook Elements

The following interactive, read-and-do features in each chapter will help you master the Outlook 2016 concepts and skills taught in this course.

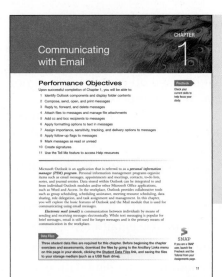

1. **Preview.** Read the **performance objectives** on the opening page of the chapter to identify the skills you will learn.

2. **Precheck.** Test your knowledge of the chapter content by taking the **Precheck** quiz. Use the results to help focus your study on the topics and skills you need to learn. The Precheck quizzes are accessed from the links menu in the *Workbook* ebook. **SNAP** users should go to their SNAP Assignments page to complete these quizzes.

3. **Prepare.** For Chapters 1 and 4, copy the **data files** necessary to complete the chapter exercises.

4. **Motivate.** Read the **chapter introduction** to learn how mastering the skills covered in the chapter will help you accomplish key tasks.

5. **Learn (Read).** Read the **description** of each tool or skill carefully.
   - Pay special attention to the **button images** and **screen visuals** provided.

6. **Reinforce.** Read each **Quick Steps** summary in the margin to focus on the essential steps for completing a task.

7. **Apply (Do).** Complete each **exercise** to gain hands-on practice with the skill you just learned.
   - Before beginning an exercise, notice its **title**, which indicates your learning goal.
   - Some exercises have special **notes** at the beginning. Be sure to read them and follow the directions.
   - Follow the **steps** in each exercise carefully. Note that numbered callouts on the screen visuals point to what you should see on the screen after a particular step. If your screen does not match the display, return to that step and make sure you completed it correctly or return to the previous step and try again.
   - View **Check Your Work** images in locked PDFs to see what your completed exercise should look like.
   - At the completion of an exercise, leave Outlook open unless directed otherwise. In the next exercise, you will pick up where you left off.

   Complete each interactive **tutorial** to follow simple instructions as they guide you through the steps in a skill and then practice the skill on your own with optional help. **SNAP** users should go to their SNAP Assignments page to complete these tutorials.

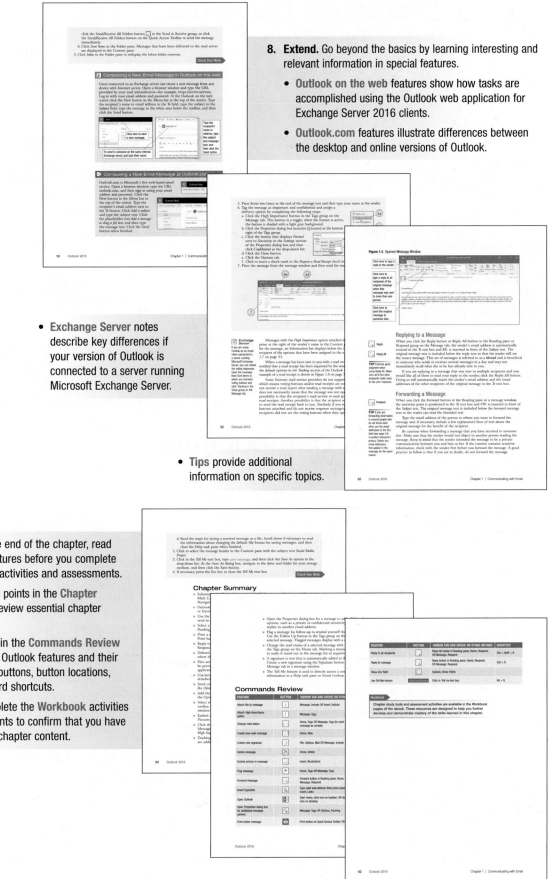

8. **Extend.** Go beyond the basics by learning interesting and relevant information in special features.

- **Outlook on the web** features show how tasks are accomplished using the Outlook web application for Exchange Server 2016 clients.

- **Outlook.com** features illustrate differences between the desktop and online versions of Outlook.

- **Exchange Server** notes describe key differences if your version of Outlook is connected to a server running Microsoft Exchange Server.

- **Tips** provide additional information on specific topics.

9. **Review.** At the end of the chapter, read the review features before you complete the workbook activities and assessments.

- The bulleted points in the **Chapter Summary** review essential chapter content.

- The entries in the **Commands Review** identify key Outlook features and their associated buttons, button locations, and keyboard shortcuts.

10. **Assess.** Complete the **Workbook** activities and assessments to confirm that you have mastered the chapter content.

Workbook Elements

Access the *Workbook* ebook through the links menu in your ebook. The *Workbook* ebook provides a variety of materials you can use to check your understanding of the concepts and features covered in the textbook. **Some activities are also offered in SNAP. Students using SNAP should go to their SNAP Assignments page to complete those activities.**

Study Tools offer multimedia and text-based review of the concepts, features, and skills taught in a chapter. These tools are accessed from the links menu in the *Workbook* ebook.

The **Concepts Check** completion activities test your recall of key points about Outlook tools and features. These activities are accessed from the links menu in the *Workbook* ebook. SNAP users should go to their SNAP Assignments page to complete these activities.

A **Recheck** quiz at the end of each chapter enables you to recheck your understanding of the chapter content. You may recheck your understanding at any time and as many times as you wish. The Recheck quiz is accessed from the links menu in the *Workbook* ebook. SNAP users should go to their SNAP Assignments page to complete the Recheck quizzes.

The **Skills Assessments** provide directions for completing tasks but do not tell you how to perform every step. If you can complete these workbook exercises successfully, then you have mastered the chapter content.

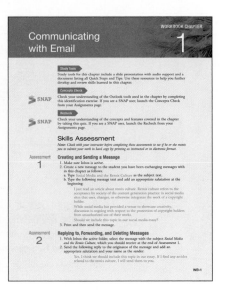

Course Components

The *Microsoft® Outlook 2016* textbook contains the essential content you will need to master the features and skills covered. Additional resources are provided by the following digital components.

SNAP Web-Based Training and Assessment for Microsoft® Office 2016

SNAP is a web-based training and assessment program and learning management system (LMS) for Microsoft Office 2016. SNAP offers rich content, a sophisticated grade book, and robust scheduling and analytics tools. SNAP courseware supports the *Outlook 2016* content and delivers interactive tutorials that increase skills-focused moments with guided training and measured practice. SNAP includes a quiz for each chapter and a final exam for the course, plus an item bank that can be used to create custom assessments. SNAP provides automatic scoring and detailed feedback on exercises and assessments to help identify areas where additional support is needed, evaluating student performance at both the individual level and the course level. The *Outlook 2016* SNAP course content is also available to export into any LMS system that supports LTI tools.

Paradigm Education Solutions provides technical support for SNAP through 24-7 chat at ParadigmEducation.com. In addition, an online user guide and other training tools for SNAP are available.

Student Ebook and *Workbook* Ebook

The student ebook and *Workbook* ebook provide access to all program content from any device (desktop, tablet, and smartphone) anywhere, through a live Internet connection. The versatile ebook platform features dynamic navigation tools including a linked table of contents and the ability to jump to specific pages, search for terms, bookmark, highlight, and take notes. The ebooks offer live links to the interactive content and resources that support the textbook, including the data files. The student ebook includes links to the interactive Precheck quizzes, interactive tutorials, Check Your Work images in downloadable PDFs, and related *Workbook* ebook.

The *Workbook* ebook includes access to Study Tools such as chapter-based slide presentations with audio support, and Quick Steps and Tips documents. It also provides access to interactive end-of-chapter Concepts Check exercises, interactive Recheck quizzes, and Skills Assessments. The *Workbook* is accessed through the links menu on the last page of each chapter in the student ebook. It may also be accessed online at **ParadigmEducation.com/ebooks** or from your SNAP course.

SNAP users should go to their SNAP Assignments page to complete the interactive quizzes, tutorials, and exercises.

Instructor eResources

All instructor resources are available digitally through a web-based ebook online at **ParadigmEducation.com/ebooks** or from your SNAP course. The materials are organized by type and also by chapter, and can be previewed from the ebook or downloaded. The instructor materials include the following items:

- Grading rubrics and model answers for evaluating responses to chapter exercises and Skills Assessments
- A grading sheet and assignment sheets
- Lesson blueprints with teaching hints
- Discussion questions
- A sample syllabus and course planning resources
- An MOS Specialist Objectives chart
- Chapter-based PowerPoint presentations with lecture notes
- A final exam
- A Capstone Project complete with instructions, model answers, and a grading rubric

About the Author

Denise Seguin served on the faculty of business at Fanshawe College of Applied Arts and Technology in London, Ontario, from 1986 until her retirement from full-time teaching in December 2012. She developed curriculum and taught a variety of office technology, software applications, and accounting courses to students in postsecondary Information Technology diploma programs and Continuing Education courses. Seguin served as Program Coordinator for Computer Systems Technician, Computer Systems Technology, Office Administration, and Law Clerk programs and was acting Chair of the School of Information Technology in 2001.

Along with authoring *Microsoft® Outlook*, 2000 to 2016 editions, she has also authored *Seguin's COMPUTER Concepts & Applications with Microsoft Office* (first and second editions, 2013 and 2016). Seguin has co-authored *Our Digital World*, (first to fourth editions), *Benchmark Series: Microsoft® Excel®* (2007, 2010, and 2013 editions), *Benchmark Series: Microsoft® Access®* (2007, 2010, and 2013 editions), *Marquee Series: Microsoft® Office* (2000 to 2016 editions), and *Using Computers in the Medical Office* (2003 to 2010 editions).

In 2007, Seguin earned her Masters in Business Administration specializing in Technology Management, choosing to take her degree at an online university. She has an appreciation for those who are juggling work and life responsibilities while furthering their education, and she has taken her online student experiences into account when designing instructions and assessment activities for this textbook.

In 2016, Seguin returned to part-time teaching at Fanshawe College choosing to teach online courses. She returned to teaching to connect with today's virtual students and to keep up to date with best practices in online teaching.

Getting Started

Microsoft Outlook 2016 is part of the Microsoft Office suite, which includes Word, Excel, PowerPoint, OneNote, Access, and Publisher. The Office suite is sold in various collections such as Office Home & Business 2016, Office 365 Home, and Office Professional 2016 to name a few. The software is included as part of the Office 365 subscription paid monthly or annually, or as one-time purchased software for installation on one PC only. Outlook is also included in the Office Home & Business 2016 for Mac collection and as an app for Android or Apple smartphones.

Outlook.com is the free, web-based version of Outlook for accessing email, calendar, contacts, and tasks. Outlook.com links to the data stored on your desktop edition of Outlook so that you can view the same data from any other device connected to the Internet.

In the workplace, Outlook is often used in conjunction with a Microsoft Exchange Server to provide workplace collaboration and sharing features not available to home users. Those who use Outlook connected to an Exchange server may choose to use Outlook via their web browser and the Outlook Web App called Outlook on the web.

The user interface for Outlook when you are using the software from an edition designed for a PC, a Mac, a smartphone, or a web browser may vary. Some editions may also offer a limited set of commands or options. The desktop edition offers the complete set of commands and options.

Using Outlook 2016 with This Textbook

This textbook is intended for use with the desktop edition of Microsoft Outlook installed on a PC running Windows. If you have another edition of Microsoft Outlook or are using Outlook on a Mac, you can still use this textbook to learn about the features and options. However, be aware that the interface may vary from the illustrations shown in this book and in some cases, functionality may be limited or an option may not be available.

Screen captures in this book were created using the Windows 10 operating system and a screen resolution display setting of 1920 x 1080. Your resolution may differ and should be optimized for your display size and personal preferences. Be aware that some screens may not match the illustrations in this book for displays set to a resolution other than 1920 x 1080 and/or if the Outlook window has been resized to a width that causes the ribbon to display buttons differently. For example, a button may display with an icon and text label below the icon, an icon and text label adjacent to the icon, or an icon only, depending on the window size.

Adding a Picture to Your Outlook Profile

People like to display photos next to their name in email messages and in the People panes of other Outlook items. The Exchange server administrator usually configures Outlook to populate each person's photograph from an employee database to the person's contact record in the global address list (GAL). An individual can also add or change the photograph associated with the Exchange server mailbox using Outlook on the web. If you are not connected to Outlook where the mail administrator automatically populates the photographs for each person, you can add your picture to your Microsoft account profile so that the same image displays in all Microsoft applications, such as Word and Excel, as well as Outlook.

The various methods for adding a picture are described next in this introduction because of the complexity of writing a single exercise for the variety of configurations encountered in school settings.

Adding a Picture in Outlook on the Web

Complete these steps to add a photo of yourself to your profile on the Exchange server if no picture is present:

1. Open a browser window, navigate to the URL for Outlook on the web provided by your mail administrator, and then sign in to your account.
2. Click the image control near the top right of the browser window and then click *Change* below your name and email address in the drop-down list.
3. Click the Choose photo control (displays as a file folder) in the right pane.

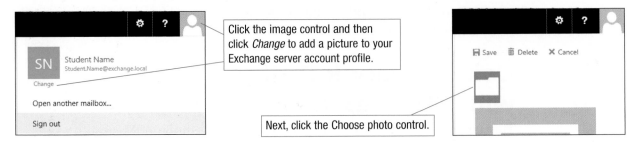

4. At the Choose File to Upload dialog box, navigate to the drive and/or folder in which the desired image file is stored and then double-click the file name for the photo.
5. When the photo finishes uploading and the thumbnail image appears in the image control in the right pane, click the Save button.

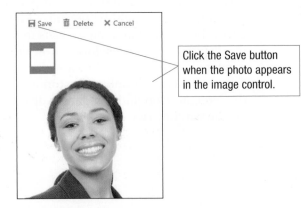

Adding a Picture to Your Microsoft Account Profile

Complete these steps to add a photo of yourself to your Microsoft account profile, which also displays your photo in other Microsoft applications:

1. Open a browser window and go to Outlook.com.
2. If necessary, sign in to your Microsoft account.
3. Click your name or image control near the top right of the browser window and then click *Edit profile* at the drop-down list.
4. Click *Change picture* at the Profile page.
5. Click the Browse button next to the Choose picture text box.

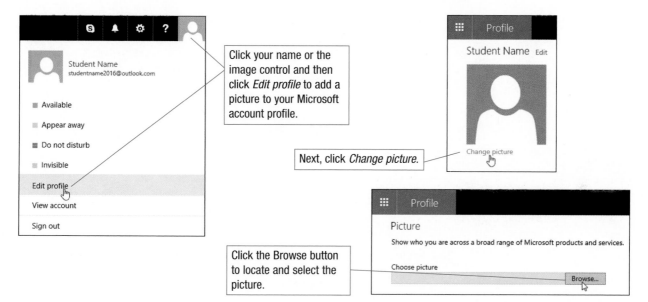

Click your name or the image control and then click *Edit profile* to add a picture to your Microsoft account profile.

Next, click *Change picture.*

Click the Browse button to locate and select the picture.

6. At the Open dialog box, navigate to the drive and/or folder in which the desired image file is stored and then double-click the file name for the photo.
7. If necessary, drag the image inside the box in the larger-sized preview to choose the area for your picture that you want to show. Watch the image in the smaller-sized preview to help you choose the area.
8. Click the Save button when finished.
9. Click the Microsoft Apps button (Waffle icon) to go back to the Outlook.com inbox.

Drag the image inside the preview box until the smaller-size preview at the top left displays the desired area, and then click the Save button.

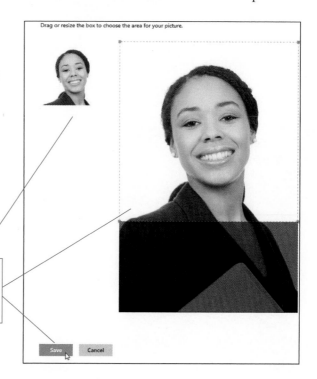

Communicating with Email

Performance Objectives

Upon successful completion of Chapter 1, you will be able to:

1 Identify Outlook components and display folder contents

2 Compose, send, open, and print messages

3 Reply to, forward, and delete messages

4 Attach files to messages and manage file attachments

5 Add cc and bcc recipients to messages

6 Apply formatting options to text in messages

7 Assign importance, sensitivity, tracking, and delivery options to messages

8 Apply follow-up flags to messages

9 Mark messages as read or unread

10 Create signatures

11 Use the Tell Me feature to access Help resources

Precheck

Check your current skills to help focus your study.

Microsoft Outlook is an application that is referred to as a *personal information manager (PIM) program*. Personal information management programs organize items such as email messages, appointments and meetings, contacts, to-do lists, notes, and journal entries. Data stored within Outlook can be integrated to and from individual Outlook modules and/or other Microsoft Office applications, such as Word and Access. In the workplace, Outlook provides collaborative tools such as group scheduling, scheduling assistance, meeting resource scheduling, data sharing, role delegation, and task assignment and management. In this chapter, you will explore the basic features of Outlook and the Mail module that is used for communicating using email messages.

Electronic mail (email) is communication between individuals by means of sending and receiving messages electronically. While text messaging is popular for brief messages, email is still used for longer messages and is the primary means of communication in the workplace.

Data Files

Three student data files are required for this chapter. Before beginning the chapter exercises and assessments, download the files by going to the Ancillary Links menu on this page in your ebook, clicking the <u>Student Data Files</u> link, and saving the files to your storage medium (such as a USB flash drive).

SNAP

If you are a SNAP user, launch the Precheck and the Tutorial from your Assignments page.

Setting Up Outlook

The screen you see when you start Outlook 2016 for the first time will be determined by whether a prior version of Outlook existed on the computer you are using. If a prior version of Outlook existed, you will see a message indicating that Outlook is migrating the information from the old Outlook data file to the new Outlook data file. Existing messages are transferred to Outlook 2016 because you already have an *email profile* (a file that stores the configuration of your email account, data files, and other Outlook settings).

On a computer for which no prior version exists, you will be presented with the Welcome to Outlook 2016 screen at startup. Click Next at the welcome screen and click Next at the second screen to set up your email account. At the Add Account screen, enter your name, email address, and email password two times and then click Next. In most cases, Outlook can set up your email account with these three items. If Outlook cannot configure the email account successfully, you will have to manually enter the mail server settings, such as the messaging protocol, the server name for incoming and outgoing messages, and other information. Your Internet Service Provider (ISP) provides you with these settings.

Exploring the Outlook Window

Outlook

To start Outlook, click the Start button, and then click the Outlook 2016 tile, or click All apps in the left pane, scroll down the program list, and then click *Outlook 2016*. You may also be able to start Outlook 2016 by clicking the Outlook icon on the taskbar or by double-clicking the icon on the desktop.

The Microsoft Outlook application window appears similar to the one shown in Figure 1.1. Buttons within the ribbon interface are used to access commands

Figure 1.1 Microsoft Outlook 2016 Window

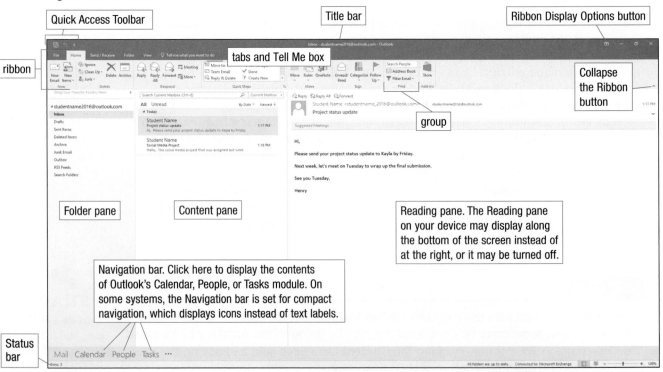

and features, such as New Email to start a new email message. The ribbon is divided into individual tabs, and each tab is split into groups of related buttons.

Outlook has five tabs—File, Home, Send / Receive, Folder, and View—for each of its modules (Mail, Calendar, People, and Tasks). However, the groups and available buttons within each tab vary depending on the module you are viewing.

The first tab in the ribbon is the File tab, which displays the backstage area. Use the backstage area to manage your account and account settings; to open, export, save, and print items; and to customize the Outlook environment.

The Quick Access Toolbar, located at the top left of the Outlook window, contains a Send/Receive All Folders button and an Undo button by default. You can add buttons (such as Print) to the toolbar by clicking the Customize Quick Access Toolbar button ⊟ located at the end of the toolbar and then clicking the desired command at the drop-down list.

By default, when you start Outlook, Mail is the active module and Inbox is the active folder within Mail. Outlook information items for each module are stored within a separate folder for that module. For example, when mail messages are received, they are initially stored within the Inbox folder. Click the Mail, Calendar, People, or Tasks text label or icon on the Navigation bar to display the folder's items within the Content pane. Table 1.1 describes the types of items that are stored within each Outlook module.

A folder in Outlook is not the same as a folder created on a storage device. Outlook folders are not separate items viewable in a Documents window. Instead, folders in Outlook are used to organize data within a single data file called a *store*. The data file for Outlook may have the file extension *.pst* (for *personal information store*) or *.ost* (for *offline store*). Think of an Outlook folder as a single drawer inside a filing cabinet. The filing cabinet (Outlook data store) stores everything you need in one place. The drawers (folders) are used to organize items in separate containers. An item such as an appointment can be stored only within the Calendar drawer, and when you open the Calendar drawer, you can see only appointments.

Table 1.1 Outlook Modules

Folder or module name	Contents stored within folder or module
Inbox	Email messages that have been received. Other folders used in the Mail module for mail messages are Drafts, Sent Items, Deleted Items, Archive, Junk Email, and Outbox. These folder names display in the Folder pane below the email name or email address when Mail is active.
Calendar	Scheduled appointments, events, and meetings.
People (Contacts)	Information such as name, address, telephone number, email address, and other data about the individuals with whom you regularly communicate.
Tasks	Descriptions of activities that you need to complete and want to keep track of to manage your time and to-do list.
Notes	Reminders and other pieces of unstructured information that you want to store for later use.

Navigating Outlook Modules

The Navigation bar contains text labels or icons for the four commonly used modules in Outlook: Mail, Calendar, People, and Tasks. Click a text label or icon on the Navigation bar to change the active module and display the module's contents in the Content pane.

Exercise 1 Viewing Module Contents

1. Click the Start button and then click the Outlook 2016 tile in the right pane of the Start menu, or click All apps in the left pane of the Start menu, scroll down the program list, and then click *Outlook 2016*. You may also be able to start Outlook by clicking an icon on the taskbar, or by double-clicking an icon on the desktop.
2. If necessary, type your user name and password to connect to the mail server. *Note: Following this exercise, instructions will assume that Outlook is running and you are connected to the mail server.*
3. Change the active module using the Navigation bar by completing the following steps:
   a. Click the Calendar text label or icon on the Navigation bar. The current day displays with scheduled appointments, if any exist, in Day, Week, or Month view. The top section in the Folder pane changes to the *Date Navigator*, which contains a calendar for the current and next months.
   b. Click the People text label or icon on the Navigation bar and view the layout of the Outlook window.

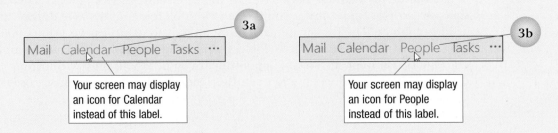

   c. Click the Tasks text label or icon on the Navigation bar and view the layout of the Outlook window.
   d. Click the Navigation Options button (three dots) on the Navigation bar and then click *Notes* at the pop-up list. View the layout of the Outlook window.

4. Click the Mail text label or icon on the Navigation bar to change the active module back to the Mail module with the Inbox folder active.

Creating and Sending Email Messages

Email has become the business standard for communication because it allows a message to be delivered within seconds anywhere in the world. The business community embraced email many years ago because of its speed of delivery and low cost. Correspondence is now conducted mostly electronically, replacing paper-based letters and memos. Individuals also use email to communicate with relatives and friends all around the world.

To send and receive email, you need to have an account on a *mail server*. The mail server acts as the post office, routing messages from their senders to the recipients. The software on your PC that you use to send the messages that you compose and to read the messages that you receive is called the *mail client*. Connection to a mail server from your PC can be through a local area network that is connected to the mail server or through a high-speed network device such as a DSL or cable modem.

Just as one post office serves many people in a community, one mail server connects multiple users. Each individual connected to the mail server is assigned a *user name* and *password* for unique identification and security in accessing mail services.

Using Outlook Connected to Microsoft Exchange Server

Outlook can be used as an email client connected to a mail server running Exchange Server or to an Internet mail server. Organizations use Microsoft Exchange Server on their internal networks to provide employees with additional options such as the scheduling assistant to plan and schedule meetings, assign and delegate tasks to teams, and post notices in public folders. Users connected to an Exchange server can view all the other internal users in a global address list and send a message to someone else in the organization by typing that person's name. Messages sent externally require the recipient's full email address, such as *name@server.net*.

Outlook on the web for Exchange Server allows employees to work in Outlook from their home or another location with Internet access using a web browser. From a browser, employees can read, edit, and create new messages, appointments, contacts, and tasks using a secure web-based interface that connects them to their workplace account and mail server.

If you are using Outlook with an *outlook.com* or a *live.com* account, you are using Outlook as a Microsoft Exchange client by default.

Using Outlook Connected to an Internet Mail Server

If you are not using Outlook as an Exchange server client, then you are using Outlook as an Internet mail client. When creating your email profile, you have to specify one of the following *mail protocols* (sets of standards that define how the mail is managed):

- **POP3** *Post Office Protocol 3* accounts download messages to the local computer when the user logs in to the mail server. The advantage of using POP3 is that once the messages are downloaded, you can read them even if you are offline. POP3 accounts are not as useful for someone who wants to access the same email account from multiple devices. Depending on the server options, messages may be deleted from the server once downloaded.

- **IMAP** *Internet Message Access Protocol* accounts store messages on the email server. IMAP is a popular choice for individuals who want to access email on multiple devices because messages are kept on the mail server. For example, you can read a

Quick Steps

Create and Send a Message
1. Click New Email button in New group on Home tab.
2. Type address in *To* text box.
3. Type brief description in *Subject* text box.
4. Type content in message window.
5. Click Send.

TIP Follow proper business etiquette when using email for business purposes. Many employees mistakenly perceive email as casual correspondence. Keep in mind that your workplace email records are the property of the employer and can also be used as evidence in legal proceedings.

message on a computer at work and also read and respond to the same message later in the evening from a different computer at home.

The exercises and assessments in this chapter assume that you are already connected to your mail server in a computer facility at your school or from your home or another location. If necessary, start Outlook and connect to the ISP that provides your email account before starting an exercise or assessment.

Composing a New Email Message

New Email

TIP As a courtesy to the recipient, always include a brief description in the *Subject* text box that accurately describes the content of the message.

To create a new message, click the New Email button in the New group on the Home tab with Mail as the active module and Inbox as the active folder. A message window opens similar to the one shown in Figure 1.2.

The address that you type in the *To* text box is either the user name of the recipient, if you are sending the message to someone on the same mail server as you, or the full Internet address of the recipient, such as *name@server.net*, if you are sending the message to someone outside your network. When typing multiple addresses, separate them with a semicolon and one space—for example, *JDoe@emcp.net; MSmith@paradigm.net; GAdams@mailserver.com.*

Figure 1.2 New Email Message Window

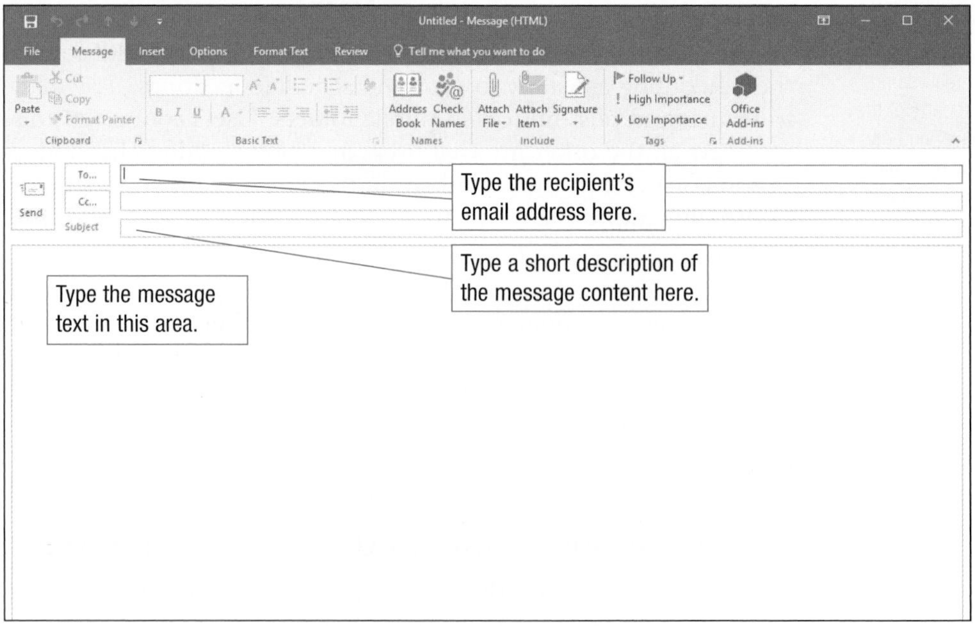

Type the recipient's email address here.

Type a short description of the message content here.

Type the message text in this area.

Exercise 2 Creating and Sending a Message

Note: Check with your instructor for specific instructions on the recipient name and address you should use. Your instructor may designate email partners for sending and receiving messages, or you may be instructed to send messages to yourself.

1. With Inbox active, complete the following steps to create and send a message:

   a. Click the New Email button in the New group on the Home tab.

1a

b. Type the email address for the recipient in the *To* text box—for example, *Student Name* (if you are communicating with someone connected to the same Exchange server as you) or *studentname@server.net*.

c. Press Tab two times or click in the *Subject* text box.

d. Type Social Media Essay and then press Tab or press Enter to move the insertion point to the message text window below *Subject*.

e. Type the message text below. Press Enter two times to end a paragraph and insert a blank line between each set of paragraphs. The text within each paragraph may wrap to the next line at a different location than shown below depending on the size of your message window.

> First name, [Substitute the first name of the message recipient for *First name*.]
>
> Let me know what you think of the following paragraph as the introduction in our essay on social media.
>
> Social media refers to online technologies such as message boards, blogs, podcasts, wikis, and vlogs with which users can interact by sharing experiences, opinions, pictures, and other electronic content with each other. These exchanges take place in websites such as YouTube, Facebook, Twitter, Tumblr, and Flickr to name a few. The ease with which information can be shared and made accessible to a large community has led to the rapid acceptance of these technologies by people of all ages.

f. Press Enter two times at the end of the message and then type your name as the sender.

g. Click the Send button. The message automatically closes once you have clicked Send.

2. The message will be placed in one of two folders. If the mail server is busy, you are offline, or your computer does not send messages immediately, the message will be queued in the Outbox folder; otherwise, the message will be placed in the Sent Items folder. Complete the following steps to check the mail folders to see where the message has been placed:

a. Look next to the Outbox in the Folder pane. If a message is queued in the Outbox, the folder name is displayed in bold and the number of queued messages is noted in blue text. Click *Outbox* in the Folder pane, click the Send / Receive tab, and then click the Send/Receive All Folders button ⊞ in the Send & Receive group, or click the Send/Receive All Folders button on the Quick Access Toolbar to send the message immediately.

   b. Click *Sent Items* in the Folder pane. Messages that have been delivered to the mail server are displayed in the Content pane.

3. Click *Inbox* in the Folder pane to redisplay the Inbox folder contents.

> **Check Your Work**

◻ Composing a New Email Message in Outlook on the web

Users connected to an Exchange server can create a new message from any device with Internet access. Open a browser window and type the URL provided by your mail administrator—for example, https://server.net/owa. Log in with your email address and password. At the Outlook on the web screen click the New button in the Menu bar at the top of the screen. Type the recipient's name or email address in the *To* field, type the subject in the *Subject* field, type the message in the white area below the toolbar, and then click the Send button.

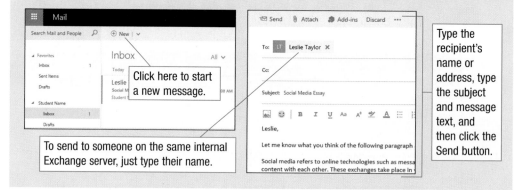

Click here to start a new message.

To send to someone on the same internal Exchange server, just type their name.

Type the recipient's name or address, type the subject and message text, and then click the Send button.

◻ Composing a New Email Message at Outlook.com

Outlook.com is Microsoft's free web-based email service. Open a browser window, type the URL outlook.com, and then sign in using your email address and password. Click the New button in the Menu bar at the top of the screen. Type the recipient's email address next to the *To* button. Click *Add a subject* and type the subject text. Click the placeholder text *Add a message or drag a file here* and then type the message text. Click the Send button when finished.

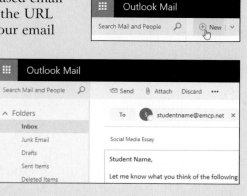

Opening, Printing, Replying to, and Forwarding Messages

Quick Steps

Print a Message
1. Select or open message.
2. Click File tab.
3. Click *Print.*
4. Click Print button.
5. If necessary, close message.

Reply to a Message
1. Click Reply button in Reading pane.
2. Type reply message.
3. Click Send.

Forward a Message
1. Click Forward button in Reading pane.
2. Type recipient's address.
3. Type message.
4. Click Send.

Unread inbox messages display with a vertical blue bar at the left of the message header and with the subject and time (or date) in bold blue text. The sender's name, the subject, and the first line of message text appear in the message header. By default, messages are arranged by date with the most recent message displayed at the top of the list.

If you are online when a new message is received, a chime will sound and a *desktop alert*, similar to the one shown in Figure 1.3, will appear near the bottom right of your screen. Click the alert to open the message or rest the pointer over the alert to keep it visible longer.

Figure 1.3 Desktop Alert for New Message Received

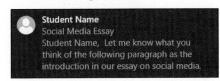

Reading and Printing Messages

In many cases, you can read, reply to, or forward a message directly from the Reading pane. If the Reading pane is turned off on the computer you are using, click the View tab, click the Reading Pane button in the Layout group, and then click *Right* at the drop-down list to show the pane in the same location as shown in Figure 1.4. Open a long message by double-clicking the message header in the Content pane to open the message in a window similar to the window shown in Figure 1.5 on page 20.

Print the active message by clicking the File tab, clicking *Print* at the backstage area, and then clicking the Print button. Most people add the Print button to the Quick Access Toolbar if they often print messages by clicking the Customize Quick Access Toolbar button located at the end of the toolbar and then clicking *Print*.

Print

Figure 1.4 Viewing Messages in the Reading Pane

If you are using Outlook connected to a server running Microsoft Exchange Server, the name of your mailbox on the server displays here instead of the email address.

A feature called *inline replies* allows you to reply or forward a message directly from the Reading pane.

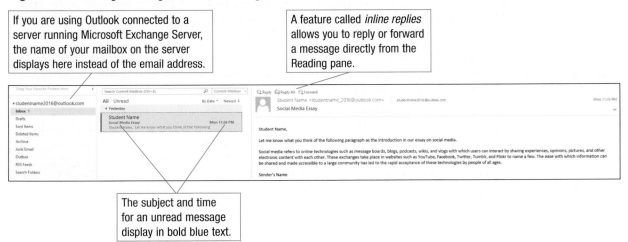

The subject and time for an unread message display in bold blue text.

Figure 1.5 Opened Message Window

Click here to type a reply to the sender.

Click here to type a reply to all recipients of the original message when that message was sent to more than one person.

Click here to send the original message to someone else.

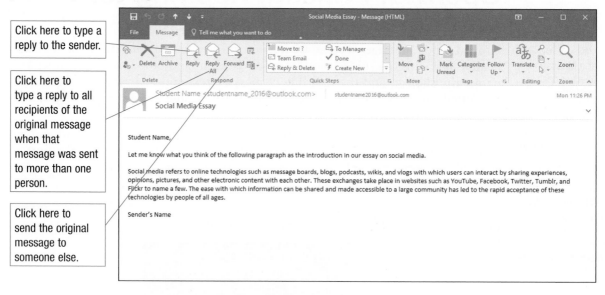

Replying to a Message

 Reply

 Reply All

TIP Exercise good judgment when using Reply All. Make sure *all* of the other recipients really need to see your response.

When you click the Reply button or Reply All button in the Reading pane or Respond group on the Message tab, the sender's email address is automatically entered in the *To* text box and *RE:* is inserted in front of the *Subject* text. The original message text is included below the reply text so that the reader will see the source message. This set of messages is referred to as a ***thread*** and is beneficial to someone who sends or receives several messages in a day and may not immediately recall what she or he has already sent to you.

If you are replying to a message that was sent to multiple recipients and you would like all of them to read your reply to the sender, click the Reply All button. Doing so will automatically insert the sender's email address and the email addresses of the other recipients of the original message in the *To* text box.

Forwarding a Message

 Forward

TIP If you are forwarding information to several people who do not know each other, put the email addresses in the *Bcc* field (see page 24) to protect everyone's privacy. Delete any email addresses that appear in the message for the same reason.

When you click the Forward button in the Reading pane or a message window, the insertion point is positioned in the *To* text box and *FW:* is inserted in front of the *Subject* text. The original message text is included below the forward message text so the reader can read the threaded text.

Type the email address of the person to whom you want to forward the message and, if necessary, include a few explanatory lines of text above the original message for the benefit of the recipient.

Be cautious when forwarding a message that you have received to someone else. Make sure that the sender would not object to another person reading the message. Keep in mind that the sender intended the message to be a private communication between you and him or her. If the content contains sensitive information, check with the sender first before you forward the message. A good practice to follow is that if you are in doubt, do not forward the message.

Exercise 3 Printing, Replying to, and Forwarding a Message

Note: To complete this exercise, you must first receive the message created in Exercise 2, either from another student or from yourself.

1. Make sure that Inbox is active and that the message sent to you in Exercise 2 appears in the Content pane with the Reading pane open at the right. If necessary, click the View tab, click the Reading Pane button in the Layout group, and then click *Right* at the drop-down list.

2. Print and reply to the message by completing the following steps:

   a. If necessary, click to select the message header for the message with the subject *Social Media Essay* in the Content pane.

   b. Click the Print button 🖶 on the Quick Access Toolbar, and then click *Print*. **Note:** *If necessary, add the Print button to the Quick Access Toolbar by clicking the Customize Quick Access Toolbar button* ⬇ *at the right end of the Quick Access Toolbar and then clicking* Print *at the drop-down list.*

   c. Click the Reply button in the Reading pane.

   d. With the insertion point automatically positioned at the top left of the message text in the Reading pane, type the following reply text:

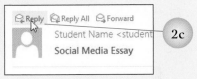

   First name, [Substitute the first name of the person from whom you received the message for *First name*.]

   I like the introductory paragraph for our essay. I have been hearing that protecting one's privacy when communicating using social media is a concern. We should investigate this further so that we can include information to safeguard our personal information when using social media.

   e. Press Enter two times at the end of the reply message and then type your name as the sender.

   f. Click Send.

Pop Out opens the message in a separate message window.

Discard cancels the reply and closes the message.

2f — Send

    📄 Pop Out ✕ Discard

    To...   Student Name <studentname_2016@outlook.com>
    Cc...
    Subject RE: Social Media Essay

    Student Name,

2d I like the introductory paragraph for our essay. I have been hearing that protecting one's privacy when communicating using social media is a concern. We should investigate this further so that we can include information to safeguard our personal information when using social media.

    Sender's Name

2e From: Student Name [mailto:studentname_2016@outlook.com]
    Sent: Monday, May 30, 2018 11:26 PM
    To: studentname2016@outlook.com
    Subject: Social Media Essay

    Student Name,

---

3. Now that you have read and replied to the message, you decide to send both the original message and your reply to someone else by completing the following steps:

   a. Click *Sent Items* in the Folder pane.

   b. If necessary, click to select the message header in the Content pane for the message you just sent in Step 2, and then click the Forward button in the Reading pane.

Note: If the message does not appear in the Sent Items folder, it is in the Outbox folder. Click the Send/Receive All Folders button on the Quick Access Toolbar. In a few seconds, the message should appear in the Content pane.

c. With the insertion point positioned in the *To* text box, type the email address of the person that you want to forward the message to. *Note: The AutoComplete feature matches entries in the AutoComplete cache with the text you type. If the person's information appears in a drop-down list, accept the highlighted name in the list by pressing Enter, or select another name in the list.*

d. Click at the top of the message text window and then type the following text:

First name, [Substitute the first name of the person to whom you are forwarding the message for *First name*.]

I thought you might be interested in reading this information on social media.

e. Press Enter two times and then type your name as the sender.
f. Click Send.
4. Click Inbox in the Folder pane.

Check Your Work

◻ Replying to and Forwarding Messages in Outlook on the web

Click to select a message header in the Content pane and then use the Reply all button located near the top right of the message in the Reading pane. Click the Reply all button arrow and then click *Reply* or *Forward* if you do not want to use the *Reply all* option.

◧ Opening, Replying to, and Forwarding Messages at Outlook.com

Click a message header in the Content pane to open the message. Click the Reply button located near the top right of the message to respond to a message. Find the *Reply all* and *Forward* options by clicking the Reply button arrow.

Social Media Essay

Student Name
To: studentname2016@outlook.com;

Click here to close the message.

Student Name,

Reply
Reply all
Forward

Deleting Messages

After a period of time, the Inbox and Sent Items folders become filled with messages that are no longer needed and should be deleted. To delete a message, click to select the message header and then press the Delete key or click the Delete button in the Delete group on the Home tab. The message will be moved to the Deleted Items folder where it can be restored if necessary.

Delete

Quick Steps

Delete a Message
1. Click message header in Content pane.
2. Click Delete button in Delete group on Home tab.

Empty the Deleted Items Folder
1. Right-click *Deleted Items* in Folder pane.
2. Click *Empty Folder*.
3. Click Yes.

You can use the mouse to select more than one message for deletion by following standard Windows conventions:

- If the messages to be deleted are next to each other in the list, click to select the first message header, hold down the Shift key, and then click the last message header.

- If the messages to be deleted are not next to each other in the list, click to select the first message header and then hold down the Ctrl key while clicking the remaining message headers.

From time to time, the Deleted Items folder should be emptied to permanently remove the messages. To do this, complete the following steps:

1. Right-click *Deleted Items* in the Folder pane.
2. Click *Empty Folder* at the shortcut menu.
3. Click Yes at the message box asking if you are sure you want to continue to permanently delete everything in the Deleted Items folder.

Exercise 4 Deleting Messages and Emptying the Deleted Items Folder

1. With Inbox active, display the contents in the Sent Items folder.
2. Delete the message that you sent in Exercise 2 by completing the following steps:
   a. If necessary, click to select the message header in the Content pane for the message you sent in Exercise 2.
   b. If necessary, click the Home tab on the ribbon.
   c. Click the Delete button in the Delete group.
3. Delete the two messages that you sent in Exercise 3 by completing steps similar to Steps 2a to 2c.
4. Empty the Deleted Items folder by completing the following steps:
   a. Click *Deleted Items* in the Folder pane.
   b. Notice that the messages you deleted in Steps 2 and 3 are displayed in the Content pane.
   c. Right-click *Deleted Items* in the Folder pane.
   d. Click *Empty Folder* at the shortcut menu.

e. Click Yes at the message asking to continue to permanently delete everything in the Deleted Items folder.

5. Change the active folder to Inbox.

4e

Microsoft Outlook ✕

! Everything in the "Deleted Items" folder will be permanently deleted. Continue?

Yes   No

Deleting Messages in Outlook on the web

Select the message or group of messages to be deleted in the Content pane and then click the Delete button in the Menu bar along the top of the screen.

⊕ New | ∨   🗑 Delete   Archive   Junk   Sweep   Move to ∨   Categories ∨   •••

Inbox   All ∨

Social Media Essay

Today

☐ Student Name
Social Media Essay   11:17 AM
Leslie, Let me know what you think of the following para...

SN   Student Name
To: Leslie Taylor; ✉

Leslie,

Attaching Files to Messages

 Attach File

TIP New to Outlook 2016 is the *Recent Items* section in the Attach File drop-down list. Files worked on recently appear in the list and can be attached to the message with just one click.

Quick Steps

Attach a File to a Message
1. Click Attach File button in Include group on Message tab or on Insert tab in message window.
2. Click file name in *Recent Items* list, or click *Browse This PC*, navigate to the location of the file, and then double-click file name.

Display the *Bcc* Text Box
1. Open message window.
2. Click Options tab.
3. Click Bcc button in Show Fields group.

 Bcc

Office documents, pictures, and other types of files are routinely distributed by email. To attach a file to an open message, click the Attach File button in the Include group on the Message tab or on the Insert tab. Next, click a file name in the *Recent Items* section of the drop-down list, or click *Browse This PC* to open the Insert File dialog box to browse to the storage medium and/or folder containing the file that you want to attach to the message and then double-click the file name.

When you receive an email message with a file attached, you can preview, open, save, or print the file from the Reading pane or message window. When you click the file name in the Reading pane, the message text disappears and is replaced with the contents of the attached file. Some files cannot be viewed in the Reading pane. For those files, double-click the file name to open the file attached to the message in the source application. When a file is selected in the Reading pane or message window, the Attachment Tools Attachments tab becomes active with buttons to open, print, save, remove, select, and copy a file.

Word, Excel, and PowerPoint open file attachments in Protected view, used to read the contents of the file; editing the file is prevented until you click the Enable Editing button in the Protected view Message bar. This feature helps protect you from a malicious code infection.

Sending Copies of Messages to Other People

Use the *Cc* text box in the message window to send a copy of the message to one or more other people. *Cc* stands for *carbon copy*. All the message recipients can view all the other names and email addresses included as *To* and *Cc* recipients.

Add an email address to the *Bcc* text box to send a copy of a message to someone else and prevent all other recipients from seeing that person's name in the message. *Bcc* stands for *blind carbon copy*. Only the sender can see the identity of a bcc recipient. Click the Options tab in the message window and then click the Bcc button in the Show Fields group to display the *Bcc* text box.

Exercise 5 Attaching a File to a Message and Sending a Copy to Someone Else

Note: Make sure you have copied the student data files for this chapter to your storage medium before completing this exercise.

1. With Inbox active, click the New Email button in the New group on the Home tab.
2. With the insertion point positioned in the *To* text box, type the email address for the recipient.
3. Press Tab or click in the *Cc* text box and type the email address of the student you forwarded a message to in Exercise 3, Step 3.
4. Click the Options tab and then click the Bcc button in the Show Fields group. *Note: Skip this step if the Bcc text box is already visible in your message window.*
5. Click in the *Bcc* text box and then type the email address of another student in your class.
6. Press Tab or click in the *Subject* text box and then type Social Media Privacy Tips.
7. Press Enter or click in the message text box and then type the following message text:

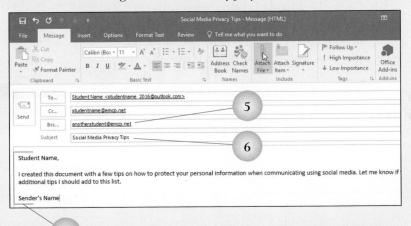

> First name, [Substitute the first name of the message recipient for *First name*.]
>
> I created this document with a few tips on how to protect your personal information when communicating using social media. Let me know if you have additional tips I should add to the list.

8. Press Enter two times at the end of the message text and then type your name as the sender.
9. Attach the Word document named ***SocialMediaPrivacy.docx*** to the message by completing the following steps:
   a. Click the Message tab and then click the Attach File button in the Include group.
   b. Click *Browse This PC* at the drop-down list. At the Insert File dialog box, navigate to the location on your storage medium where the student data files are stored for Chapter 1, and then double-click the file ***SocialMediaPrivacy.docx*** in the Content pane.
   c. Look below the *Subject* text box. Notice the Attached field added to the message with the name of the file and the file size displayed with a Word document icon.
   d. Click the File tab in the message window, click *Print*, and then click the Print button.
10. Click Send.

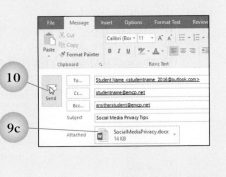

Check Your Work

Exercise 6 Previewing File Attachments and Using File Attachment Tools

Note: *To complete this exercise, you must first receive the message created in Exercise 5, either from another student or from yourself.*

1. With Inbox active, look at the message header in the Content pane for the message received with the subject *Social Media Privacy Tips*. Notice the paper clip graphic at the right of the sender's name indicating that the message has a file attachment.
2. If necessary, click to select the message header and then look at the message in the Reading pane. Attachments can be previewed and/or opened directly from the Reading pane.
3. Click the file name **SocialMediaPrivacy.docx** in the Reading pane. Outlook removes the message text and displays in the Reading pane a preview of the Microsoft Word document. The Attachment Tools Attachments tab also becomes active.
4. Read the document in the Reading pane.
5. Open and then save the document to your storage medium by completing the following steps:
   a. Click the Open button in the Actions group on the Attachment Tools Attachments tab. Microsoft Word opens with the document opened in Protected view.
   b. Click the Enable Editing button in the PROTECTED VIEW message bar. The message bar closes and the full ribbon now displays with the Word document.

   c. Exit Microsoft Word by clicking the Close button at the top right corner of the Word document window.
   d. In the Outlook window, with the Word document still displayed in the Reading pane, click the Save As button in the Actions group on the Attachment Tools Attachments tab.
   e. With **SocialMediaPrivacy.docx** selected in the *File name* text box at the Save Attachment dialog box, navigate to the drive and folder in which you want to save the document, and then click the Save button.

6. With the file attachment still open in the Reading pane, click the Remove Attachment button in the Actions group on the Attachment Tools Attachments tab.

7. Click Remove Attachment at the Microsoft Outlook message box asking if you are sure you want to remove the attachment from the message. Since you have a copy of the file saved to your storage medium, you can remove the attachment from the message and thus save storage space for your email folder on your hard disk.

Quick Steps

Format the Text in a Message
1. Select message text to be formatted.
2. Apply format option in Basic Text group on Message tab OR click Format Text tab and apply desired format option.

Embed an Image in a Message
1. Click Insert tab.
2. Click Pictures button in Illustrations group.
3. Navigate to location of image file on storage medium.
4. Double-click image file name.

Insert a Hyperlink in a Message
In message text window, type a valid web address and then press spacebar or Enter; OR
1. Click Insert tab.
2. Click Hyperlink button in Links group.
3. Type web address.
4. Click OK.

Attaching Files and Showing *Bcc* in Outlook on the web

Click the Attach button in the Menu bar along the top of the screen to add a file attachment. To add the *Bcc* option, click *Bcc* at the end of the To field.

Click the Attach button to add a file to the message.

Click here to add a Bcc address to the message.

Attaching Files and Showing *Bcc* at Outlook.com

Click *Cc* and/or *Bcc* at the right end of the To field to add the fields to the message. Attach a file to the message by clicking the Attach button on the Menu bar. At the next screen, click Computer in the left navigation pane, navigate to the drive and folder, and then double-click the file name. Click the Attach as a copy button to send a copy of the file to the recipient; or, if you want to collaborate online with the recipient to make changes to the file attachment, choose the Upload and attach as a OneDrive file button. The file is uploaded to the Email attachments folder in your OneDrive account.

Click the Attach button to add a file to the message.

Click here to add Cc and Bcc addresses.

Pictures

Hyperlink

Applying Formatting Options in Messages

By default, new messages are composed and sent using HTML format. HTML features allow you to apply formatting—such as font options, paragraph alignment, bullets, styles, backgrounds, and other graphic elements commonly found in web pages—to selected text.

The Basic Text group on the Message tab of a message window contains many of the typical font and paragraph formatting options applied to text in messages. Click the Format Text tab to access more text formatting options, including the *Styles* gallery (with predefined font and paragraph options) and editing tools such as Find and Replace, as shown in Figure 1.6. Buttons on the Insert tab of a message window are used to embed tables, pictures, graphics, hyperlinks, and symbols in a message.

Be cautious not to overuse formatting and graphics in messages. When used appropriately, formatting options help to emphasize key points in your message, and graphics help to illustrate a concept or show an item, feature, or process.

Figure 1.6 Format Text Tab in a Message Window

Choose the Plain Text or Rich Text button to change the mail format for an individual message. Plain text does not allow any formatting or graphic options. Rich text is used when sending messages to others on the same Microsoft Exchange server.

Find is used to locate all occurrences of specified text in the message window. Replace changes all occurrences of the specified text to something else automatically. Use the Select button to assist with selecting text or objects.

Exercise 7 Formatting Text in a Message and Inserting a Hyperlink and an Image

1. With Inbox active, click the New Email button.
2. With the insertion point positioned in the *To* text box, type the email address for the recipient.
3. Click in the *Subject* text box and then type Social Media Project.
4. Press Enter or click in the message text box and then type the following message text:

    First name, [Substitute the first name of the message recipient for *First name.*]

    Here is a picture for our presentation and some information about two social media attacks that we can include in the essay.

    Sophos network security reported fake messages sent to Twitter users. The messages claimed that video of the user was posted on Facebook. When the user clicked the posted link, a Trojan virus was installed on the unsuspecting user's PC.

    Numerous Pinterest accounts have been hacked to post image spam on pinboards and other social networks linked to the user's account.

    Facebook remains the top target for hackers because the social network has surpassed one billion users.

5. Press Enter two times at the end of the message text and then type your name as the sender.

6. Apply formatting options to the message text using buttons in the Basic Text group on the Message tab by completing the following steps:

   a. Select the last three paragraphs of text in the message window above your name.

   b. Click the Bullets button in the Basic Text group on the Message tab. Do not click the Bullets button arrow.

   c. Deselect the paragraphs and then select *Twitter* in the first bulleted paragraph.

   d. Click the Font Color button arrow in the Basic Text group.

   e. Click *Light Blue* in the *Standard Colors* section (fourth square from right).

   f. With *Twitter* still selected, click the Bold button in the Basic Text group.

   g. Select *Pinterest* in the second bulleted paragraph and then apply bold formatting and the same font color that you applied to *Twitter*. Consider using the buttons on the Mini toolbar that appears when text has been selected to apply the formatting options.

   h. Select *Facebook* in the third bulleted paragraph and then apply bold formatting and the same font color that you applied to *Twitter*.

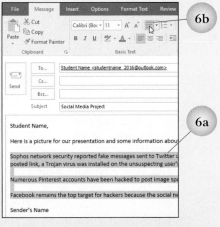

7. Apply formatting options to the message text using buttons on the Format Text tab by completing the following steps:

   a. Select the first paragraph of text, beginning with *Here is a picture*.

   b. Click the Format Text tab.

   c. Click the More button to expand the *Styles* gallery ▽. **Note:** *If the More button is not visible, widen the message window to expand the ribbon and show the* Styles *gallery in the Styles group.*

   d. Click the *Heading 2* style in the drop-down gallery.

   e. Click in the message window to deselect the text.

f. Click the Change Styles button in the Styles group, point to *Style Set*, and then click *Shaded* at the drop-down gallery (fourth button in third row of *Built-In* section).

g. Deselect the text and notice the change in the appearance of the message text. Each style set applies different options for text elements in each style. The available style formats depend on the active theme, which can be changed using the Themes button in the Themes group on the Options tab.

8. Insert a hyperlink and picture into the message text by completing the following steps:

a. Click after your name at the bottom of the message text, press Enter to insert a blank line, and then type the following text:

Image below courtesy of Chris2d via Wikimedia Commons [press the spacebar]

b. Click the Insert tab and then click the Hyperlink button in the Links group.

c. With the insertion point positioned in the *Address* text box of the Insert Hyperlink dialog box, type commons.wikimedia.org and then press Enter or click OK. Note that Outlook can also automatically format a web address as a hyperlink when you type text in the message window recognized by Outlook as a valid web address.

d. Click the Pictures button in the Illustrations group on the Insert tab.

e. At the Insert Picture dialog box, navigate to the location on your storage medium where the student data files are stored for Chapter 1.

f. Double-click the file *Social_Network_Security.png*.

g. Scroll down to view the picture embedded in the message.

9. Print the message from the message window and then send the message.

Check Your Work

Applying Formatting Options in Outlook on the web

Formatting options for messages in Outlook on the web are accessed from the toolbar that appears below the *Subject* text. Click the down-pointing arrow at the right end of the toolbar to choose additional options. Styles and other advanced formatting options available in the desktop version of Outlook are not available in Outlook on the web.

Applying Formatting Options at Outlook.com

Format text using the buttons on the Formatting toolbar located at the bottom of the message window. Styles and other advanced formatting options available in the desktop version of Outlook are not available for Outlook.com messages.

[!] High Importance

Quick Steps

Assign Importance to a Message

With message window open, click High Importance or Low Importance button in Tags group on Message tab.

Request a Read Receipt

1. Click Options tab in message window.
2. Click *Request a Read Receipt* check box in Tracking group.

Assign Other Message Options

1. Click Properties dialog box launcher in Tags group on Message tab OR in Tracking or More Options group on Options tab in message window.
2. Add required options.
3. Click Close button.

Tagging and Assigning Message Options in the Message Window

The Tags group on the Message tab of a message window contains High Importance and Low Importance buttons. Attaching one of these options to a message indicates the priority of the message to the recipient.

Click the Options tab to assign tracking options such as voting responses, read receipts, and delivery receipts. You can also choose to delay the delivery of the message or have replies directed to someone else.

Click the Properties dialog box launcher located at the bottom right in the Tags group on the Message tab, or Tracking group or More Options group on the Options tab, to open the Properties dialog box. The dialog box contains additional options such as changing *Sensitivity* from *Normal* to *Personal*, *Private*, or *Confidential*.

Voting buttons display Approve/Reject or Yes/No/Maybe buttons in the message when received. The recipient clicks his or her response and a message is returned to the sender with the response. Delivery and read receipts can be attached to the message so the sender will be notified when the message is delivered to the recipient's mailbox and/or when the recipient opens the message.

In the *Delivery options* section of the Properties dialog box, you can direct replies to your message to someone else. For example, if you are going to be away and want a message that is replied to looked at in your absence, type an assistant's email address in the *Have replies sent to* text box.

When you are done selecting options, click the Close button to close the Properties dialog box.

Exercise 8 Tagging a Message and Assigning Message Options

1. With Inbox active, open a new message window.
2. Type the email address for the recipient.
3. Click in the *Subject* text box and then type Social Media Essay.
4. Press Enter or click in the message text box and then type the following message text:

First name, [Substitute the first name of the message recipient for *First name*.]

We need to be sure we have all the latest information on techniques to protect our personal information and privacy when using social media. I suggest we each research the topic and get together next week to share information.

5. Press Enter two times at the end of the message text and then type your name as the sender.
6. Tag the message as important and confidential and assign a delivery option by completing the following steps:

   a. Click the High Importance button in the Tags group on the Message tab. This button is a toggle; when the feature is active, the button is shaded with a light gray background.

   b. Click the Properties dialog box launcher located at the bottom right of the Tags group.

   c. Click the button that displays *Normal* next to *Sensitivity* in the *Settings* section of the Properties dialog box and then click *Confidential* at the drop-down list.

   d. Click the Close button.

   e. Click the Options tab.

   f. Click to insert a check mark in the *Request a Read Receipt* check box in the Tracking group.

7. Print the message from the message window and then send the message.

This option was changed in Step 6a by the High Importance button.

Check Your Work

Exchange Server

If you are using Outlook as an email client connected to a server running Microsoft Exchange Server, you can review the voting responses. Open the message from Sent Items in which you included voting buttons and click *Tracking* in the Show group on the Message tab.

Messages with the *High Importance* option attached display a red exclamation point at the right of the sender's name in the Content pane. In the Reading pane for the message, an Information bar displays below the sender's name informing the recipient of the options that have been assigned to the message, as shown in Figure 1.7 on page 33.

When a message has been sent to you with a read receipt attached, you will be notified that a read receipt has been requested by the sender unless you have modified the default options in the *Tracking* section of the Outlook Options dialog box. An example of a read receipt is shown in Figure 1.8 on page 33.

Some Internet mail service providers do not support email tracking options, which means voting buttons and/or read receipts are not processed. If you do not receive a read report after sending a message with a read receipt attached, it does not necessarily mean that the message was not opened by the recipient. One possibility is that the recipient's mail service or mail application does not support read receipts. Another possibility is that the recipient selected *No* when prompted to send the read receipt back to you. Similarly, if you send a message with voting buttons attached and do not receive response messages, it may be because some recipients did not see the voting buttons when they opened the message.

Figure 1.7 Message Tags Information Bar in Reading Pane

Message tags are shown in the Information bar in the Reading pane.

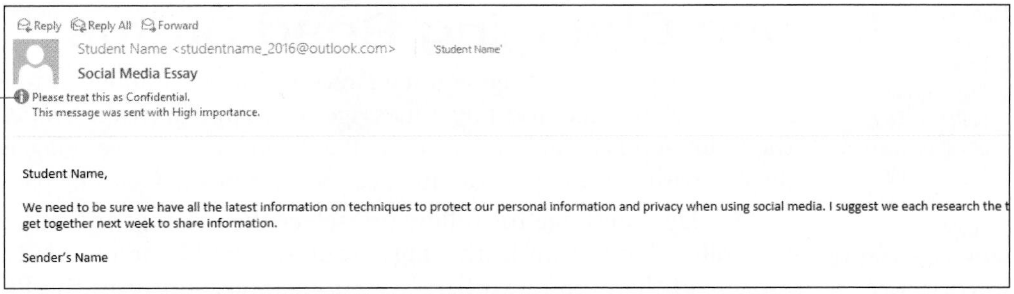

> Reply Reply All Forward
>
> Student Name <studentname_2016@outlook.com>   'Student Name'
> Social Media Essay
> ⓘ Please treat this as Confidential.
> This message was sent with High importance.
>
> Student Name,
>
> We need to be sure we have all the latest information on techniques to protect our personal information and privacy when using social media. I suggest we each research the t get together next week to share information.
>
> Sender's Name

Figure 1.8 Read Report Message Sent to Sender

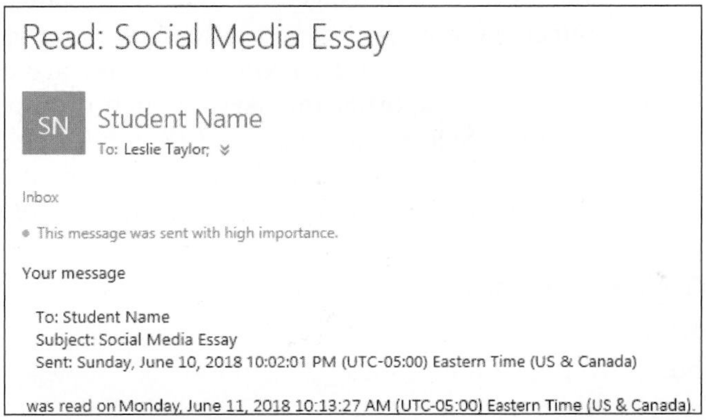

> Read: Social Media Essay
>
> SN   Student Name
>   To: Leslie Taylor; ⌄
>
> Inbox
>
> • This message was sent with high importance.
>
> Your message
>
> To: Student Name
> Subject: Social Media Essay
> Sent: Sunday, June 10, 2018 10:02:01 PM (UTC-05:00) Eastern Time (US & Canada)
>
> was read on Monday, June 11, 2018 10:13:27 AM (UTC-05:00) Eastern Time (US & Canada).

Tagging and Assigning Message Options in Outlook on the web

Click the More commands button (three dots), point to *Set importance*, and then click *High* or *Low* to attach an importance level to the message. Click *Show message options* at the drop-down list to change the sensitivity option or to request a read receipt.

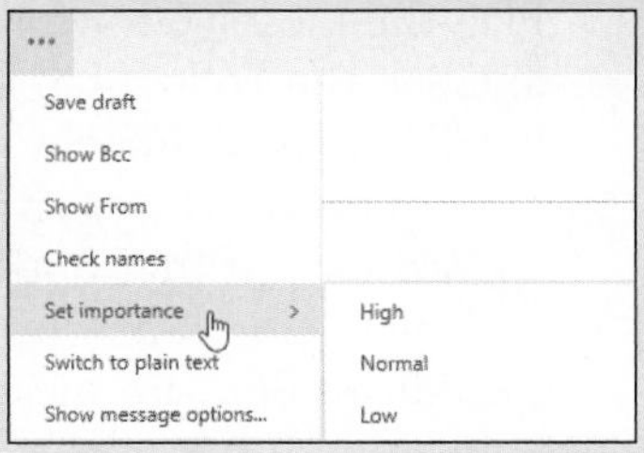

| ••• |
| Save draft |
| Show Bcc |
| Show From |
| Check names |
| Set importance >   High |
| Switch to plain text   Normal |
| Show message options...   Low |

Tagging and Assigning Message Options at Outlook.com

Attach a priority indicator to a message by clicking the More commands button (three dots) on the Menu bar, pointing to *Set importance*, and then clicking *High* or *Low*.

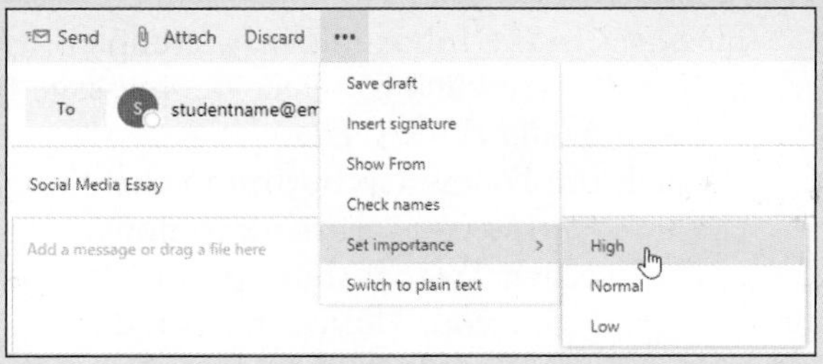

| ✉ Send   📎 Attach   Discard   ••• |
| |
| To   Ⓢ studentname@em   Save draft |
| Insert signature |
| Show From |
| Social Media Essay   Check names |
| Add a message or drag a file here   Set importance >   High |
| Switch to plain text   Normal |
| Low |

Quick Steps

Flag a Message
1. Select message header.
2. Click Follow Up button in Tags group on Home or Message tab.
3. Click desired flag option.

Mark a Message as Unread or Read
1. Select message header.
2. Click Unread/Read button in Tags group on Home tab.

⚑ Follow Up

✉ Unread/Read

Flagging Messages and Changing Read Status

Assign a flag to a message you have received as a reminder to follow up on something. You can also flag a message for follow-up while you create it. When the follow-up is complete, clear the flag from the message. Flagged messages display with a red flag in the message header in the Content pane.

To flag a message for follow-up, select the message in the Content pane, click the Follow Up button in the Tags group on the Home tab, and then click *Flag Message* at the drop-down list. If your email account uses the POP3 mail protocol with messages downloaded to the local PC, the Follow Up drop-down list displays the options *Today, Tomorrow, This Week, Next Week, No Date*, and *Custom*.

The status of a message automatically changes to *Read* as soon as you open it or select the message with the Reading pane open and then move to another message in the message list. Marking a message as unread makes the message stand out from the other messages, which prompts you to revisit the message in the future. Select a message and then click the Unread/Read button in the Tags group on the Home tab to change the read status. The Unread/Read button toggles back and forth between *Read* and *Unread* statuses.

Exercise 9 Flagging Messages

1. With Inbox active, open a new message window.
2. Type the email address for the recipient.
3. Click in the *Subject* text box and then type Privacy and Protection Strategy.
4. Type the following text in the message window and then add your name as the sender.
   First name, [Substitute the first name of the message recipient for *First name*.]
   Let's meet next week to discuss the Social Media Privacy Tips document and work on the final draft of our essay.
5. Flag the message for follow-up by completing the following steps:
   a. Click the Follow Up button in the Tags group on the Message tab.
   b. Click *Flag Message* at the drop-down list, or click *Next Week* if that option displays for you. Outlook adds a follow-up message in the information bar above the recipient's name.

> ⚑ Follow Up ▾ — 5a
> ⚑ Flag Message
> Clear Flag
> Tags — 5b

This is the Follow Up drop-down list that displays for users with their email account set as IMAP.

This is the Follow Up drop-down list that displays for users with a POP3 mail account (messages downloaded to local device).

> ⚑ Follow Up ▾ — 5a
> ⚑ Today — 5b
> ⚑ Tomorrow
> ⚑ This Week
> | Next Week
> ⚑ No Date
> ⚑ Custom...
> 🔔 Add Reminder...
> Clear Flag

6. Print and then send the message.
7. Apply follow-up flags to messages in the Inbox folder by completing the following steps:
   a. If necessary, click to select the message header for the message with the subject text *Social Media Privacy Tips*.
   b. Click the Follow Up button in the Tags group on the Home tab.
   c. Click *Flag Message* at the drop-down list, or click *Today* if that option displays for you. Notice that a red flag appears in the message header in the Content pane.

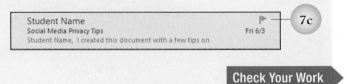

Student Name   ⚑ — 7c
Social Media Privacy Tips   Fri 6/3
Student Name, I created this document with a few tips on

Check Your Work ▸

Exercise 10 Clearing a Flag and Changing Read Status

1. With Inbox active, assume that you have finished reviewing the privacy tips document that was flagged for follow-up in the previous exercise. Clear the flag on the message by completing the following steps:

   a. If necessary, select the message header in the Content pane for the flagged message with the subject text *Social Media Privacy Tips*.

   b. Right-click the red flag in the message header to display the Flag shortcut menu and then click *Clear Flag*.

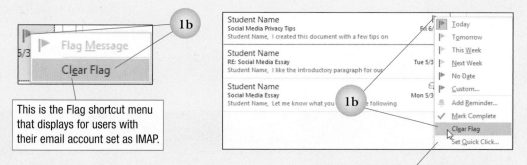

This is the Flag shortcut menu that displays for users with their email account set as IMAP.

This is the Flag shortcut menu that displays for users with a POP3 mail account and messages stored on the local device.

2. Select the message header for the message sent to you in Exercise 7 with the subject text *Social Media Project*. Assume that you want to mark this message as unread so that you are prompted to review the information again.

3. Click the Unread/Read button in the Tags group on the Home tab. The Unread/Read button toggles the read status back and forth between *Unread* and *Read* each time the button is clicked. If the message was originally marked as unread, the message is now marked as read. In that case, click the Unread/Read button a second time to mark the message as unread.

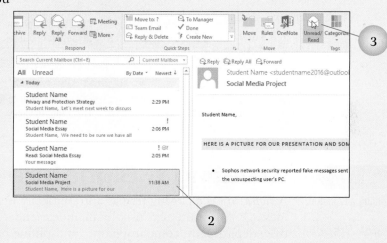

4. Double-click to open the message with the subject text *Privacy and Protection Strategy* in a message window.

5. Click the Mark Unread button in the Tags group on the Message tab.

6. Close the message window.

Flagging Messages and Changing Read Status in Outlook on the web

Flag a message by moving the mouse into the message header above the time the message was received, and then click the flag icon that appears to assign a *Today* flag. Right-click the flag icon to set a different flag. A Mark as read or Mark as unread icon appears in the same area. You can also delete the message or use the push pin icon to pin the message to the top of the list.

Click here to flag a message. Right-click to choose the flag option.

Click here to change the read status.

Flagging Messages and Changing Read Status at Outlook.com

At Outlook.com, point to a message in the message list to display the icons used to change the read status or to flag the message. Two other icons that appear are used to delete the message or pin the message to the top of the folder.

Click here to delete the message.

Click here to pin the message to the top of the folder.

You can also flag/unflag, change the read status, or pin/unpin the message from the More commands drop-down list.

Click here to change the read status.

Click here to flag the message.

Tutorial

Creating a Signature

Quick Steps

Create a Signature
1. Open message window.
2. Click Signature button in Include group on Message tab.
3. Click *Signatures*.
4. Click New button.
5. Type name for signature.
6. Click OK.
7. Type signature text and format as desired.
8. Click OK.

Signature

Creating a Signature

A *signature* is a closing that is automatically inserted at the bottom of each sent message. Signature text usually includes sender contact information, such as name, title, department, company name, and phone numbers. Some people include additional information, such as office hours, an assistant's name, and/or a security disclaimer message. Another use of signatures is to add a company logo or motto to the ends of messages.

An advantage to creating a signature is that each message contains a consistent closing. You can create multiple signatures for the different types of messages that you send. For example, create one signature for mail sent to people outside your organization that contains your complete contact information and another signature for mail sent to people within your organization that contains only your title and extension number.

To create a signature, open a message window and click the Signature button in the Include group on the Message tab. Click the *Signatures* option to open the Signatures and Stationery dialog box. Click the New button, type a name to associate with the signature text, and then click OK. Type and format the signature text in the *Edit signature* text box and then click OK.

Exercise 11 Creating a Signature

1. With Inbox active, open a new message window.
2. Click the Signature button in the Include group on the Message tab and then click *Signatures* at the drop-down list.

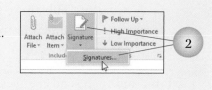

3. Create a new signature by completing the following steps:
    a. At the Signatures and Stationery dialog box with E-mail Signature the active tab, click the New button.
    b. Type External in the *Type a name for this signature* text box at the New Signature dialog box and then click OK.

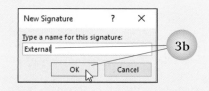

   c. Click in the *Edit signature* text box and then type the following text, substituting your name, school name, and school address for those shown:

    Student Name
    School Name
    City, State or Province ZIP Code

   d. Select the text typed in the *Edit signature* text box, click the Font button arrow, and then click *Book Antiqua* at the drop-down list.
   e. With the text still selected, click the Font Size button arrow and then click *10* at the drop-down list.
   f. With the text still selected, click the Font Color button arrow and then click *Dark Red* (first color in *Standard Colors* section) at the drop-down palette.
   g. Click to deselect the text.

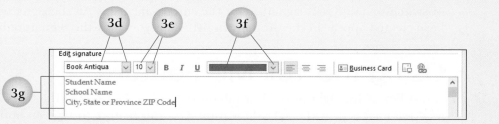

   h. Click the *New messages* option box arrow in the *Choose default signature* section of the Signatures and Stationery dialog box and then click *External* at the drop-down list.
   i. Click OK to close the Signatures and Stationery dialog box.
   j. Close the message window.

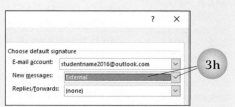

4. Create and send a message with the external signature by completing the following steps:
   a. Open a new message window. Notice that the *External* signature text is automatically inserted in the message window.
   b. Enter the email address for the recipient in the *To* text box.

c. Type Outlook Signatures in the *Subject* text box.

d. Click above the signature text in the message text box and then type the following text:

First name, [Substitute the first name of the message recipient for *First name*.]

A signature similar to the one at the bottom of this message can be created in Microsoft Word and copied and pasted into the *Edit signature* text box. Signatures can also include graphics, hyperlinks, or vCard attachments.

5. Print and then send the message.

The *External* signature is automatically added at the bottom of a new message.

Check Your Work

Open the Signatures and Stationery dialog box to create another new signature, edit the text in an existing signature, or delete a signature. Assign a different signature to replied or forwarded messages by adding the signature and then selecting the signature name at the *Replies/forwards* option box. You can also add a new signature and assign it to a different email account.

Use the Signature button in a message window to manually insert a signature or switch to a different signature for the current message. All the signatures you have created appear in the drop-down list when you click the Signature button.

Using the Tell Me Feature

Quick Steps

Use Tell Me
1. Click in *Tell Me* text box (displays *Tell me what you want to do*).
2. Type option, feature, or a short description of the task you want to do.
3. Click option in drop-down list to access the feature; open the Help task pane; or, perform a Smart Lookup.

A text box at the right of the last tab on the ribbon containing the text *Tell me what you want to do* is the Tell Me feature. Use this feature to type an option and quickly access the feature directly from the *Tell Me* text box instead of navigating the ribbon tabs. You can also use the *Tell Me* text box to type a word or phrase and search resources in a Help task pane.

Outlook 2016 Help searches the resources available from Office.com as long as you are connected to the Internet. If you are not connected to the Internet, topics from the Outlook Help feature on your computer will be displayed. The search results for Outlook Help on your computer are not as extensive as the resources available at Office.com. Click a hyperlinked topic in the search results list to navigate to an article or video on the topic. Continue using links until you find the information that you need. Use buttons at the top of the Help task pane to navigate back one topic, or search for help articles on another topic.

The Smart Lookup option on the Tell Me drop-down list opens a task pane that lets you explore Internet links related to the search term or look up a definition.

Creating a Signature in Outlook on the web

Click the Settings button (gear icon near top right of the screen) and then click *Options*. Click *Email signature* in the *Layout* section of the Options list. Create and format the signature text in the *Email signature* text box. Click the check box to automatically include the signature in new messages. Click the Save button, then click the Back arrow to close the Options list.

Creating a Signature at Outlook.com

Click the Settings button (gear icon near the top right of the screen) and then click *Options*. Click *Email signature* in the *Layout* section of the Options list and then create and format the signature text in the *Email signature* text box. Click the *Automatically include my signature on new messages I compose* check box to insert a check mark and then click the Save button. Click the Back arrow to return to messages.

Exercise 12 Using Tell Me to Learn How to Save a Message as a File

1. Search Help resources to learn how to save a message as a file by completing the following steps:
   a. Click in the *Tell Me* text box at the right of the View tab on the ribbon (displays *Tell me what you want to do*), type save message, point to *Get Help on "save message"* at the drop-down list, and then click *Save a message*.
   b. Read the paragraph below the heading *Save a message* in the Help task pane at the right side of the window.
   c. Click the link <u>Save a received message as a file</u> in the *What do you want to do?* section of the help article in the Help task pane.

d. Read the steps for saving a received message as a file. Scroll down if necessary to read the information about changing the default file format for saving messages, and then close the Help task pane when finished.
2. Click to select the message header in the Content pane with the subject text *Social Media Project*.
3. Click in the *Tell Me* text box, type save message, and then click the *Save As* option in the drop-down list. At the Save As dialog box, navigate to the drive and folder for your storage medium, and then click the Save button.
4. If necessary, press the Esc key to close the *Tell Me* text box.

Check Your Work

Chapter Summary

- Information in Outlook is organized in folders grouped by the modules Mail, Calendar, People, and Tasks. Click the module text label or icon on the Navigation bar to view the corresponding contents in the Content pane.

- Outlook can be used as an email client that is connected to an Exchange Server or Internet mail server that supports the POP3 or IMAP mail protocol.

- Use the New Email button in the New group on the Home tab to create and send an email message.

- Select a message header in the Content pane to read the message text in the Reading pane.

- Print a message using the Print button on the Quick Access Toolbar or at the Print backstage area.

- Reply to or forward a message using buttons in the Reading pane or in the Respond group on the Message tab in a message window.

- Deleted messages are moved from the current folder to the Deleted Items folder, where they remain until you empty that folder.

- Files are routinely attached to email messages. A file attached to a message can be previewed in the Reading pane or opened in Protected view in the source application.

- Use buttons on the Attachment Tools Attachments tab to manage a file attached to a message.

- Send copies of a message to other individuals using the *Cc* (carbon copy) and *Bcc* (blind carbon copy) fields. The identities of bcc recipients are kept private.

- Add the *Bcc* field to a message with the Bcc button in the Show Fields group on the Options tab in a message window.

- Select message text and apply formatting options using buttons on the Mini toolbar, Basic Text group on the Message tab, or Format Text tab of a message window.

- Embed a copy of a picture within a message or add a hyperlink using the Pictures or Hyperlink button on the Insert tab in a message window.

- Click the High Importance or Low Importance button in the Tags group on the Message tab to indicate to the recipient the message's priority. Messages tagged *High Importance* show a red exclamation point in the message header.

- Tracking options such as voting responses, delivery receipts, and read receipts are added to messages with buttons in the Tracking group on the Options tab.

- Open the Properties dialog box for a message to add additional message options, such as a private or confidential sensitivity setting, or to redirect replies to another email address.
- Flag a message for follow-up to remind yourself that it requires further action. Use the Follow Up button in the Tags group on the Home tab to flag the selected message. Flagged messages display with a red flag icon.
- Change the read status of a selected message with the Unread/Read button in the Tags group on the Home tab. Marking a message as unread is another way to make it stand out in the message list as requiring further action.
- A signature is text that is automatically added to the end of each message. Create a new signature using the Signature button in the Include group on the Message tab in a message window.
- The Tell Me feature is used to directly access a command or look up information in a Help task pane or Smart Lookup task pane.

Commands Review

FEATURE	BUTTON	RIBBON TAB AND GROUP, OR OTHER METHOD	SHORTCUT
Attach file to message		Message, Include OR Insert, Include	
Attach *High Importance* option		Message, Tags	
Change read status		Home, Tags OR Message, Tags (to mark open message as unread)	Ctrl + U (Unread) Ctrl + Q (Read)
Create new mail message		Home, New	Ctrl + N
Create new signature		File, *Options*, *Mail* OR Message, Include	
Delete message		Home, Delete	Ctrl + D, OR; Delete key
Embed picture in message		Insert, Illustrations	
Flag message		Home, Tags OR Message, Tags	
Forward message		Forward button in Reading pane; Home, Respond; OR Message, Respond	Ctrl + F
Insert hyperlink		Type valid web address then press spacebar OR Insert, Links	Ctrl + K
Open Outlook		Start menu; click icon on taskbar; OR double-click icon on desktop	
Open Properties dialog box for additional message options		Message, Tags OR Options, Tracking	
Print active message		Print button on Quick Access Toolbar OR File, *Print*	Ctrl + P

FEATURE	BUTTON	RIBBON TAB AND GROUP, OR OTHER METHOD	SHORTCUT
Reply to all recipients		Reply All button in Reading pane; Home, Respond; OR Message, Respond	Ctrl + Shift + R
Reply to message		Reply button in Reading pane; Home, Respond; OR Message, Respond	Ctrl + R
Show *Bcc* field		Options, Show Fields	
Use Tell Me feature	Tell me what you want to do	Click in *Tell me* text box	Alt + Q

Workbook

Chapter study tools and assessment activities are available in the *Workbook* pages of the ebook. These resources are designed to help you further develop and demonstrate mastery of the skills learned in this chapter.

Managing and Archiving Email Messages

Performance Objectives

Upon successful completion of Chapter 2, you will be able to:

1 Find messages using Instant Search

2 Use Search Tools to modify the scope of a search or refine search criteria

3 Create a search folder for repetitive searches

4 Arrange and sort messages in the Content pane

5 Arrange and manage messages using Conversations view

6 Apply color categories to messages

7 Create folders and move messages from one folder to another

8 Create a rule to move messages to a folder automatically

9 Modify the settings for junk email

10 Archive messages and perform mailbox maintenance

Precheck

Check your current skills to help focus your study.

Many inboxes quickly become filled with numerous messages, which makes locating a message and managing the quantity of messages time consuming. In this chapter, you will learn techniques to find messages quickly, manage messages by conversations or categories, move messages into topic-related folders, and create rules to automate message management. You will also learn about the junk email settings that will help you block a specific sender and allow legitimate mail to be placed in your inbox. In addition, you will learn about moving older messages that are no longer needed to archive folders to reduce the mailbox size. Finally, you will learn about the Mailbox Cleanup tools that can assist you in keeping your mail folders to a manageable size.

Data Files

No student data files are required for this chapter.

SNAP

If you are a SNAP user, launch the Precheck and the Tutorial from your Assignments page.

Finding Messages
Using Search Techniques

Quick Steps
Use Instant Search
1. Click in *Instant Search* box.
2. Type search word(s).
3. Review items in search results list.
Clear Search Results
Click Close Search button.

At the top of the Content pane is the *Instant Search* box that displays with the entry *Search Current Mailbox*. Instant Search is used to filter the Content pane to show only messages that meet a search criterion. To find a message in the current folder, type a keyword or phrase to identify the message in the *Instant Search* box. Outlook begins filtering the messages to show only those items that match your search text. Outlook highlights in yellow the matched search text in each message header and in the message text within the Reading pane.

To narrow the results list, type additional search words to filter out more messages. To widen the focus if the message you need to locate does not appear in the results list, delete search words. Click the Close Search button (displays as ×) at the right end of the *Instant Search* box to redisplay all messages in the Content pane.

The Instant Search feature is also part of the Windows operating system. Near the top right of all File Explorer windows, you will notice a similar *Instant Search* box that is used to locate documents, pictures, music, videos, or other types of files.

Exercise 1 Finding Messages Using Instant Search

1. With Inbox active, click in the *Instant Search* box located at the top of the Content pane that displays *Search Current Mailbox* and then type essay. Outlook displays messages in the search results list in the Content pane that contain matches to the search word. The search word is highlighted in each message header and within the Reading pane.
2. Click the Close Search button (displays as ×) located at the right of the *Instant Search* box. The Content pane is restored to show all items in the Inbox folder.

The search word is highlighted wherever it occurs in the Content pane and Reading pane.

Your search results list may vary.

3. Click in the *Instant Search* box and then type Outlook Options.
4. Click each message header that displays in the search results list and read through the message in the Reading pane, locating the highlighted words in each message. Outlook highlights matches in the *From* and *Subject* fields as well as within the message text.
5. Click the Close Search button.

Using Search Tools to Refine a Search

TIP Search results appear almost immediately as you type a search word. Outlook maintains an index in the background while you work. When you type an entry in the *Instant Search* box, Outlook consults the index rather than conducting a search of the entire folder.

You can refine the scope or criteria for a search to shorten the number of messages returned in the search results list. The Search Tools Search tab, shown in Figure 2.1, becomes active as soon as you begin typing an entry in the *Instant Search* box.

Use buttons in the Scope group to search only the current folder, to search all folders in Outlook (All Outlook Items), or to expand the search to include subfolders in the current folder. By default, the current mailbox folders are searched, but you can expand the search to include folders in other email accounts you have set up in Outlook.

Buttons in the Refine group are used to narrow the search results to specific message properties or options, as described in Table 2.1. The Recent Searches button in the Options group displays a history of your recent search requests, allowing you to locate and repeat a prior search request. Use the Search Tools button to display the indexing status of your Outlook items, to add or remove email accounts in a search, to open the Advanced Find dialog box, or to modify search options at the Outlook Options dialog box. For example, you can change the highlight color applied in the search results.

Figure 2.1 Search Tools Search Tab

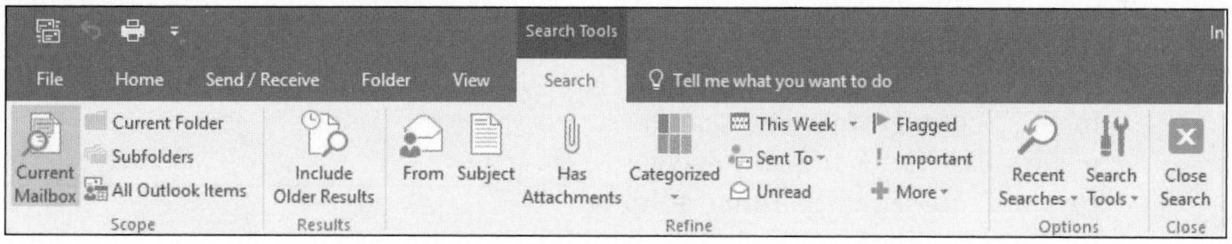

Table 2.1 Refine Group Buttons on the Search Tools Search Tab

Button	Modifies the current search to perform this function
From	Show only messages sent by a specific individual.
Subject	Restrict the search to the subject lines of the messages.
Has Attachments	Include only messages with attachments.
Categorized	Show messages assigned to a specific color category. (You will learn later in this chapter how to assign a color category to a group of related messages.)
This Week	Search messages received within a timeframe. The default is *This Week*. Use the This Week button arrow to select other timeframes, such as *Today*, *Yesterday*, *Last Week*, *This Month*, *Last Month*, *This Year*, and *Last Year*.
Sent To	Show only messages sent to a specific individual. The Sent To button drop-down list displays the options *Sent to Me or CC: Me*, *Not Sent Directly to Me*, and *Sent to Another Recipient*.
Unread	Show only unread messages.
Flagged	Show only flagged messages.
Important	Show only messages tagged with the *High Importance* option.
More	Add advanced search criteria from a list of common properties, such as *Bcc*, *Cc*, *Due Date*, *Sensitivity*, and *Message Size*.

Exercise 2 Using Search Tools to Modify a Search

1. With Inbox active, click in the *Instant Search* box located at the top of the Content pane (displays the text *Search Current Mailbox*) to display the Search Tools Search tab.
2. Practice refining the search results list using options in the Refine group on the Search Tools Search tab by completing the following steps:
   a. Click the Subject button in the Refine group and then type essay in the *Instant Search* box with *keywords* already selected within the entry *subject: "keywords"*. Only those messages with *essay* in the subject line are shown.

   b. Click the Important button in the Refine group. The list is refined further to show only messages with the *High Importance* tag from the first list.

   c. Click the Close Search button in the Close group.
3. Practice refining the search results list using options in the Scope group on the Search Tools Search tab by completing the following steps:
   a. Click in the *Instant Search* box and then type social media.

   b. Click the Current Folder button in the Scope group. The search results list shows fewer messages. In a default search, all mail folders for your mailbox are included, which means messages from *Sent Items* and *Deleted Items* are included in the search results list. By selecting Current Folder, you are limiting the search results to those messages in the Inbox folder.
   c. Click the Close Search button.

Searching Messages in Outlook on the web

The search box is located at the top of the Folder pane in Outlook on the web (displays the text *Search Mail and People*). Type search keywords in the box and then press Enter or click the Search button (magnifying glass). The Search pane replaces the Folder pane and has options to refine the search to folders or the timeframes: *All, This week, Last week, This month*, or *Select range*. Click *Exit search* to restore the full message list and Folder pane.

Searching Messages at Outlook.com

Type keyword(s) in the search box located above the folder list and then press Enter or click the Search button (magnifying glass). Refine a search using options in the search pane (left pane that replaces folder list). Options are available to restrict the search to a folder, to a person, or by a timeframe. Click *Exit search* to restore the message list and folder pane.

Using Search Folders for Repetitive Searches

New Search
Folder

Search folders provide a tool for organizing and locating messages. The search folders do not physically store messages; instead, the folders store filter and search settings. When you click the search folder name, Outlook displays in the Content pane those messages that meet the saved criteria. For example, you could create a search folder to display messages sent to you by your manager.

To create a search folder, click the Folder tab and then click the New Search Folder button in the New group. At the New Search Folder dialog box, shown in Figure 2.2, select the desired search folder option in the *Select a Search Folder* list box. Search folders are organized into four sets: *Reading Mail*, *Mail from People and Lists*, *Organizing Mail*, and *Custom*. The *Customize Search Folder* section in the New Search Folder dialog box displays further search criteria depending on the chosen search folder. For example, if you select *Mail from specific people*, the *Customize Search Folder* section displays a Choose button to select the name of the person.

Once you have created search folders, you can review updated message lists that meet the search criteria by selecting the search folder name in the Folder pane, as shown in Figure 2.3.

Quick Steps

Create a Search Folder
1. Click Folder tab.
2. Click New Search Folder button in New group.
3. Click desired search folder option.
4. If necessary, add criterion in *Customize Search Folder* section.
5. Click OK.

TIP To open the New Search Folder dialog box, you can also right-click *Search Folders* in the Folder pane and then click *New Search Folder* at the shortcut menu.

Figure 2.2 New Search Folder Dialog Box

Figure 2.3 Showing and Hiding Search Folders

Click here to show or hide the *Search Folders* list.

Messages shown in a search folder are not duplicates. A search folder is simply a saved search. Create a search folder if you repeat the same search often.

1. With Inbox active, create a search folder for high-priority messages by completing the following steps:
   a. Click the Folder tab.
   b. Click the New Search Folder button in the New group.
   c. At the New Search Folder dialog box, click *Important mail* in the *Reading Mail* section in the *Select a Search Folder* list box.
   d. Click OK. Outlook adds an Important Mail folder below Search Folders in the Folder pane and displays in the Content pane only those messages that have been tagged *High Importance*.
2. Create a second search folder for messages with attachments by completing the following steps:
   a. Right-click *Search Folders* in the Folder pane and then click *New Search Folder* at the shortcut menu.
   b. Scroll down the *Select a Search Folder* list box and then click *Mail with attachments* in the *Organizing Mail* section.
   c. Click OK. Outlook adds a With Attachments folder below the Important Mail search folder and displays in the Content pane only those messages that have files attached.
3. After you have created search folders, Outlook adds an Expand/Collapse button next to Search Folders in the Folder pane. Use the button to show or hide the *Search Folders* list by completing the following steps:
   a. Click the black, right-and-down-pointing arrow (called the *Collapse button*, which turns blue when the pointer is resting on it) next to Search Folders in the Folder pane. Outlook hides the search folders in the Folder pane. Notice that the black, right-and-down-pointing arrow changes to a white, right-pointing arrow.
   b. Click the white, right-pointing arrow (called the *Expand button*) next to Search Folders in the Folder pane. Outlook expands the folder list to show the search folders.
   c. Click *With Attachments* below Search Folders in the Folder pane.
4. Click *Inbox* in the Folder pane.

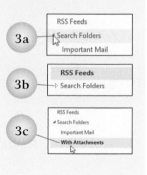

Grouping and Sorting Messages in the Content Pane

By default, Outlook displays messages in the Content pane grouped by the dates received and sorted with the most recent message at the top of the list. A Collapse button appears next to the heading for each day or other timeframe group (for example, *Today* or *Last Week*). Click the Collapse button (black, right-and-down-pointing arrow) to hide the messages for that time period. The Collapse button changes to an Expand button (white, right-pointing arrow) when messages have been collapsed. Click the Expand button to redisplay the messages below the group heading.

Click *Newest* (Sort order control) at the top of the Content pane to reorder the messages to *Oldest*. Click *Oldest* to change the sort order back to *Newest*.

Click *By Date* (Group control) at the top of the Content pane to display a drop-down list of options for grouping messages, or click the View tab and then click the desired option in the Arrangement group option box, as shown in Figure 2.4. For example, you can group the messages in the Content pane by the *From* field, which means the messages will be arranged in alphabetical order by the sender's name. Each sender's name will become a group heading with a Collapse button.

Figure 2.4 Arrangement Group on View Tab

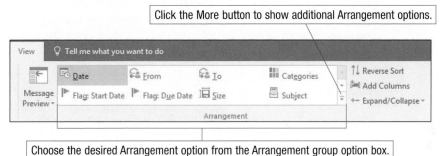

Click the More button to show additional Arrangement options.

Choose the desired Arrangement option from the Arrangement group option box.

Exercise 4 Arranging Messages in the Content Pane

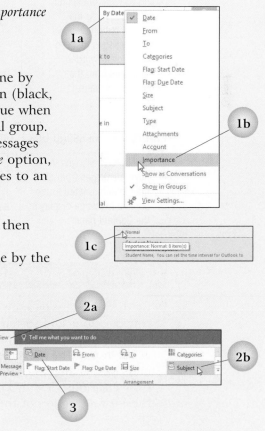

1. With Inbox active, group the messages by the *Importance* option by completing the following steps:
   a. Click *By Date* at the top of the Content pane.
   b. Click *Importance* at the drop-down list.
   c. With the messages grouped in the Content pane by the *Importance* option, click the Collapse button (black, right-and-down-pointing arrow, which turns blue when the pointer is resting on it) next to the Normal group. The Content pane now displays only those messages that have been tagged with the *High Importance* option, and the Collapse button next to *Normal* changes to an Expand button (white, right-pointing arrow).
   d. Restore the full list of messages by clicking *By Importance* at the top of the Content pane and then clicking *Date* at the drop-down list.
2. Group and sort the messages in the Content pane by the subject text by completing the following steps:
   a. Click the View tab.
   b. Click *Subject* in the Arrangement group option box. If necessary, click the More button to locate the *Subject* option. Review the new order of the messages displayed in the Content pane.
3. Click *Date* in the Arrangement group option box to restore the Content pane to the default view.

Managing Messages Using Conversations View

Quick Steps

Arrange Messages by Conversations
1. Click View tab.
2. Click *Show as Conversations* check box in Messages group.
3. Click All mailboxes or This folder button.

A *conversation* consists of a message with all replies and forwards that share the same subject line threaded to the original message. When you display the Content pane in Conversations view, each original message that has replies or forwards attached is shown with an Expand button. Expanding the conversation causes all the messages in the thread to appear below the original message, as shown in Figure 2.5.

To organize messages by conversations, click the View tab and then click the *Show as Conversations* check box in the Messages group. You are then prompted to organize the messages in all mailboxes or only in the current folder at the message box shown in Figure 2.6. Choosing All mailboxes allows the Conversations view to work similarly to a search folder, because all messages connected to the original message (regardless of which mail folder they actually reside in) are shown threaded to the original message.

Figure 2.5 Messages Grouped by Conversations

In Conversations view, each message thread is shown with an Expand button. Clicking the Expand button displays the messages that are replies or forwarded messages from the original message.

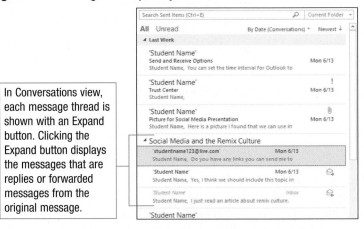

Figure 2.6 Message Box Prompting for Folders in Conversations View

Select All mailboxes to have messages from all mail folders related to the original message display in the Content pane.

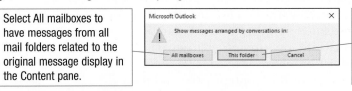

Select This folder to organize only messages in the active folder into conversations in the Content pane.

Using Conversations View in Outlook on the web

By default, messages are arranged in conversations and sorted by date in the Content pane. Click the All button arrow at the top of the message list to filter messages, change the sort order, or turn off Conversations view by clicking *Messages* in the *View as* section of the drop-down list.

Click here to display a drop-down list of view options. Click *Messages* to turn off Conversations view.

Exercise 5 Arranging Messages in Conversations

Note: To perform Steps 2 and 3 of this exercise, you must have completed Chapter 1, Assessment 1 and Assessment 2, in the workbook.

1. With Inbox active, group messages in the Sent Items folder into conversations by completing the following steps:
   a. Click *Sent Items* in the Folder pane.
   b. If necessary, click the View tab.
   c. Click to insert a check mark in the *Show as Conversations* check box in the Messages group.
   d. Click the This folder button at the Microsoft Outlook message box. Outlook arranges the Content pane to show messages that have threaded replies or forwards in groups. Each group has an Expand button next to the message header in the Content pane.

2. Locate the conversation with the subject *Social Media and the Remix Culture*. The message with the conversation thread will have an Expand button (white, right-pointing arrow) next to it in the Content pane. Click the Expand button to view the threaded messages. You may need to click the Expand button a second time to expand the list. *Note: You will not have this conversation if you did not complete Assessments 1 and 2 in the workbook for Chapter 1. In that case, skip to Step 4.*

3. Click each message in the conversation and then read the message in the Reading pane.

4. Click to remove the check mark from the *Show as Conversations* check box in the Messages group and then click the This folder button. The messages are no longer grouped by conversations.

5. Click *Inbox* in the Folder pane.

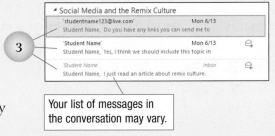

Your list of messages in the conversation may vary.

Modifying Conversation Settings

When Conversations view is active, clicking the Conversation Settings button in the Messages group on the View tab displays the drop-down list shown in Figure 2.7 on page 52. Click *Show Messages from Other Folders* to toggle the view to group conversations in other folders or only in the active folder. Click *Show Senders Above the Subject* to turn on or off the display of the sender's name above the grouped conversation's subject line. Click *Always Expand Selected Conversation* to instruct Outlook to show threaded messages without having to expand the message with the conversation thread yourself. Select *Use Classic Indented View* to have messages indented in the expanded view to show the hierarchy of the messages (the order in which you received the messages).

Figure 2.7 Conversation Settings Drop-down List

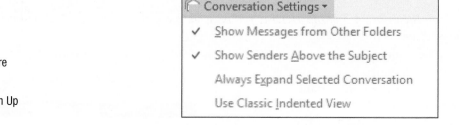

Ignore

Clean Up

Quick Steps

Clean Up a Conversation
1. Select conversation to be cleaned up.
2. Click Home tab.
3. Click Clean Up button in Delete group.
4. Click *Clean Up Conversation*.
5. Click *Clean Up*.

TIP Use the Ignore button to disregard a message that someone accidentally sent to you as part of a group email when you do not need to follow the conversation as recipients respond.

Ignoring and Deleting Messages in a Conversation

Two buttons in the Delete group on the Home tab work with conversations: Ignore and Clean Up. The Ignore button moves messages in the selected conversation to the Deleted Items folder. Future messages that are threads of the selected conversation will also be automatically placed in the Deleted Items folder. Use the Ignore button if you are copied on a message by mistake and do not want to follow the thread.

The Clean Up button displays a drop-down list with the options *Clean Up Conversation*, *Clean Up Folder*, and *Clean Up Folder & Subfolders*. Use these options to instruct Outlook to search through the selected conversation(s) and delete the messages with duplicate content. For example, assume that you sent a message to a person and he or she replied to you. Next, you replied to the person's reply and then he or she replied to your reply. By default, each reply received contains all the message thread text. Since the last message received contains the original message and all the replies that were exchanged, you really only need to save the last message. Clicking the *Clean Up Conversation* option will automatically move messages with duplicated text to the Deleted Items folder.

Exercise 6 Cleaning Up a Conversation

Note: To complete this exercise, you must have completed Chapter 1, Assessment 1 and Assessment 2, in the workbook.

1. With Inbox active, group Sent Items by conversations and then clean up a conversation to remove the duplicated messages by completing the following steps:
   a. Click *Sent Items* in the Folder pane.
   b. If necessary, click the View tab.
   c. Click to insert a check mark in the *Show as Conversations* check box in the Messages group and then click the This folder button.
   d. Expand the conversation with the subject *Social Media and the Remix Culture* (remember that you may need to click the Expand button two times to see all the messages in the conversation).

1d

Social Media and the Remix Culture

'studentname123@live.com'   Mon 6/13
Student Name, Do you have any links you can send me to

'Student Name'   Mon 6/13
Student Name, Yes, I think we should include this topic in

Student Name   Inbox
Student Name, I just read an article about remix culture.

Your list of messages in the conversation may vary.

e. With the first message selected in the *Social Media and the Remix Culture* conversation, click the Home tab.

f. Click the Clean Up button in the Delete group.

g. Click *Clean Up Conversation* at the drop-down list.

h. At the Clean Up Conversation message box, click the Clean Up button. Click OK if a second message box appears (see *Note*). Outlook moves the messages with duplicated content in the conversation to the Deleted Items folder.

Note: Click OK and then proceed to Step 3 if you receive the message informing you that no messages were cleaned up. You may or may not have duplicated content, depending on how you completed the assessments in the workbook page for Chapter 1.

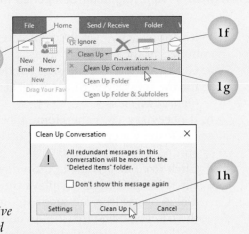

2. Click *Deleted Items* in the Folder pane. Notice the message(s) in the Conversation group with the subject *Social Media and the Remix Culture* that were moved to the Deleted Items folder.

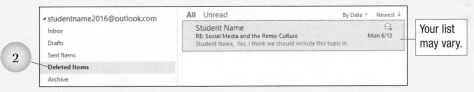

3. Click *Sent Items* in the Folder pane.
4. Click the View tab, click the *Show as Conversations* check box to remove the check mark, and then click the This folder button at the Microsoft Outlook message box.
5. Click *Inbox* in the Folder pane.

Applying Color Categories to Messages

Organize messages by assigning categories to those messages that can be grouped by a common characteristic. You can arrange the Content pane to display messages grouped by category. This allows you to view a series of related messages together. For example, you can assign a category to all messages about a project and then view the messages by arranging the Content pane by Categories view.

Outlook provides six color categories. You can assign a category to existing messages or assign a category as you are creating a new message. A category color label can be edited to provide a description of the topic to which the category relates. For example, you can rename *Blue Category* as *BEA Conference*. The same color category can be applied to other Outlook items so that related appointments, contacts, and tasks are easy to identify. The first time you apply a color category, Outlook prompts you to rename the category.

In a Message window, open the Properties dialog box and assign a color category using the Categories button near the bottom left of the dialog box.

Exercise 7 Applying Color Categories to Messages

1. With Inbox active, apply color categories to message headers in the Content pane by completing the following steps:

    a. Click to select the message header for the message with the subject text *Outlook Signatures*.

    b. If necessary, click the Home tab.

    c. Click the Categorize button in the Tags group.

    d. Click *Red category* at the drop-down list.

    e. Click No if Outlook displays the Rename Category dialog box with a message asking if you want to rename the category. The first time you use a color category, Outlook may display the Rename Category dialog box. (You will rename the categories in Step 2.) Outlook assigns Red category to the message and displays a *Red category* bar in the Reading pane and a red rectangle in the message header.

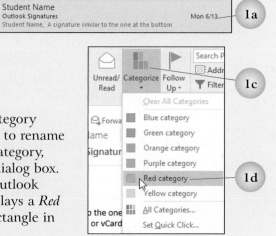

    f. Right-click any one of the message headers with the subject text *Social Media Essay*, point to *Categorize*, and then click *Blue category* at the shortcut menu. Click No if the Rename Category dialog box displays.

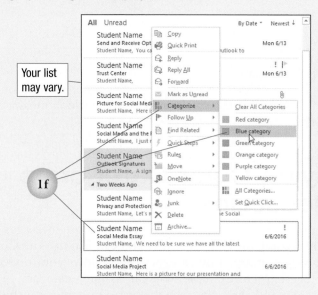

    g. Assign the Blue category to all the other messages with the subject text *Social Media Essay* by completing steps similar to Steps 1a through 1d or Step 1f. **Note:** *You will not be prompted to rename the category, since this is not the first time you are using the blue color category.*

2. Edit the labels to create descriptive titles for the color categories by completing the following steps:

    a. Click the Categorize button in the Tags group and then click *All Categories* at the drop-down list.

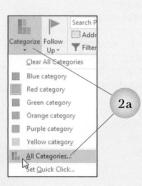

b. With *Blue category* selected in the *Name* list box, click the Rename button.

c. Type Social Media Essay and then press Enter.

d. Click *Red category* in the *Name* list box and then click the Rename button.

e. Type Outlook Tips and then press Enter.

f. Click OK. Notice that the colored category bar in the Reading pane for the selected message now displays the descriptive label for the color category.

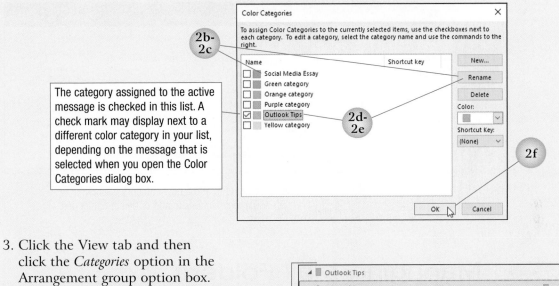

The category assigned to the active message is checked in this list. A check mark may display next to a different color category in your list, depending on the message that is selected when you open the Color Categories dialog box.

3. Click the View tab and then click the *Categories* option in the Arrangement group option box.

4. Review the arrangement of messages in the Content pane. Notice that all the messages you assigned the blue color category are grouped in an expanded list with the heading *Social Media Essay* next to a blue rectangle. The message assigned the red color category is grouped and shown expanded below the heading *Outlook Tips*. Messages with no color category assigned are displayed at the top of the list.

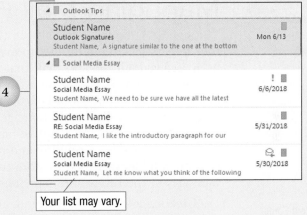

Your list may vary.

5. Restore the messages back to the default date arrangement by clicking the *Date* option in the Arrangement group option box on the View tab.

Applying Categories to Messages in Outlook on the web

Right-click a message in the Content pane and then assign a color category from the *Categorize* option on the shortcut menu. You can also select the message in the Content pane, click the Categories button at the top of the Reading pane, and then click the desired color category.

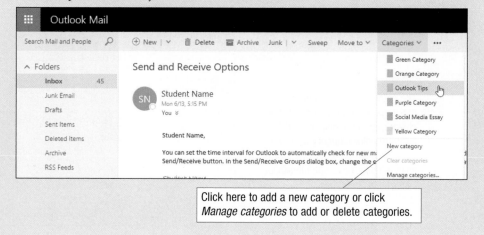

Applying Categories to Messages at Outlook.com

The same color categories used in the desktop version of Outlook can be assigned to a message at Outlook.com. Click a message header to open the message and display message options in the Menu bar. Click the Categories button and then click the desired color category. Color categories renamed in the desktop edition carry over to Outlook.com.

Click here to add a new category or click *Manage categories* to add or delete categories.

Tutorial

Managing Mail Folders

Managing Mail Folders

Throughout Chapter 1 and also in this chapter, you have been working with four folders set up in Outlook to organize mail messages: Inbox for mail that has been received, Outbox for mail that has been created but not yet uploaded to the mail server, Sent Items for messages that have been uploaded to the server and delivered to recipients, and Deleted Items for messages that have been deleted. Frequently, you will want to manage messages by putting related items in a separate folder with a descriptive name. For example, if you are working on a large project and have been sending and receiving several messages about it, consider creating a folder in which to store those messages separately from the other messages in the Inbox and Sent Items folders.

Creating a folder and then moving related messages to it organizes the messages in a separate container. Selecting the folder name in the Folder pane allows you to view the group or project messages independently from other messages.

Expanding Folders and Creating a New Folder

The folder list in the Folder pane displays the names of the Outlook mail folders in a hierarchical arrangement. A white, right-pointing arrow (Expand button) next to a folder name in the list indicates that the folder contains subfolders. Click the Expand button to show the names of the subfolders.

Complete the following steps to create a new folder or subfolder:

1. Right-click the name of the Outlook folder in the Folder pane in which you want the new folder created as a subfolder. For example, right-click *Inbox* if you want to create a new subfolder within the Inbox folder.
2. Click *New Folder* at the shortcut menu.
3. Type the name for the new folder and then press Enter.

Quick Steps

Create a Folder
1. Right-click name of Outlook folder in which to create new subfolder.
2. Click *New Folder*.
3. Type name for new folder.
4. Press Enter.
OR
1. Click Folder tab.
2. Click New Folder button in New group.
3. Type name for new folder.
4. Select name of folder in which to place new folder.
5. Click OK.

New Folder

To create a new folder using the ribbon, click the New Folder button in the New group on the Folder tab. This opens the Create New Folder dialog box, shown in Figure 2.8. Type the name for the new folder in the *Name* text box and then click the name of the folder in which the new folder should be placed. For example, to create a new folder as a subfolder in the Inbox, click *Inbox* in the *Select where to place the folder* list box and then click OK. To create the new folder at the same level in the folder hierarchy as Inbox, click the email account name at the top of the folder list.

Figure 2.8 Create New Folder Dialog Box

Moving Messages

Before you move messages, expand the folders in the Folder pane if necessary. Once you have created new folders in which to organize messages, Outlook provides several methods for moving messages from one folder to another:

- With the message headers selected in the Content pane, drag the message headers from their current location to the desired folder name in the Folder pane.

Move

- With the message headers selected in the Content pane, click the Move button in the Move group on the Home tab and then click the desired folder name at the drop-down list.
- With one or more message headers selected in the Content pane, right-click one of the selected headers, point to *Move* at the shortcut menu, and then click the desired folder name. Click *Other Folder* if the desired folder name does not appear in the list of folders. At the Move Items dialog box, select the destination folder name in the *Move the selected items to* list box and then click OK.
- Select the message headers in the Content pane and then click the Move to button (first button) in the Quick Steps group on the Home tab. The Move to button displays a folder name if the button has already been assigned to a folder.

The first time the Move to button in the Quick Steps group is used, the First Time Setup dialog box opens. At the dialog box, click the *Move to folder* option box arrow (displays *Choose folder*), click the desired folder name, or click *Other Folder* and then double-click the desired folder name in the Select Folder dialog box. Click Save when finished. The Move to button displays the folder name. The next time you need to move a message to the same folder, select the message and then click the folder name button in the Quick Steps group.

To change the destination folder displayed on the Move to button in the Quick Steps group, display the shortcut menu for the button and then click *Edit [folder name]*. At the Edit Quick Step dialog box, click the current folder name option box, click the desired folder, or click *Other Folder* and then double-click the desired folder name at the Select Folder dialog box. Click the Save button when finished.

Multiple messages can be moved in one operation with a mouse by using the multiple select keys Ctrl + click for messages that are not next to each other in the message list, and Shift + click for messages next to each other in the message list.

Exercise 8 Creating a New Folder and Moving Messages

1. With Inbox active, create a subfolder within the Inbox folder by completing the following steps:
   a. Click the Folder tab and then click the New Folder button in the New group.
   b. At the Create New Folder dialog box with the insertion point positioned in the *Name* text box, type Social Media.
   c. With *Folder contains* already set to *Mail and Post Items* and *Inbox* already selected in the *Select where to place the folder* list box, click OK.
2. Move messages from the Inbox folder to the Social Media folder by completing the following steps:
   a. Select the message header in the Content pane for the first message assigned the blue *Social Media Essay* category.
   b. Hold down the Ctrl key and click each additional message header assigned the blue *Social Media Essay* category. If you click a message by mistake, click the message header a second time while holding down the Ctrl key and the message will be deselected. If you are using a tablet with a touchscreen and cannot select multiple messages, proceed to Step 2c and move each message individually.
   c. Drag the selected message headers from the Content pane to the *Social Media* folder name in the Folder pane. If you are using a tablet with a touchscreen, you may need to slide each message header individually to the *Social Media* folder name.

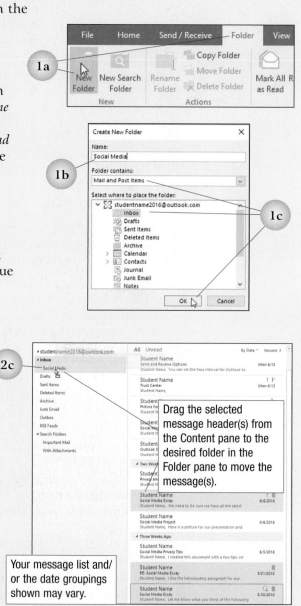

Drag the selected message header(s) from the Content pane to the desired folder in the Folder pane to move the message(s).

Your message list and/or the date groupings shown may vary.

3. Move a message to the Social Media folder using the Move to button by completing the following steps:

a. If necessary, select the message header for the message with the subject text *Social Media Privacy Tips* and then click the Home tab.

b. Click the Move to: ? button in the Quick Steps group. ***Note:*** *Your button may display a folder name instead of* Move to: ? *if this feature has already been used. In that case, right-click the folder name button and then click* Edit [folder name] *at the shortcut menu.*

c. The First Time Setup or Edit Quick Step dialog box opens. For the First Time Setup dialog box, click the *Move to folder* option box arrow (the box currently displays *Choose folder*), click *Social Media* at the drop-down list, and then click the Save button. For the Edit Quick Step dialog box, click the folder name's option box arrow, click *Social Media*, and then click the Save button.

d. Look at the first button in the Quick Steps group. Notice that the Move to button now displays *Social Media* next to the folder icon.

e. With the *Social Media Privacy Tips* message still selected, click the Social Media button in the Quick Steps group. The message is moved to the Social Media folder.

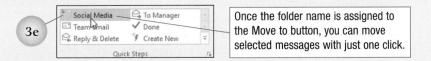

Once the folder name is assigned to the Move to button, you can move selected messages with just one click.

4. Click *Social Media* in the Folder pane to view the folder contents.

5. Click *Inbox* to make Inbox the active folder. Notice that the quantity of messages you need to manage in the Inbox is much smaller now that you have moved messages to a subfolder.

📧 Managing Messages in Outlook on the web

Right-click the mailbox name in the Folder pane, to create a new folder. Move messages by dragging message headers from the Content pane to folder names as described in Exercise 8, Step 2. Right-click a folder name instead of the mailbox name to create a subfolder. For example, to create a subfolder from Inbox, right-click *Inbox* and then click *Create new subfolder* at the shortcut menu.

Create new folder
Rename
Delete
Empty folder
Add to Favorites
Move...

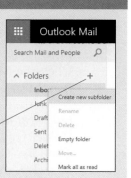
TIP Set aside a time on the same day each week to clean up your Inbox by deleting unneeded messages and moving messages to folders. Doing this will help to keep your Inbox a manageable size. If you receive several emails a day you may need to do this more than once per week.

A common method used to manage mail messages is to organize messages in folders in a similar manner to how you organize documents on your hard disk or storage medium. Create folders and/or subfolders and routinely move related messages from the Inbox to these other folders. Use the buttons in the Actions group on the Folder tab to manage folders. Options include renaming, copying, moving, and deleting folders.

Make deleting messages when they are no longer needed and emptying the Deleted Items folder part of your message management routine. Consider that in a month's time (assuming a standard five-day work week), the number of messages in your Inbox will grow to 200 if you receive 10 messages a day, and after five months, you will be trying to manage over 1,000 messages!

Creating a Rule to Move Messages to a Folder Automatically

Quick Steps

Create a Rule
1. Select message header that meets condition.
2. Click Rules button in Move group on Home tab.
3. Click *Create Rule*.
4. Change condition options as required.
5. Click *Move the item to folder* check box.
6. If necessary, expand folder list.
7. Click desired folder name.
8. Click OK three times.

 Rules

A *rule* is an action that is performed on messages based on a condition that you specify. Rules can be created that instruct Outlook to move messages to specific folders automatically. The condition that makes the messages move can be based on a name, a subject, or a message setting such as the *Importance* option.

The easiest method for creating a rule based on a sender's name or subject is to select a message in the Content pane that meets the condition, click the Rules button in the Move group on the Home tab, and then click *Create Rule* at the drop-down list. Outlook opens the Create Rule dialog box, where you can choose the condition and the action you want performed. Information from the active message is inserted next to the appropriate Create Rule condition options, as shown in Figure 2.9.

Figure 2.9 Create Rule Dialog Box

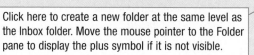

Exercise 9 Creating a New Folder and Message Rule

1. With Inbox the active folder, create a new subfolder within Inbox by completing the following steps:
    a. Right-click *Inbox* in the Folder pane and then click *New Folder* at the shortcut menu.
    b. Type Outlook Tips in the blank text box that appears below *Inbox* in the Folder pane and then press Enter.

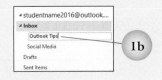

2. Create a rule to move messages received in the Inbox that have information about using the Outlook application to the Outlook Tips folder by completing the following steps:
    a. Select the message header in the Content pane with the subject *Outlook Signatures*.
    b. Click the Rules button in the Move group on the Home tab and then click *Create Rule* at the drop-down list.
    c. Click to insert a check mark in the *Subject contains* check box in the *When I get Email with all of the selected conditions* section in the Create Rule dialog box.
    d. Click to place an insertion point in the *Subject contains* text box and then delete the word *Signatures* so that the entry in the text box consists of only the word *Outlook*.
    e. Click to insert a check mark in the *Move the item to folder* check box in the *Do the following* section in the Create Rule dialog box.
    f. Click the Select Folder button. At the Rules and Alerts dialog box, click the Expand button next to *Inbox* in the *Choose a folder* list box, click *Outlook Tips*, and then click OK. This will place the text *Outlook Tips* in the *Move the item to folder* text box in the Create Rule dialog box.
    g. Click OK at the Create Rule dialog box to complete the rule.

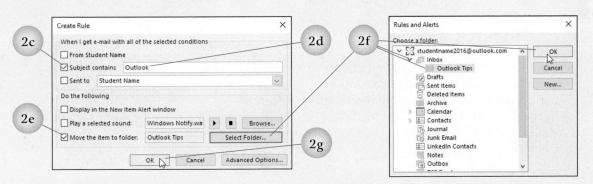

    h. Click OK at the Success message box indicating that the rule has been created.

3. New rules that are created are applied automatically to messages as they are received. Manually apply the message rule created in Step 2 to existing messages in the Inbox by completing the following steps:
   a. Click the Rules button in the Move group and then click *Manage Rules & Alerts* at the drop-down list.
   b. At the Rules and Alerts dialog box with the Email Rules tab active, click the Run Rules Now button.

3b

Click a rule in the *Rule* list box to view a description of the condition and the action that will be performed. You can also edit a rule by clicking the blue underlined condition or action and changing the rule's parameters.

   c. At the Run Rules Now dialog box, click to insert a check mark in the *Outlook* check box in the *Select rules to run* list box and then click the Run Now button. Outlook applies the rule to the existing messages and moves messages that meet the specified condition.

3c

   d. Click the Close button to close the Run Rules Now dialog box.
   e. Click OK to close the Rules and Alerts dialog box.

3d

4. Click *Outlook Tips* in the Folder pane to view the folder contents. Notice that Outlook moved the message with the subject *Outlook Signatures* to the Outlook Tips folder. In the future, any message received with the word *Outlook* in the subject field will be placed in the Outlook Tips folder automatically.
5. Click *Inbox* to make Inbox the active folder.

TIP Consider creating a rule that will move messages received from your manager to an Action folder so important messages from him or her are not lost in your Inbox.

Creating rules is a powerful message management tool for controlling the size of your Inbox. If you receive many messages in a day and several that are related in some way, consider creating folders and rules to direct the messages to specific locations where you can easily view and manage the content. Outlook displays folder names that have new messages in bold and indicates a count of the unread emails in blue text in the folder list. When using rules to automatically direct messages to folders, periodically look at the folder list to see if you have new email that needs to be read.

Open the New inbox rule panel by right-clicking a message header that meets your condition for a new rule and then clicking *Create rule*.

Type a name for the rule in the *Name* text box. Select the appropriate options in the *When the message arrives, and it matches all of these conditions*, and the *Do all of the following* sections. Click OK when finished, then click Back.

To manage rules, click the Settings button (gear icon near top right of screen), click *Options* at the drop-down list, and then click *Inbox and sweep rules* at the Options pane.

✓ OK   ✗ Cancel
New inbox rule
Name
It was received from...
When the message arrives, and it matches all of these conditions *
It was received from... ▼   Student Name
It was sent to... ▼   Leslie Taylor
It includes these words in the subject... ▼   Outlook Signatures
Add condition
Do all of the following *
Move the message to folder... ▼   Select one...
Add action
Except if it matches any of these conditions
Add exception
✓ Stop processing more rules (What does this mean?)

Display the New inbox rule panel by clicking the Settings button (gear icon located near the right end of the Outlook Mail banner), clicking *Options* at the drop-down list, clicking *Inbox and sweep rules* in the *Mail* section of the Options pane, and then clicking the Add button (plus symbol).

Type a name for the new rule in the *Name* text box and then select the appropriate options in the *When the message arrives, and it matches all of these conditions* and the *Do all of the following* sections. Click OK when finished, and then click the Back button to close the Options pane.

🖫 OK   ✗ Cancel
New inbox rule
Name
When the message arrives, and it matches all of these conditions
Select one... ▼
Add condition
Do all of the following
Select one... ▼
Add action
Except if it matches any of these conditions
Add exception
✓ Stop processing more rules (What does this mean?)

Creating a New Rule Using the Rules Wizard

In Exercise 9, the new rule was created by selecting a message header for a message that met the condition. In some cases, you may want to create a new rule from scratch. The Rules Wizard, shown in Figure 2.10 on page 64, helps you to create a new rule based on templates for the most frequently used rules grouped into two types: organization and notification.

Templates in the *Stay Organized* section help you move messages to folders or follow up on messages that require further action. For example, if a message arrives in your Inbox with a certain project name in the subject text, you can have it automatically flagged for follow up and moved to a project folder. Templates in the *Stay Up to Date* section prompt you with a notification alert when a certain type of message arrives in your Inbox. For example, a message can be automatically sent to your smartphone if a message from your manager arrives in your Inbox.

Complete the following steps to create a new rule using the Rules Wizard:

1. Click the File tab.
2. Click the Manage Rules & Alerts button at the backstage area.
3. Click the New Rule button in the Rules and Alerts dialog box with the Email Rules tab active.
4. Select the rule template and customize the rule description at the Rules Wizard dialog box, shown below. Use the Next button in the Rules Wizard to specify multiple conditions and/or exceptions to the rule and to assign a name for the rule.
5. Click Finish when you are done.

Figure 2.10 The Rules Wizard

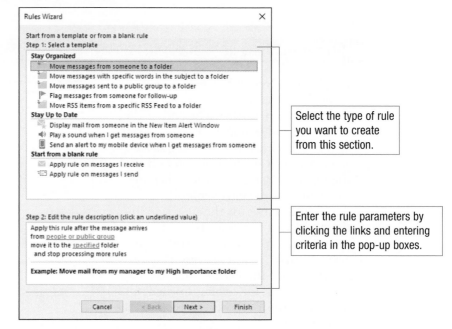

Understanding the Junk Email and Phishing Filters

You have probably noticed the Junk Email folder in the Folder pane. It is a good idea to check this folder periodically to review its contents and see if legitimate messages have been moved to Junk Email by mistake. In an attempt to protect you from spam and malicious phishing messages, Outlook automatically screens all new messages as they are received. Messages that are deemed to be spam are moved to the Junk Email folder, and you are prompted that this action has taken place. Messages that are deemed to be phishing are placed in the Inbox but have attachments, links, and Reply and Reply to All buttons disabled.

Managing Messages that Junk Email Filters Mishandle

Messages that appear in your Inbox that are not screened correctly by the junk email filters can be marked as junk so that future messages from the same sender are moved to the Junk Email folder. To do this, select the message that was missed by the junk filters, click the Junk button in the Delete group on the Home tab, and then click *Block Sender* at the drop-down list.

At times, legitimate messages are routed to the Junk Email folder by mistake. When that happens, select the message in the Junk Email folder, click the Junk button in the Delete group on the Home tab, and then click *Never Block Sender*, *Never Block Sender's Domain (@example.com)*, or *Never Block this Group or Mailing List* at the drop-down list.

Modifying Junk Email Filter Settings

Quick Steps

Change Junk Email Filter Settings
1. Click Junk button in Delete group on Home tab.
2. Click *Junk E-mail Options.*
3. Change options as required.
4. Click OK.

By default, junk email protection is set to *Low*, which moves the most obvious spam messages to the Junk Email folder. This setting also moves messages from blocked senders to the Junk Email folder. Junk filters work on two levels: first, lists of email addresses and Internet domains known to be associated with spam or malware, and second, artificial intelligence technology that evaluates a message based on factors such as the time sent and keywords within the message that indicate a high probability of spam.

To view and/or change the filter settings, click the Junk button in the Delete group on the Home tab and then click *Junk E-mail Options* at the drop-down list. Doing so opens the Junk Email Options dialog box, shown in Figure 2.11.

With the Options tab selected, you can change the protection level from *Low* to *No Automatic Filtering, High,* or *Safe Lists Only*. You can also choose to have messages identified as junk email permanently deleted instead of moved to the Junk Email folder.

Figure 2.11 Junk Email Options Dialog Box with Options Tab Selected

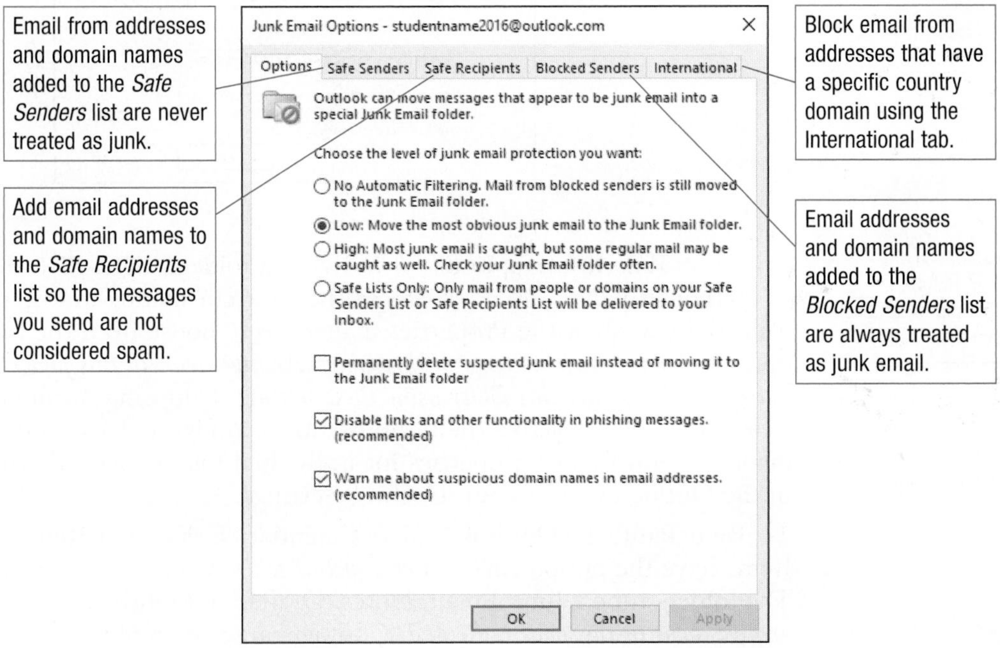

TIP A new feature in Outlook 2016 for Office 365 subscribers only is called *Clutter*. Once Clutter is turned on, the program keeps track of messages you don't open. As new email arrives in the Inbox, messages that you are likely to ignore are moved into the Clutter folder automatically. The program adjusts its settings when you move a message into or out of the Clutter folder.

Email from addresses and domain names added to the *Safe Senders* list are never treated as junk.

Add email addresses and domain names to the *Safe Recipients* list so the messages you send are not considered spam.

Block email from addresses that have a specific country domain using the International tab.

Email addresses and domain names added to the *Blocked Senders* list are always treated as junk email.

Junk Email Options - studentname2016@outlook.com

Options | Safe Senders | Safe Recipients | Blocked Senders | International

Outlook can move messages that appear to be junk email into a special Junk Email folder.

Choose the level of junk email protection you want:

○ No Automatic Filtering. Mail from blocked senders is still moved to the Junk Email folder.

◉ Low: Move the most obvious junk email to the Junk Email folder.

○ High: Most junk email is caught, but some regular mail may be caught as well. Check your Junk Email folder often.

○ Safe Lists Only: Only mail from people or domains on your Safe Senders List or Safe Recipients List will be delivered to your Inbox.

☐ Permanently delete suspected junk email instead of moving it to the Junk Email folder

☑ Disable links and other functionality in phishing messages. (recommended)

☑ Warn me about suspicious domain names in email addresses. (recommended)

OK | Cancel | Apply

Archiving Folders

Quick Steps

**Change Global
AutoArchive Settings**
1. Click File tab.
2. Click *Options*.
3. Click *Advanced*.
4. Click AutoArchive
   Settings button.
5. Change settings as
   required.
6. Click OK two times.

Over time, your mail folders grow larger in size due to the accumulation of stored messages. If you use email for essential records of transactions, agreements, plans, or other details, you should archive the messages instead of deleting them. An ***archive*** is a file containing old messages that have been purged from the mail folder. The archived messages can be retrieved, if necessary, by expanding the archive folder that displays in the Content pane when an archive file has been opened.

You can manually transfer old items to the archive file or you can turn on and then rely on the global AutoArchive feature to have Outlook transfer the items automatically. Items are considered for archiving when they reach a specified age. When active, the default setting is for AutoArchive to run every 14 days and clean out items that are older than six months. You can change the AutoArchive options for each Outlook folder. AutoArchive can either delete items or move old items to the storage file. The default setting moves old items to a file named *archive.pst*.

To turn on and/or change the default options for AutoArchive, click the File tab and then click *Options* to display the Outlook Options dialog box. Click *Advanced* in the left pane and then click the AutoArchive Settings button. In the AutoArchive dialog box, shown in Figure 2.12, change the options as required and then click OK.

TIP When activated, AutoArchive runs automatically whenever you start Outlook and prompts you to act on archiving messages after 14 days.

Figure 2.12 AutoArchive Dialog Box

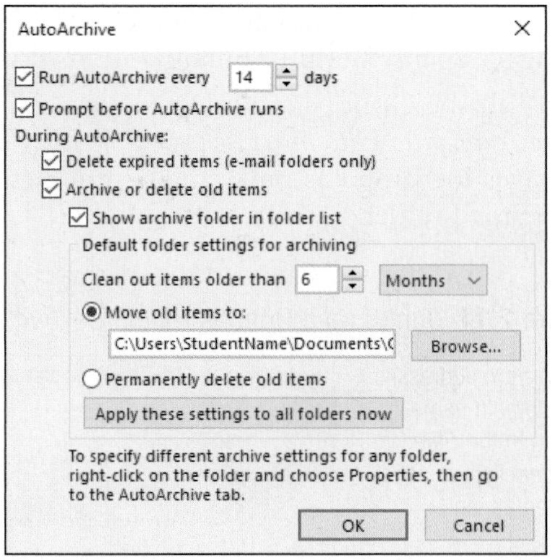

TIP Before archiving, clean out from mail folders any messages that do not need to be retained, to avoid storing messages unnecessarily.

To set *AutoArchive* options for individual folders, right-click the folder name in the Folder pane, click *Properties* at the shortcut menu, and then click the AutoArchive tab at the Properties dialog box. Choose from the following three options: *Do not archive items in this folder, Archive items in this folder using the default settings*, and *Archive this folder using these settings*. Choosing *Archive this folder using these settings* makes active the options shown in Figure 2.13 on page 67. Changes made to AutoArchive properties for individual folders override the global settings in the Outlook Options AutoArchive Settings.

By default, the Outlook folders Calendar, Tasks, Sent Items, and Deleted Items have the option *Archive items in this folder using the default settings* selected. The folders Inbox, Junk Email, Notes, Drafts, and Outbox have the option *Do not archive items in this folder* selected. Contacts are not archived.

Figure 2.13 Inbox Properties Dialog Box with AutoArchive Tab Selected

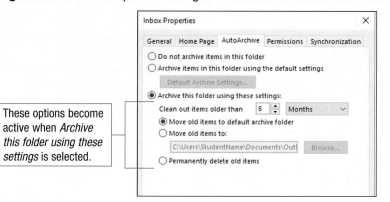

TIP In a business environment, email messages must be saved according to the record retention rules that apply to any other business document. Check with your manager before manually archiving messages, in case a corporate archive system is already in place and personal archiving will violate the company's security policies.

These options become active when *Archive this folder using these settings* is selected.

 Archive

 Tools

Quick Steps

Perform a Manual Archive

1. Click to select message(s).
2. Click Archive button in Delete group on Home tab.

OR

1. Click File tab.
2. Click Tools button at backstage area.
3. Click *Clean Up Old Items*.
4. If necessary, click *Archive this folder and all subfolders*.
5. Click folder name to archive.
6. Enter date in *Archive items older than* text box.
7. Click Browse button.
8. Navigate to drive and/or folder and type archive file name.
9. Click OK two times.

Manually Archiving Items

To move an individual message to the Archive folder, select the message header in the Content pane and then click the Archive button in the Delete group on the Home tab. You can also select multiple messages and move them in one step. Note that when you archive items manually, the size of your mailbox file is not reduced.

To have Outlook perform an archive by examining messages during a specified timeframe, click the File tab, click the Tools button at the backstage area, and then click *Clean Up Old Items* at the drop-down list to open the Archive dialog box, shown in Figure 2.14. Click *Archive all folders according to their AutoArchive settings* to archive all folders based on each folder's AutoArchive properties, or click *Archive this folder and all subfolders* to choose the folder and timeframe you want to process. For the latter option, you next click the folder name in the folders list box, change the date in the *Archive items older than* text box, and use the Browse button to specify the drive, folder, and file name for the archive file. Clicking OK starts the archive process. Click the Back button to close the backstage area.

The Status bar displays the message *Archiving [folder name]* near the right end of the Status bar as messages are archived. You will also see the messages in the folder being removed if the folder is active in the Content pane.

Figure 2.14 Archive Dialog Box

Archive	×
○ Archive all folders according to their AutoArchive settings	
● Archive this folder and all subfolders:	
˅ ✖ studentname2016@outlook.com	
> Inbox	
Drafts	
Sent Items	
Deleted Items	
Archive	
> Calendar	
> Contacts	
Journal	
Junk Email	

Archive items older than: Thu 5/10/2018

☐ Include items with "Do not AutoArchive" checked

Archive file:

C:\Users\StudentName\Documents\OutlookAr

[OK]   [Cancel]

Exercise 10 Turning On AutoArchive Settings and Manually Archiving Sent Items

1. With Inbox active, check the global AutoArchive settings on the computer you are using by completing the following steps:
   a. Click the File tab and then click *Options* in the left pane at the backstage area.
   b. Click *Advanced* in the left pane at the Outlook Options dialog box.
   c. Click the AutoArchive Settings button in the *AutoArchive* section.

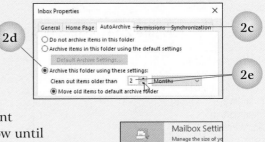

   d. Click to insert a check mark in the *Run AutoArchive every [ ] days* check box to turn AutoArchive on. **Note:** *Skip this step if the option is already active.*
   e. Review the default AutoArchive settings with AutoArchive active. For example, note that with the AutoArchive feature turned on, the default option prompts you before AutoArchive cleans out items that are older than six months.
   f. Click OK to close the AutoArchive dialog box and then click OK to close the Outlook Options dialog box.
2. View and change AutoArchive settings for the Inbox folder by completing the following steps:
   a. Right-click *Inbox* in the Folder pane.
   b. Click *Properties* at the shortcut menu.
   c. Click the AutoArchive tab at the Inbox Properties dialog box. The default AutoArchive option for this folder is *Do not archive items in this folder*.
   d. Click *Archive this folder using these settings* to make it active. **Note:** *Skip this step if the option is already active.*
   e. Click the *Clean out items older than* measurement box increment (up) or decrement (down) arrow until the number *2* appears in the box.
   f. Click OK.
3. Manually archive the Sent Items folder by completing the following steps:
   a. Click the File tab.
   b. Click the Tools button and then click *Clean Up Old Items* at the drop-down list.

c. If necessary, click *Archive this folder and all subfolders* at the Archive dialog box to make that option active.

d. Click *Sent Items* in the folder list box.

e. Click the *Archive items older than* option box arrow and then click a date in the drop-down calendar that is two days before the current date.

f. Click the Browse button. At the Open Outlook Data Files dialog box, navigate to the drive for your storage medium, select and delete the current file name in the *File name* text box, and then type SentItemsArchive-YourName-[CurrentDate] where *[CurrentDate]* is replaced by today's date and your first and last names are substituted for *YourName*.

g. Click OK to close the Open Outlook Data Files dialog box.

h. Click OK to close the Archive dialog box. Depending on the number of messages in Sent Items, archiving may take a few moments to complete.

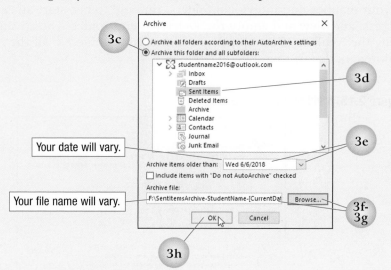

4. Click the Back button at the backstage area. Notice the new *archives* entry in the Folder pane.

5. Display Sent Items in the Content pane. Only messages sent in the last two days are shown; the list may be empty if you have not sent any messages in the last two days.

6. Click the Expand button next to *archives* in the Folder pane. The list expands and displays a Sent Items folder. Notice also that Outlook added Deleted Items and Search Folders folders.

7. Click *Sent Items* in the expanded folder list below *archives* in the Folder pane. Outlook displays in the Content pane the messages that were moved from the main Sent Items folder in Step 3. *Note: The Content pane may be empty if you do not have messages in your Sent Items folder that are more than two days old. If that is the case, return to Step 3 and redo the steps, changing the date at Step 3e to today's date.*

8. Make Inbox the active folder.

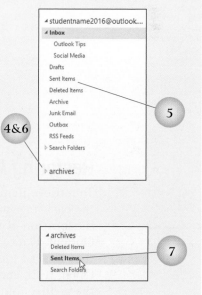

If you create an archive file on your computer's hard drive, make a copy of the archive on a removable storage medium (such as an external hard drive or USB drive) for backup and record retention purposes. Alternatively, consider saving a copy of the archive in cloud storage (such as OneDrive), where the file can be accessed from any device with an Internet connection. Email archiving and records management are critical functions in today's workplace, which relies on email for transactions, instructions, meeting notes, and other communications.

Using the Mailbox Cleanup Tool

Click the File tab, click the Tools button at the backstage area, and then click *Mailbox Cleanup* at the drop-down list to open the Mailbox Cleanup dialog box, shown in Figure 2.15. From this dialog box, you can view the current sizes of your mailbox and individual folders, find old items, start an AutoArchive process, and view and empty the Deleted Items folder. The advantage of using the Mailbox Cleanup feature is that you can access all the mail folder maintenance tools from one dialog box.

Figure 2.15 Mailbox Cleanup Dialog Box

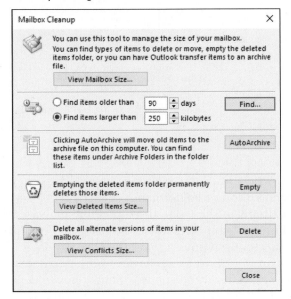

Restoring Archived Items

To retrieve items saved in an archive file, click the File tab, click *Open & Export* at the backstage area, and then click the Open Outlook Data File button. Browse to the location of the archive file and then double-click the file name at the Open Outlook Data File dialog box. Expand *archives* in the Folder pane and then click the name of the folder in the expanded list that contains the archived messages. Open, read, and print messages as required. You can also copy or move items from the archive folder to current folders if necessary.

When finished, right-click *archives* in the Folder pane and then click *Close "Archives"* at the shortcut menu.

Chapter Summary

- Find messages by typing a keyword or phrase in the *Instant Search* box at the top of the Content pane. Buttons in the Scope and Refine groups on the Search Tools Search tab are used to reduce the number of messages in the search results.

- A search folder stores search settings and is used for searches that are often repeated. Create a new search folder using the New Search Folder button in the New group on the Folder tab or by selecting *New Search Folder* from the *Search Folders* shortcut menu.

- Messages in the Content pane are grouped by date, with the most recent messages placed at the top of the list by default.

- Click *By Date* at the top of the Content pane to change how messages are grouped and sorted, or select an option from the Arrangement group option box on the View tab.

- In Conversations view, Outlook groups the original message with all the threaded replies and forwarded messages. Insert a check mark in the *Show as Conversations* check box on the View tab and then choose the current folder or all mailboxes to group messages by conversations.

- The Conversation Settings button in the Messages group on the View tab provides options for grouping and displaying conversations.

- Ignoring a conversation means that current and future messages in the thread are deleted.

- The Clean Up button in the Delete group on the Home tab automatically analyzes all the messages in a conversation and deletes duplicated messages.

- Apply color categories to messages as a method of organizing related messages.

- Create new folders to organize related messages. Folders can be created as subfolders within existing folders.

- Move messages by dragging them from the Content pane to other folder names in the Folder pane.

- A *rule* stores conditions that instruct Outlook to move messages to a specific folder as soon as they are received. Create a new rule based on an existing message that meets the condition or by using the Rules Wizard.

- Outlook automatically screens new messages and moves messages considered spam to the Junk Email folder. Junk email filters work on two levels: first, lists of email addresses and Internet domains known to be spam or malware, and second, artificial intelligence that indicates a message is likely to be spam or phishing.

- A message that is not handled properly by the junk email filters can be redirected by selecting the message and using options from the Junk button in the Delete group on the Home tab and/or by modifying options in the Junk Email Options dialog box.

- An archive is a file containing old items that have been purged from the active folder. Use the AutoArchive dialog box to set global archive options. Individual folders can have their own AutoArchive options.

- Perform a manual archive by selecting a message and then clicking the Archive button in the Delete group on the Home tab, or by opening the Archive dialog box from the Tools button at the backstage area.

- The Mailbox Cleanup dialog box provides all folder maintenance features in one location.

- Open an Archive file to view, print, and/or restore an archived message.

Commands Review

FEATURE	BUTTON	RIBBON TAB AND GROUP, OR OTHER METHOD	SHORTCUT
Archive messages	OR	Home, Delete OR File, Tools	
Arrange messages		View, Arrangement OR click *By Date* at top of Content pane	
Assign color category		Home, Tags	
Change AutoArchive settings		File, *Options*, *Advanced*	
Clean up conversation		Home, Delete	
Create message rule		Home, Move OR File, Manage Rules & Alerts	
Create new folder		Folder, New Folder	Ctrl + Shift + E
Find message		Click in *Instant Search* box	Ctrl + E
Ignore conversation		Home, Delete	Ctrl + Delete
Modify junk email options		Home, Delete	
Move messages		Home, Move OR Home, Quick Steps	
Search folders		Folder, New Search Folder	
Use Conversations view		View, Messages	
Use search tools		Click in *Instant Search* box	

Workbook

Chapter study tools and assessment activities are available in the *Workbook* pages of the ebook. These resources are designed to help you further develop and demonstrate mastery of the skills learned in this chapter.

Using Calendar for Scheduling

Performance Objectives

Upon successful completion of Chapter 3, you will be able to:

1 Schedule, edit, move, and delete appointments and events

2 Schedule recurring appointments

3 View and print daily, weekly, and monthly calendars

4 Change the Calendar view to show only active appointments

5 Turn on the Reading pane and view appointment details

6 Apply color categories to appointments and view appointments by category

7 Create conditional formatting rules

8 Schedule meetings by sending meeting requests

9 Accept, decline, and update meeting requests

10 Change calendar options

11 Display and work with multiple calendars

12 Share a calendar

13 Delete a calendar

Precheck

Check your current skills to help focus your study.

The Calendar module in Outlook is used to schedule appointments and events such as conferences and meetings. An appointment or meeting that occurs on a regular basis can be created as a recurring item that is entered only once. The Reminder feature sounds a chime and displays a reminder message at a set interval before the appointment, event, or meeting time.

Meetings are integrated with email so that an individual can send a meeting request to others as an email message. When the invitee responds to the message by accepting a meeting request, the details are automatically added to his or her calendar. In this chapter, you will use Calendar to schedule multiple appointments, events, and meetings and explore various methods of displaying, printing, and viewing calendar information.

SNAP

If you are a SNAP user, launch the Precheck and the Tutorial from your Assignments page.

Data Files

No student data files are required for this chapter.

Scheduling Appointments and Events

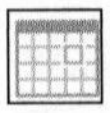

New Appointment

Click the Calendar text label or icon on the Navigation bar to display the contents of the Calendar module. Initially, the calendar opens in Month view, as shown in Figure 3.1; however, if the view is changed during an Outlook session, the calendar remains in the last view shown when Outlook is restarted. The top section in the Folder pane is the Date Navigator, which shows the current month with directional arrows that allow you to browse forward and backward to previous and upcoming months. The current month or current date has the background shaded blue in the Date Navigator.

Schedule a new appointment by first displaying the month, week, or day of the appointment in the Appointment area. To do this, click the appointment date in the Date Navigator or click the Back or Forward button (left- or right-pointing arrow) next to the date displayed at the top of the Appointment area and then scroll one month, week, or day at a time. (Alternatively, click the Go To dialog box launcher 🖃, type the date, and then press Enter or click OK.) Click within the date box for the date (Month view) or next to the appointment time (Day, Work Week, or Week view) in the Appointment area, type a short description of the appointment, and then press Enter or click outside the appointment box.

Display the Appointment window, shown in Figure 3.2 on page 75, to enter more details about an appointment. To enter a new appointment using the Appointment window, click the desired day or time in the Appointment area and perform one of the following actions:

- Click the New Appointment button in the New group on the Home tab.
- Double-click next to the appointment starting time in the Appointment area.
- Right-click next to the appointment starting time in the Appointment area and then click *New Appointment* at the shortcut menu.

Quick Steps

Schedule an Appointment Using Click and Type
1. Click appointment date in Date Navigator.
2. Click next to appointment time in Appointment area.
3. Type description of appointment.
4. Press Enter.

TIP The Peek feature shows you the current day's appointments in a pop-up balloon. Point to Calendar on the Navigation bar to peek at today's schedule from another module. Within Calendar, point to a scheduled appointment to view more appointment details.

Figure 3.1 The Calendar Window

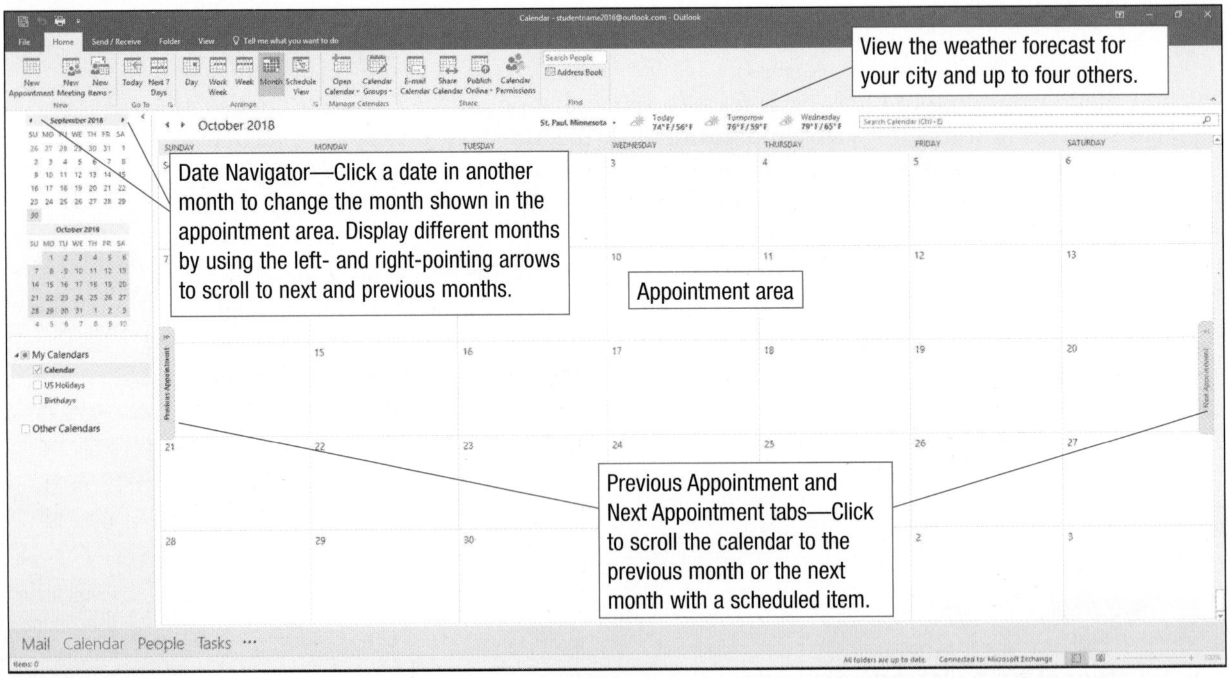

Date Navigator—Click a date in another month to change the month shown in the appointment area. Display different months by using the left- and right-pointing arrows to scroll to next and previous months.

View the weather forecast for your city and up to four others.

Appointment area

Previous Appointment and Next Appointment tabs—Click to scroll the calendar to the previous month or the next month with a scheduled item.

Figure 3.2 Appointment Window

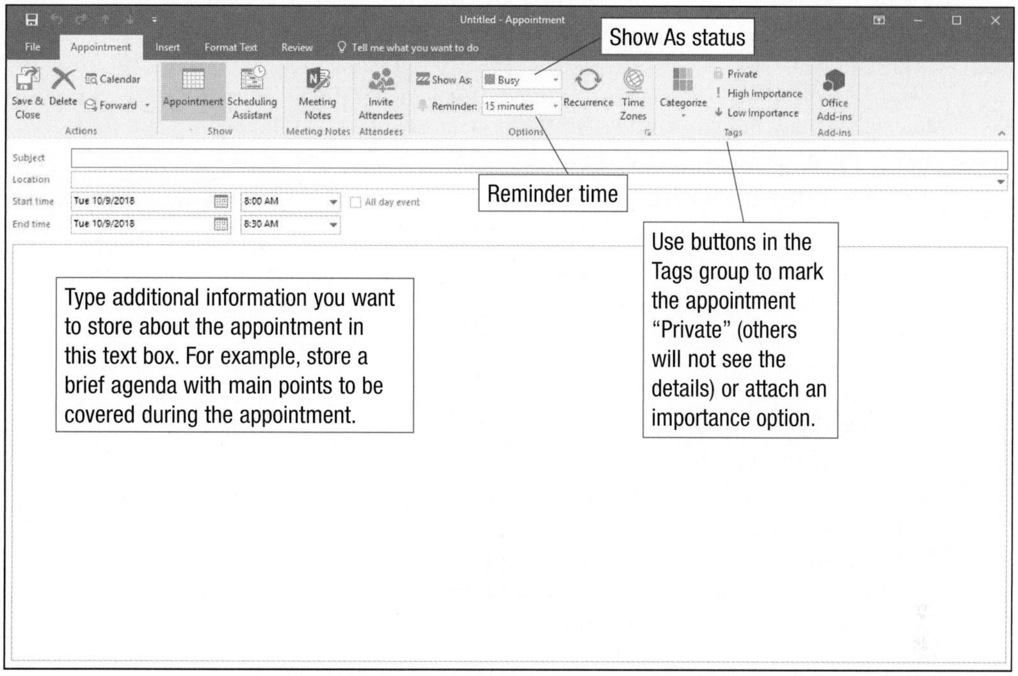

Show As status

Reminder time

Type additional information you want to store about the appointment in this text box. For example, store a brief agenda with main points to be covered during the appointment.

Use buttons in the Tags group to mark the appointment "Private" (others will not see the details) or attach an importance option.

Quick Steps

Schedule an Appointment Using the Appointment Window
1. Click appointment date in Date Navigator.
2. Click next to appointment time in Appointment area.
3. Click New Appointment button in New group on Home tab.
4. Type description in *Subject* text box.
5. Type location in *Location* text box.
6. Change other options as required.
7. Click Save & Close.

Type a description of the appointment in the *Subject* text box and the location where the appointment will take place in the *Location* text box. The *Start time* option box will display the day and time that you selected in Calendar before opening the Appointment window. Change the start day and time by clicking the *Start time* day or time option box arrow and then clicking the correct entry. If necessary, you can select the current time entry and type a specific time of your own, such as *10:50 AM*. Enter the end time for the appointment by clicking the *End time* day or time option box arrow and then clicking the correct day or time at the drop-down list.

By default, a reminder is set to display a reminder message and play a chime 15 minutes before the scheduled appointment. Click the *Reminder* option box arrow in the Options group on the Appointment tab to change the reminder time or select *None* at the drop-down list to turn off the Reminder feature.

Use the *Show As* option box arrow in the Options group on the Appointment tab to change the appointment status from the default option of *Busy* to *Free*, *Working Elsewhere*, *Tentative*, or *Out of Office* in the scheduled time slot. When other people view your calendar to plan a meeting, the time slot will appear as a colored or patterned bar, depending on the *Show As* setting.

Use the text box below *End time* to type additional information about the appointment that you want to store, such as driving directions to the location, an agenda, reminders for items to take with you to the appointment, and background information on the person with whom you are meeting, to name a few examples. When all the required entries have been made, click the Save & Close button in the Actions group on the Appointment tab.

Exercise 1 Scheduling Appointments and Navigating Using Go To Date

Note: The exercises in this chapter instruct you to schedule appointments and meetings in October 2018. Check with your instructor, if necessary, for alternative instructions that schedule these items in the current month or in October of the current year.

1. With Outlook open, click the Calendar text label or icon on the Navigation bar. If necessary, change to Day view by clicking the Day button in the Arrange group on the Home tab.

2. Add a new appointment to the calendar using the click-and-type method by completing the following steps:
   a. Click the Go to Date launcher button located at the bottom right of the Go To group on the Home tab.
   b. At the Go To Date dialog box, type 10/15/2018 and then press Enter or click OK.
   c. Click next to *10:00 AM* in the Appointment area. A blue shaded appointment box appears with a default duration set to one-half hour.
   d. Type Staff meeting for health and safety updates.
   e. Press Enter or click in the Appointment area outside the appointment box.

3. Add a new appointment using the Appointment window by completing the following steps:
   a. With *October 15, 2018* the active date, click next to *1:00 PM* in the Appointment area.
   b. Click the New Appointment button in the New group on the Home tab. An Untitled - Appointment window opens.
   c. With the insertion point positioned in the *Subject* text box, type Lunch meeting with Leslie Taylor.
   d. Press Tab or click in the *Location* text box and then type The Waterfront Bistro.
   e. Click the *End time* time option box arrow and then click *2:30 PM (1.5 hours)* at the drop-down list.
   f. Click the *Show As* option box arrow in the Options group on the Appointment tab (currently displays *Busy*) and then click *Out of Office* at the drop-down list.
   g. Click the High Importance button in the Tags group on the Appointment tab.

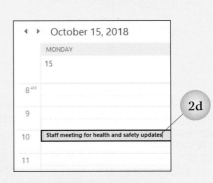

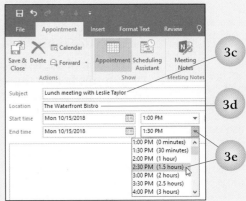

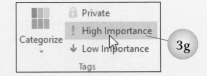

h. Click the *Reminder* option box arrow in the Options group (currently displays *15 minutes*) and then click *30 minutes* at the drop-down list.

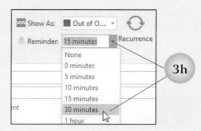

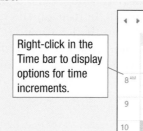

3h

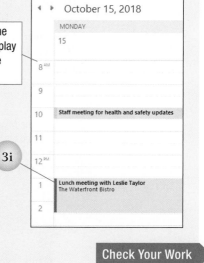

Right-click in the Time bar to display options for time increments.

i. Click the Save & Close button in the Actions group. The appointment appears in the Appointment area with a purple border at the left edge of the appointment box. Purple is the color displayed for times in the calendar that are *Out of Office*.

3i

4. Click the File tab, click *Print*, and then click the Print button at the Print backstage area with *Daily Style* already selected in the *Settings* section.

Check Your Work

Scheduling Appointments in Outlook on the web

Display the calendar by clicking the Microsoft Apps button (sometimes called the waffle button) at the top left of the screen next to Mail, and then clicking the Calendar tile at the drop-down Navigation bar.

Click *Day, Work Week, Week* or *Month* near the top right of the screen to change the display. Change the date using the Date Navigator at the top of the Folder pane. Add a new appointment using the click-and-type method described in Exercise 1, Step 2, or by clicking the New button on the Menu bar and using the text boxes and options in the Appointment panel.

The *Show as* option *Away* in Outlook on the web is the same as the *Show as* option *Out of Office* in the desktop Outlook.

To display your calendar, click the Microsoft Apps button (sometimes called the waffle button) in the upper left corner of the screen next to Outlook Mail, and then click the Calendar tile at the drop-down Navigation bar. The first time you access Calendar, you may be prompted to set your time zone. If necessary, adjust the time zone and then click the Continue to Calendar button.

Click the Microsoft Apps button and then click the Calendar tile on the drop-down Navigation bar to display the current calendar.

Click *Day*, *Work Week*, or *Week* near the top right of the screen to change the Month display. Change the date by clicking a date in the current month in the Date Navigator, or by using the Previous and Next buttons above the current month to change to the next or previous month and then clicking the desired date.

Add a new appointment in Month view by clicking to select the desired date and then clicking again to open an appointment box. In Week or Day view, navigate to the desired date and then click next to the desired time. In the pop-out option box that appears, type a subject and location in the appropriate text box, change the start or end time as needed and then click the Save button, or click *More details* to add other options in the Appointment panel. Click the Save button in the appointment box or Appointment panel when finished.

You can also add a new appointment by clicking the New button on the Calendar Menu bar. Type the details in the Appointment panel that appears, change other options as required, and then click the Save button.

Click *More details* to open the Appointment panel with additional options.

Scheduling Recurring Appointments

An appointment that occurs on a regular basis at fixed intervals needs to be entered only once, and Outlook automatically schedules the remainder of the occurrences within the recurrence pattern and range. To schedule a recurring appointment, open the Appointment window, enter the specifications for the first occurrence, and then click the Recurrence button in the Options group on the Appointment tab. The Appointment Recurrence dialog box shown in Figure 3.3 appears, in which you enter the recurring pattern details.

Recurrence

TIP Meetings and events can also be set up as recurring items. Click the Recurrence button in the Meeting or Event window.

Figure 3.3 Appointment Recurrence Dialog Box

Appointment Recurrence ×

Appointment time

Start: 3:00 PM
End: 3:30 PM
Duration: 30 minutes

Recurrence pattern

○ Daily   Recur every   1   week(s) on:
● Weekly   □ Sunday   □ Monday   ☑ Tuesday   □ Wednesday
○ Monthly   □ Thursday   □ Friday   □ Saturday
○ Yearly

Range of recurrence

Start: Tue 10/16/2018   ● No end date
     ○ End after: 10   occurrences
     ○ End by: Tue 12/18/2018

OK   Cancel   Remove Recurrence

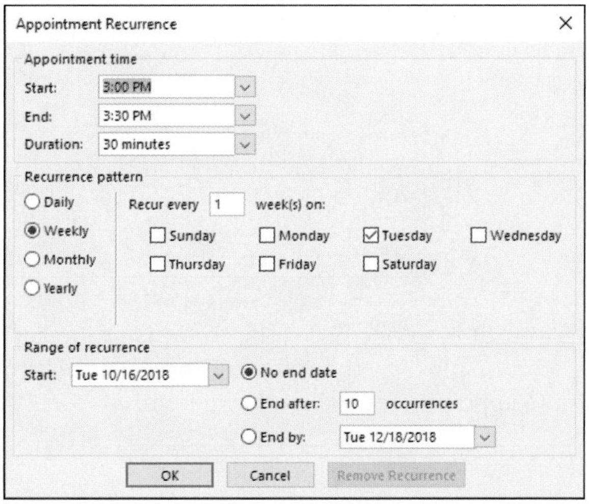

Exercise 2 Scheduling a Recurring Appointment

1. With Calendar active and the date *October 15, 2018* displayed in the Appointment area, schedule a recurring appointment by completing the following steps:
   a. Click the Forward button located next to *October 15, 2018* to display *October 16, 2018* in the Appointment area.
   b. Click next to *3:00 PM* in the Appointment area.
   c. Click the New Appointment button in the New group on the Home tab.
   d. With the insertion point positioned in the *Subject* text box, type Project status meeting.
   e. Press Tab or click in the *Location* text box and then type Meeting Room A.
   f. Click the Recurrence button in the Options group on the Appointment tab.

October 15, 2018

1a

Forward DAY

Project status meeting - Appointment

File   Appointment   Insert   Format Text   Review   ♀ Tell me what you want to do

Save & Close   Delete   Forward   Calendar   Appointment   Scheduling Assistant   Meeting Notes   Invite Attendees   Show As: Busy   Reminder: 15 minutes   Recurrence   Time Zones

Actions   Show   Meeting Notes   Attendees   Options

1d

1f

Subject   Project status meeting
Location   Meeting Room A
Start time   Tue 10/16/2018   3:00 PM   □ All day event
End time   Tue 10/16/2018   3:30 PM

1e

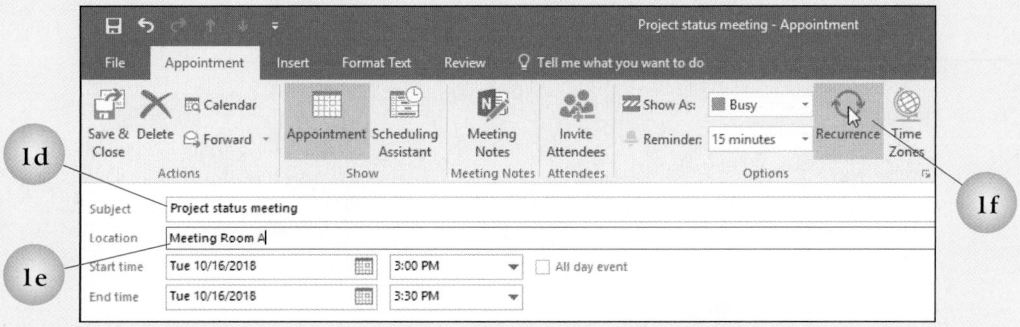

g. At the Appointment Recurrence dialog box, select the value *1* in the *Recur every [ ] week(s) on* text box in the *Recurrence pattern* section and then type *2*.

h. Click OK to accept all the other settings and close the Appointment Recurrence dialog box. Outlook adds the recurrence details in the Appointment window below the *Location* text box.

Appointment Recurrence ✕

Appointment time
Start: 3:00 PM
End: 3:30 PM
Duration: 30 minutes

1g

Recurrence pattern
○ Daily   Recur every 2 week(s) on:
● Weekly   ☐ Sunday   ☐ Monday   ☑ Tuesday   ☐ Wednesday
○ Monthly   ☐ Thursday ☐ Friday   ☐ Saturday
○ Yearly

By default, the recurrence is set to *Weekly* on the active day of the week with no end date.

Range of recurrence
Start: Tue 10/16/2018   ● No end date
                         ○ End after: 10 occurrences
                         ○ End by: Tue 12/18/2018

1h   OK   Cancel   Remove Recurrence

i. Click the Save & Close button in the Actions group on the Appointment tab. The recurrence icon displays at the right end of the appointment box in the Appointment area to indicate the appointment is a recurring item.

3   Project status meeting; Meeting Room A

4

recurrence icon

Scheduling Recurring Appointments in Outlook on the web

Open an Appointment panel and use the *Repeat* drop-down list, to select a recurrence pattern for a recurring appointment. Choose *Other* at the drop-down list to select from more patterns or to customize the frequency.

Start
Tue 10/16/2018   3:00 PM   ☐ All day

End
Tue 10/16/2018   3:30 PM   ☐ Private

Repeat   Calendar
Never   Calendar

✓ Never   Show as
Every day   Busy
Every Tuesday
Every workday
Day 16 of every month
Every third Tuesday
Every October 16
Other...

Click the *Repeat* option box arrow to open the drop-down list.

Select repeat pattern

Occurs   Daily

Every 1 days

Save   Cancel

Click *Other* to open the Select repeat pattern dialog box with more recurrence options.

Use the *Repeat* drop-down list in the Appointment panel to select a recurrence pattern. Click *Other* to open the Select repeat pattern dialog box.

Repeat

Never

✓ Never

Every day

Every Monday

Every workday

Day 15 of every month

Every third Monday

Every October 15

Other...

Select repeat pattern

Occurs | Daily

Every | 1 | days

Save | Cancel

Click *Other* to open the Select repeat pattern dialog box with more recurrence options.

Scheduling Events

An event differs from an appointment in that it is an activity that lasts an entire day or longer. Examples of an event include a seminar, training session, conference, trade show, and vacation. Other occasions that you might like to enter in the calendar as events are birthdays and anniversaries. An event does not occupy a time slot on the day it is scheduled. It appears in the banner for the scheduled day at the top of the Appointment area below the date.

To schedule an event in Day view, double-click in the white text box below the colored bar for the day of the week at the top of the Appointment area to open an Untitled - Event window. The Event window is similar to the Appointment window, except that the *All day event* check box at the right of the *Start time* and *End time* day and time option boxes is automatically checked.

Each of these other methods also opens a new Event window:

- Right-click in the white text box below the colored bar with the day of the week at the top of the Appointment area and then click *New All Day Event* at the shortcut menu.
- Click the New Items button in the New group on the Home tab and then click *All Day Event* at the drop-down list.
- Click in the white text box below the colored bar with the day of the week at the top of the Appointment area, type the event description, and then press Enter.

Exercise 3 Adding an Event

1. With Calendar active and the date *October 16, 2018* displayed in the Appointment area, schedule a one-day conference as an event by completing the following steps:
   a. Double-click in the white text box (displays *16*) below the colored bar for the day of the week (displays *TUESDAY*). An Untitled - Event window opens.

◄ ► October 16, 2018

TUESDAY

16

8 AM

1a

b. With the insertion point positioned in the *Subject* text box, type Social Media Conference.

c. Press Tab or click in the *Location* text box and then type Downtown Convention Center.

d. Click the *Show As* option box arrow in the Options group on the Event tab (currently displays *Free*) and then click *Out of Office*.

e. Click the High Importance button in the Tags group.

f. Click Save & Close in the Actions group. The event subject and location details appear below the date at the top of the Appointment area. In addition, the background color in the Appointment area for the day is shaded light purple, because the event is defined as occurring out of the office.

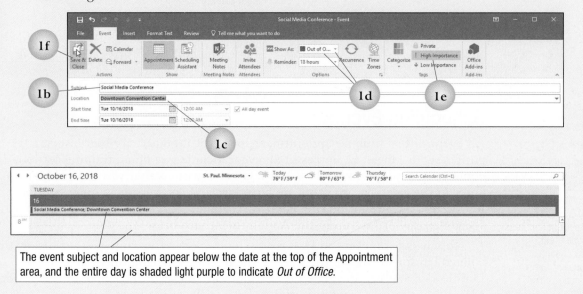

The event subject and location appear below the date at the top of the Appointment area, and the entire day is shaded light purple to indicate *Out of Office*.

TIP Create an event for any date for which you want to be reminded: birthday, anniversary, car maintenance reminder, bill payment, and so on.

Scheduling Events in Outlook on the web

In Day view, create an event by clicking in the white box below the date that displays above the Appointment area and then typing the event description. Add a location in the pop-out box that appears.

Click here to create an event.

< > Tuesday, October 16, 2018 ⌄

Tuesday, October 16, 2018

Social Media Conference

Downtown Convention Center

12:00 AM ▾   12:00 AM ▾   ✓ All day

Save   More details

Scheduling Events at Outlook.com

In Day view, click in the white box below the date at the top of the Appointment area to open an event box. Type the location and click *More details* if necessary to add more options.

< > Tuesday, October 16, 2018 ⌄

Social Media Conference

Tuesday, October 16, 2018

Social Media Conference

Downtown Convention Center

12:00 AM ▾   12:00 AM ▾   ✓ All day

Save   More details

Using Natural Language Phrases

In day or time text boxes within Appointment or Event windows, you can type natural language phrases and Outlook will convert them to the appropriate entries. For example, in the *Start time* day text box, if you type *next Monday*, Outlook automatically calculates and enters the date for the Monday following the current day. In the time text box, type *ten o'clock am* and Outlook converts the entry to *10:00 AM*.

Editing, Deleting, and Moving Appointments

TIP Click in the *Instant Search* box (displays *Search Calendar*) to locate an appointment by typing keyword(s).

Delete

Double-click an existing appointment or event in the Appointment area to open the Appointment or Event window and then change the details. To delete an appointment or event, select the appointment or event box and then press Delete or click the Delete button in the Actions group on the Calendar Tools Appointment tab.

To move an appointment, open the Appointment window and change the *Start time* and *End time* settings. You can also drag an appointment box to a new time or a new day.

Exercise 4 Editing, Deleting, and Moving Appointments

1. With Calendar active and *October 16, 2018* displayed in the Appointment area, change the starting time for the project status meeting (which you scheduled in Exercise 2) by completing the following steps:
   a. Double-click the appointment box for *Project status meeting* at 3:00 p.m.
   b. Since the appointment is one of a recurring series of appointments, Outlook displays the Open Recurring Item dialog box, asking if you want to open just this one occurrence or the entire series. Click *The entire series* to select this option and then click OK.
   c. Click the Recurrence button in the Options group on the Appointment Series tab.
   d. Click the *Start* option box arrow in the *Appointment time* section of the Appointment Recurrence dialog box and then click *4:30 PM* at the drop-down list. The *End* time automatically changes to *5:00 PM* because *Duration* is set to *30 minutes*.
   e. Click OK to close the Appointment Recurrence dialog box.
   f. Click the Save & Close button in the Actions group.

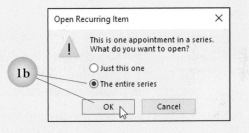

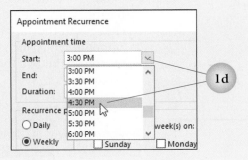

2. Delete the lunch appointment on October 15 by completing the following steps:
   a. Click *October 15* in the Date Navigator or click the Back button at the top of the Appointment area.
   b. Click to select the appointment *Lunch meeting with Leslie Taylor* in the Appointment area. When the appointment is selected, a black border surrounds the appointment box and the appointment details appear in a pop-out balloon if you rest the mouse pointer on the appointment box.
   c. Click the Delete button in the Actions group on the Calendar Tools Appointment tab.
3. Double-click the appointment box for *Staff meeting for health and safety updates* to open the Appointment window.
4. Change the *Start time* to *1:00 PM* and then click the Save & Close button in the Actions group on the Appointment tab.
5. Click the File tab and then click *Print*. At the Print backstage area, click *Weekly Calendar Style* in the *Settings* section and then click the Print button.

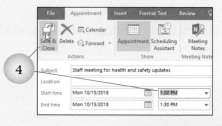

Check Your Work

Editing, Deleting, and Moving Items in Outlook on the web

Click an existing appointment to open a pop-up box with the appointment or event details that includes an Edit and Delete button. Click the Edit button to make changes to the appointment details in the Appointment panel, or click the Delete button to remove the item from your calendar.

Mon 10/15/2018 1:00p - 2:30p
The Waterfront Bistro

Lunch with Leigh Avaire

LT Leslie Taylor

✎ Edit   🗑 Delete

Editing, Deleting, and Moving Items at Outlook.com

Click an existing appointment to open a pop-up box with the appointment or event details that includes an Edit and Delete button. Click the Edit button to open the Appointment panel to make changes to the details, or click the Delete button to remove the appointment or event from your calendar.

Changing the Calendar View

TIP Before printing
your calendar, change
to the view you want
to see in the printout,
because Outlook
automatically changes
the print setting style
to match the view.

The Arrange group on the Home tab contains buttons that allow you to change
the view for the calendar to Day, Work Week, Week, or Month, as shown and
described in Figure 3.4.

Figure 3.4 Arrange Group on the Home Tab

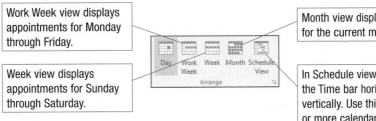

Work Week view displays appointments for Monday through Friday.

Week view displays appointments for Sunday through Saturday.

Month view displays appointments for the current month.

In Schedule view, the calendar displays the Time bar horizontally instead of vertically. Use this view to look at two or more calendars at the same time to assist with planning meetings.

Displaying the Calendar in Table Format

 Change View

Click the View tab and then click the Change View button in the Current View
group to choose *List* or *Active*, which displays appointments in a table format.
List view shows all the appointments that have been scheduled in the calendar,
whereas Active view displays only those appointments that have not yet occurred.

Appointments and events are arranged in table format sorted by the start
date in ascending order and grouped by recurrence option. Change the sort order
to sort the list by subject or location by clicking the *SUBJECT* or *LOCATION*
column heading. The list reorders in ascending order. Click the column heading a
second time to change the sort order to descending order.

Displaying the Reading Pane

Reading Pane

Click the View tab, click the Reading Pane button in the Layout group, and then
click *Right* or *Bottom* at the drop-down list to turn on the Reading pane at the right
edge or bottom of the Calendar window. Select an appointment to view the details
within the Reading pane. Figure 3.5 shows the Reading pane at the bottom of
the window with the details displayed for the recurring project status meeting on
October 16, 2018.

Quick Steps
**Change the Current
View**
Click desired button
in Arrange group on
Home tab.
OR
1. Click View tab.
2. Click Change View
   button in Current
   View group.
3. Click desired view.

**Display the Reading
Pane**
1. Click View tab.
2. Click Reading Pane
   button in Layout
   group.
3. Click *Bottom* or
   Right.

Figure 3.5 Calendar Window with Reading Pane at Bottom of Window

Display the Reading pane to view the details for a selected appointment without having to open the Appointment window.

Exercise 5 Changing the View and Displaying the Reading Pane

1. With Calendar active and *October 15, 2018* displayed in the Appointment area, change the current view to display only active appointments, increase the column width, and print the view by completing the following steps:

    a. Click the View tab, click the Change View button in the Current View group, and then click *Active* at the drop-down list. The calendar displays in a table format with the appointments grouped by the recurrence pattern. Information in some columns may not be entirely visible.

    b. If necessary, drag the column boundary at the right of *SUBJECT* approximately 1 inch to the right to expand the column width if the entire subject text for each appointment is not currently visible. Dragging a column boundary right or left increases or decreases the column width. A black, vertical line indicates the new right column boundary position as you drag the mouse.

    c. Double-click the right column boundary for the *LOCATION* column. Double-clicking adjusts the column width to the length of the longest entry. If necessary, double-click the *SUBJECT* right column boundary if the entire subject text is still not visible after completing Step 1b.

    d. Double-click the *START, END,* and *RECURRENCE PATTERN* right column boundaries.

    e. Print the current view in landscape orientation by completing the following steps:

        1) Click the File tab and then click *Print*.
        2) Click *Table Style* in the *Settings* section of the Print backstage area.
        3) Click the Print Options button.
        4) Click the Page Setup button in the *Print style* section of the Print dialog box.
        5) Click the Paper tab in the Page Setup: Table Style dialog box, click *Landscape* in the *Orientation* section, and then click OK.
        6) Click the Print button in the Print dialog box. Some columns in your printout may not display all the text even though you resized the columns. Resizing the columns improves the display, but not always the printout.

2. Click the Change View button in the Current View group on the View tab and then click *Calendar* at the drop-down list to return to the regular calendar display.

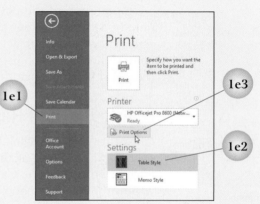

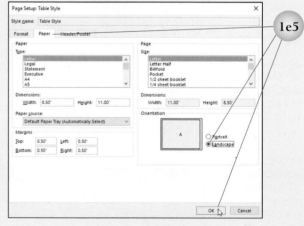

3. Display *October 15, 2018* in the Appointment area, click the Home tab, and then click the Month button in the Arrange group to view the month October 2018.
4. Turn on the display of the Reading pane, view appointment details, and resize the pane by completing the following steps:
   a. Click the View tab, click the Reading Pane button in the Layout group, and then click *Right* at the drop-down list.

   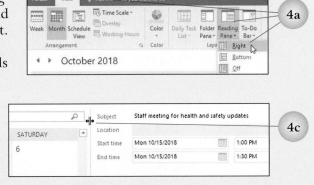

   b. Select the appointment on October 15 to display the appointment details in the Reading pane.
   c. Drag the boundary line between the Content pane and the Reading pane to the right when the pointer displays with the double vertical line and left- and right-pointing arrows to resize the pane until the Reading pane occupies approximately one-third of the window.
   d. Select the appointment on October 30 and then read the appointment details in the Reading pane.
   e. Click the View tab and then click the Week button in the Arrangement group. Review the layout of the Appointment area in Weekly Calendar style.
5. If necessary, click the View tab. Click the Reading Pane button and then click *Off* at the drop-down list.
6. Click the Home tab and then click the Day button in the Arrange group.
7. Click *October 15, 2018* in the Date Navigator.

Check Your Work

Applying Color Categories to Appointments

Quick Steps

Apply a Color Category to an Appointment
1. Select appointment.
2. Click Categorize button in Tags group on Calendar Tools Appointment tab.
3. Click desired color category.

 Categorize

The same six color categories that can be assigned to messages can be assigned to appointments. By using the same categories in all the Outlook modules, you can assign a common color to all items related to the same project or task. An appointment that has been assigned a color category has the appointment box shaded the associated color in the Appointment area.

When an appointment is selected in the Appointment area, the Calendar Tools Appointment tab appears with the Categorize button located in the Tags group. Click the button and then click a color category to assign it to the selected appointment. You can also choose *Categorize* from the shortcut menu to assign a category to an appointment. Edit the color category titles by opening the Color Categories dialog box using the same technique you learned in Chapter 2.

You can assign multiple color categories to one item. If more than one color category is assigned to an appointment, Outlook displays the appointment box shaded in the color of the last assigned color category and includes a color category icon for each of the other assigned color categories at the right end of the appointment box within the Appointment area.

Exercise 6 Applying Color Categories to Appointments, Renaming a Color Category, and Viewing Appointments by Category

1. With Calendar active and *October 15, 2018* displayed in the Appointment area, apply a color category to an existing appointment and event by completing the following steps:

   a. Display *October 16, 2018* in the Appointment area.

   b. Right-click *Social Media Conference* in the date banner at the top of the Appointment area, point to *Categorize*, and then click *Social Media Essay* (blue category) at the shortcut menu.

   c. Click to select the appointment box at *4:30 PM* for the *Project status meeting* appointment.

   d. Click the Categorize button in the Tags group on the Calendar Tools Appointment Series tab.

   e. Click *Green Category* at the drop-down list. Click No if a Rename Category dialog box appears informing you that this is the first time you have used the Green Category and asking if you want to rename it. You will rename the category in the next step.

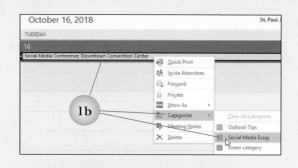

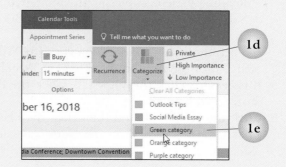

2. Rename the green color category by completing the following steps:

   a. Right-click the green-shaded *Project status meeting* appointment box, point to *Categorize*, and then click *All Categories* at the shortcut menu.

   b. At the Color Categories dialog box with *Green Category* already selected, click the Rename button.

   c. Type Conference Planning Project and then press Enter.

   d. Click OK to close the Color Categories dialog box.

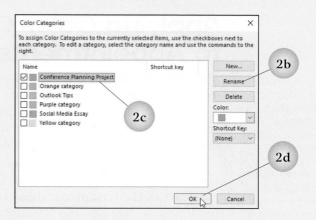

3. Schedule a new appointment and assign a category by completing the following steps:

   a. Display *October 15, 2018* in the Appointment area.

   b. Click next to *11:00 AM* in the Appointment area and then click the New Appointment button in the New group on the Home tab.

   c. Type Conference venue selection in the *Subject* text box.

   d. Press Tab and then type My office in the Location text box.

e. Click the Categorize button in the Tags group on the Appointment tab and then click *Conference Planning Project* (green category) at the drop-down list.

f. Change the *End time* to *1:00 PM (2 hours)*.

g. Click Save & Close.

4. Display the active appointments grouped by color category by completing the following steps:

   a. Click the View tab, click the Change View button in the Current View group, and then click *Active* at the drop-down list.

   b. Click the Categories button in the Arrangement group option box. Outlook displays the appointments arranged in groups by assigned color category with each category automatically expanded to display all items.

   c. Double-click the right column boundary for the *SUBJECT, LOCATION, START,* and *END* columns to adjust the width of each to the length of the column's longest entry.

SUBJECT	LOCATION	START	END	RECURRENCE PATTERN	CATEGORIES
▲ Categories: (none): 1 item(s)					
Staff meeting for health and safety updates		Mon 10/15/2018 1:00 PM	Mon 10/15/2018 1:30 PM		
▲ Categories: Conference Planning Project: 2 item(s)					
Project status meeting	Meeting Room A	Tue 10/16/2018 4:30 PM	Tue 10/16/2018 5:00 PM	every 2 week(s) on Tuesday from 4:30 PM to 5:00 PM	Conference Planning Project
Conference venue selection	My office	Mon 10/15/2018 11:00 AM	Mon 10/15/2018 1:00 PM		Conference Planning Project
▲ Categories: Social Media Essay: 1 item(s)					
Social Media Conference	Downtown Convention Center	Tue 10/16/2018 12:00 AM	Wed 10/17/2018 12:00 AM		Social Media Essay

   d. Print the calendar in Table style and with landscape orientation. Note that some columns in your printout may not display the full text.

5. Click the Change View button and then click *Calendar* at the drop-down list.

6. Display *October 15, 2018* in the Appointment area.

Check Your Work

Applying Color Categories to Appointments in Outlook on the web

Open the Appointment or Event panel to apply a color category using the Categorize button on the Menu bar. Click the Save button when finished.

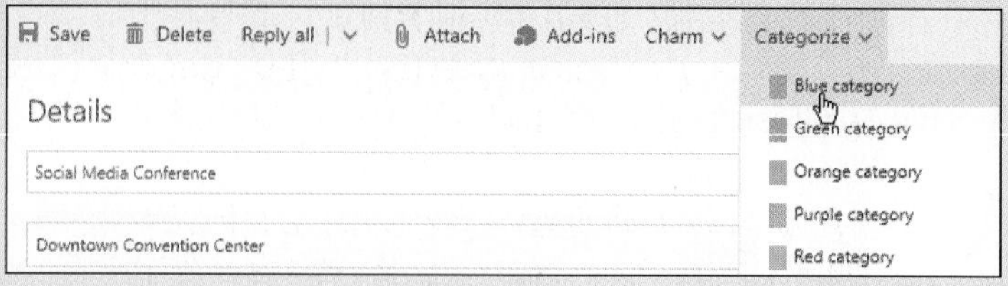

Save
Delete
Reply all
Attach
Add-ins
Charm
Categorize
Details
Social Media Conference
Downtown Convention Center
Blue category
Green category
Orange category
Purple category
Red category

Tutorial

Creating an Appointment Rule

Quick Steps

Create a Conditional Formatting Rule with Color

1. Click View tab.
2. Click View Settings button in Current View group.
3. Click Conditional Formatting button.
4. Click Add button.
5. Type name for new rule in *Name* text box.
6. Choose desired color in *Color* list box.
7. Click Condition button.
8. Choose filter criteria.
9. Click OK two times.

View Settings

Creating a Conditional Formatting Rule with Color

You can create an appointment rule (similar to a message rule) that automatically applies a color to an appointment based on a keyword that is typed in the *Subject* field. For example, if you use Outlook to enter your personal appointments as well as your business appointments, you may wish to apply a color to all of your personal appointments to make them easily identifiable in the calendar.

As you learned in Chapter 2, a rule performs an action on an item based on a condition you specify. Following the example, you would create the condition that the word *personal* exists in the *Subject* field in order for the color to be applied automatically to the appointment. To create a conditional formatting rule, click the View Settings button in the Current View group on the View tab. At the Advanced View Settings: Calendar dialog box, click the Conditional Formatting button to open the Conditional Formatting dialog box, shown in Figure 3.6.

Click the Add button to create a new rule. Outlook displays the name *Untitled* in the *Name* text box in the *Properties of selected rule* section. Type a name to identify the rule and choose the color to apply in the *Color* list. Click the Condition button to open the Filter dialog box and set the criteria on which the appointment is to be formatted. When finished, click OK to close each dialog box.

Figure 3.6 Conditional Formatting Dialog Box

Conditional Formatting
Rules for this view:
Add
Delete
Move Up
Move Down
Properties of selected rule
Name:
Color:
Condition...
OK
Cancel
These options become accessible after you click the Add button.

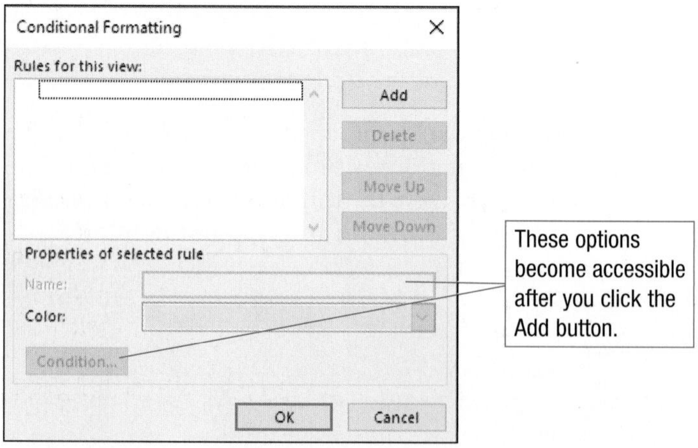

Exercise 7 Creating a Conditional Formatting Rule Using Color

1. With Calendar active in Day view and the date *October 15, 2018* displayed in the Appointment area, rename the *Orange Category* to *Personal* by completing the following steps:
   a. Right-click the *Staff meeting* appointment box at *1:00 PM*, point to *Categorize*, and then click *All Categories* at the shortcut menu.
   b. Click *Orange Category* in the *Name* list and then click the Rename button.
   c. Type Personal and then press Enter.
   d. Click OK.
2. Create a conditional formatting rule to automatically format personal appointments with the orange color by completing the following steps:
   a. Click the View tab and then click the View Settings button in the Current View group.
   b. At the Advanced View Settings: Calendar dialog box, click the Conditional Formatting button.
   c. At the Conditional Formatting dialog box, click the Add button. A new rule named *Untitled* appears checked in the *Rules for this view* list box and in the *Name* text box in the *Properties of selected rule* section.
   d. With the text *Untitled* already selected in the *Name* text box, type Personal Appointments.
   e. Click the *Color* option box arrow and then click *Orange* (second color box).
   f. Click the Condition button.
   g. At the Filter dialog box, type personal in the *Search for the word(s)* text box.
   h. With *subject field only* already selected in the *In* text box, click OK to close the Filter dialog box.
   i. Click OK to close the Conditional Formatting dialog box.
   j. Click OK to close the Advanced View Settings: Calendar dialog box.
3. Schedule a new personal appointment on October 15, 2018, and see the rule applied to the appointment by completing the following steps:
   a. Click next to *9:00 AM* in the Appointment area.
   b. Type Personal appointment (doctor) and then press Enter. As soon as you press Enter, Outlook applies the orange color to the appointment box.
4. Click the File tab and then click *Print*. With *Daily Style* selected in the *Settings* section at the Print backstage area, click the Print button.

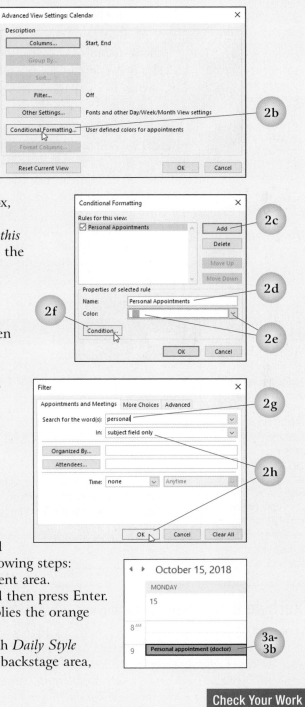

Check Your Work

Scheduling Meetings

Quick Steps

Schedule a Meeting
1. Display meeting date.
2. Click appointment time in Appointment area.
3. Click New Meeting button in New group on Home tab.
4. Add invitees' names in *To* text box.
5. Type meeting description in *Subject* text box.
6. Type location in *Location* text box.
7. Change other options as required.
8. Click Send.

New Meeting

Scheduling a meeting involves selecting the meeting day and time and opening a Meeting window in which you identify the individuals you want to attend the meeting, the subject, the location, and other options as required. Individuals are notified of the meeting via an email message once you click Send.

To begin creating a new meeting request, perform one of the following actions to open a Meeting window similar to the one shown in Figure 3.7:

- Click the New Meeting button in the New group on the Home tab.
- Click the New Items button in the New group on the Home tab and then click *Meeting* at the drop-down list.
- Open a new Appointment window and then click the Invite Attendees button in the Attendees group on the Appointment tab.
- Right-click in the Appointment area at the meeting start time and then click *New Meeting Request* at the shortcut menu.

Type the names or email addresses for the people you want to invite to the meeting in the *To* text box separated by semicolons. If you are using an internal Exchange server you can use the Scheduling Assistant button to help you find a day and time when most people are available. The meeting window changes to show you the free and busy times for each individual. Drag the vertical colored bar for the start or end time to adjust the meeting when you see a time slot that is available for everyone. If you are not connected to an Exchange Server, the Scheduling button appears in place of Scheduling Assistant.

Figure 3.7 Meeting Window

Exchange Server

Use the Rooms button at the right of the *Location* text box to reserve a meeting room. Consider also using the Room Finder pane, which shows suggested best times and available rooms. For example, click a suggestion in the Room Finder pane when most people and a room are available at the same time.

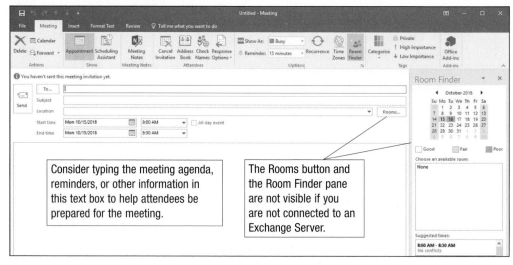

> Consider typing the meeting agenda, reminders, or other information in this text box to help attendees be prepared for the meeting.

> The Rooms button and the Room Finder pane are not visible if you are not connected to an Exchange Server.

Exercise 8 Scheduling a Meeting and Viewing Tracking Details

Note: In this exercise and in several remaining exercises and assessments, you will be sending email messages related to meeting requests to the student with whom you exchanged email in Chapter 1. Check with your instructor if necessary for alternative instructions on whom you should include in the meeting requests, because you cannot send a meeting request to yourself. Another option is to send a meeting request to an email address for yourself that is not the same as the one you are using for these exercises.

1. With Calendar active and the date *October 15, 2018* displayed in the Appointment area, schedule a meeting by completing the following steps:
   a. Click next to *3:00 PM* in the Appointment area.
   b. Click the New Meeting button in the New group on the Home tab.
   c. Type the email address for the person you are inviting to the meeting in the *To* text box.
   d. Click in the *Subject* text box and then type Conference keynote speaker planning meeting.
   e. Click in the *Location* text box and then type Meeting Room B.
   f. Click the *End time* time option box arrow and then click *4:00 PM (1 hour)* at the drop-down list.
   g. Click the Send button. The meeting is scheduled in your calendar and an email message is sent to the student who was invited to the meeting.

2. View the Scheduling and Tracking information in the Meeting window by completing the following steps:
   a. Double-click the *Conference keynote speaker planning meeting* appointment box at *3:00 PM*.
   b. Click the Scheduling Assistant button (Exchange users) or Scheduling button (non-Exchange users) in the Show group on the Meeting tab. The Meeting window shows the *All Attendees* list and calendar entries for each attendee. At the bottom of the window are options to add more attendees, change calendar options, change the meeting day and/or time, or add a room.

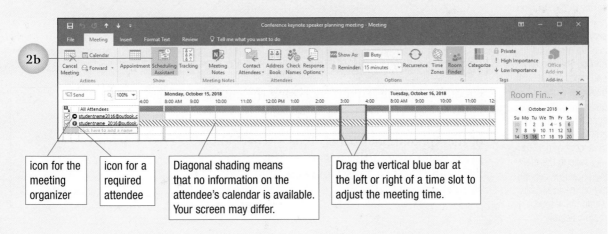

icon for the meeting organizer

icon for a required attendee

Diagonal shading means that no information on the attendee's calendar is available. Your screen may differ.

Drag the vertical blue bar at the left or right of a time slot to adjust the meeting time.

c. Click the Tracking button in the Show group on the Meeting tab. (Do not click the button arrow.) Notice the Response column where Outlook logs responses received from each attendee.

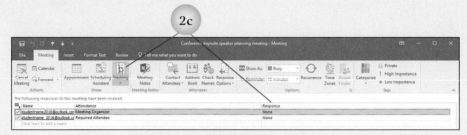

d. Click the Close button on the Meeting window Title bar.
3. View the meeting request email message sent by completing the following steps:
a. Click the Mail text label or icon on the Navigation bar.
b. Click *Sent Items* in the Folder pane.
c. Double-click the message header for the meeting request sent in Step 1 to open the meeting request message.
d. Click the File tab within the message window, click *Print*, and then click the Print button.
e. Close the message window.
4. Click *Inbox* in the Folder pane.

Check Your Work

Scheduling Meetings in Outlook on the web

Add meeting participants to the *People* text box at the top right of the Appointment panel to create a meeting request. Outlook for the web tracks responses automatically for attendees on the same server.

Click the plus (+) symbol to select people from Contacts or the global address list for the server.

Exchange Server

Resources such as meeting rooms and equipment can be automatically scheduled by including the resource as an invitee in the meeting request. The Exchange server administrator sets up a mailbox for each resource and room and allows bookings in the calendar for authorized schedulers. Outlook automatically sends an accept or decline message to the meeting organizer, depending on the availability within the resource or room calendar.

Scheduling Meetings at Outlook.com

Create a meeting request by typing the email address of the person you want to invite to the meeting in the *People* text box at the right side of the Appointment panel. Type a semicolon or press Enter to add the person to the Attendees list below the text box. Continue adding people as needed.

Responding to Meeting Requests

TIP Always respond promptly to meeting requests so the meeting organizer is not left wondering if you are attending or not.

Quick Steps

Accept a Meeting Request
1. Display Inbox.
2. Select or open meeting request message.
3. Click Accept button.
4. Click *Edit the Response before Sending* or *Send the Response Now.*
5. If editing response, type message and then click Send.

A meeting request message has buttons for responding to the meeting organizer in the Respond group on the Meeting tab (Figure 3.8). Respond buttons are also included along the top of a message in the Reading pane. The invitee can choose to click Accept, Tentative, Decline, or Propose New Time. Click the desired Respond button to send a reply message to the meeting organizer. Outlook also includes a preview of your calendar for the meeting day and time within the message so that you can easily determine if you have a conflicting appointment.

When the invitee chooses Accept, Tentative, or Decline, a drop-down list appears below the button with three options: *Edit the Response before Sending*, so that a few words of explanation can be provided; *Send the Response Now*, so that the meeting organizer receives the default response message of *User name has accepted*; and *Do Not Send a Response*. Accept or Tentative responses schedule the meeting in your calendar. If you choose Decline, the message is moved to the Deleted Items folder and the meeting is not scheduled.

The meeting organizer receives the responses by means of email messages. In addition, Outlook updates the Tracking page in the Meeting window so that the organizer can view all the invitation responses in one place.

If an invitee is unavailable at the requested meeting day and time, he or she can propose a new time for the meeting rather than decline the invitation. In this case, the invitee selects the Propose New Time button and chooses *Tentative and Propose New Time* or *Decline and Propose New Time*. At the Propose New Time dialog box, the invitee enters the new start time and end time meeting parameters and then clicks the Propose Time button. The invitee types a short explanation in the message window and then sends the reply. The meeting organizer sees the original day and time and the proposed new day and time particulars in the response message.

Figure 3.8 Respond Buttons in Meeting Request Message

Use these buttons to respond to the meeting organizer.

Exercise 9 Accepting a Meeting Request

Note: To complete this exercise, you must have received a meeting request from another student for Exercise 8. If you sent the request to yourself at a secondary email address, you will need to sign in to your other email account to complete this exercise.

1. With Inbox active, accept a meeting request by completing the following steps:
   a. Double-click the message header in the Content pane for the message with the subject *Conference keynote speaker planning meeting*.
   b. Click the Accept button in the Respond group on the Meeting tab.
   c. Click *Edit the Response before Sending* at the drop-down list.

d. Type the following text in the message window:

The latest budget for the conference provides $5,000 to cover keynote speaker costs.

e. Print the response message.

f. Send the message. A message is sent to the meeting organizer with the subject text *Accepted: Conference keynote speaker planning meeting* below the attendee's name. Outlook also deletes the meeting request message from the Inbox once you have responded.

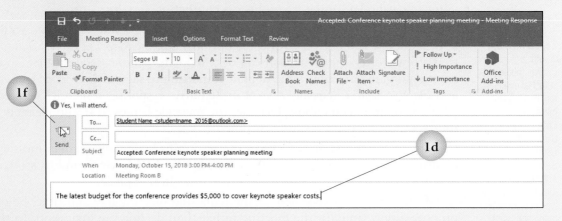

2. Display the calendar with the active date *October 15, 2018*. Outlook added the meeting to your calendar. ***Note:*** *You will have two meetings scheduled for 3:00 p.m. on October 15 if you have completed both Exercises 8 and 9—one as a meeting organizer and the other as a meeting attendee. If you completed this exercise from a secondary email account, sign out and return to the account you normally use for this textbook.*

Check Your Work

TIP You can forward a calendar item via an email message. Select the calendar item and then click the Forward button in the Actions group on the Calendar Tools Appointment tab. A message window opens with the item details in a file attachment.

If you send a meeting request to someone who does not use Outlook and whose email program does not process Outlook requests, Outlook sends an email invitation message that includes the meeting details and attaches to the message an iCalendar text file (*.ics* file). The individual can use the file attachment to import the meeting into his or her scheduling program. For example, an *.ics* file can be imported into Google Calendar. An invitee who receives this type of request does not see the meeting respond buttons. He or she will use the Reply button to send an email back to the meeting organizer indicating his or her attendance.

Responding to Meeting Requests in Outlook on the web

Respond to the meeting organizer using the Accept, Tentative, and Decline buttons along the top of the message in the Reading pane. Choose to edit or send the response or send no response from the button's drop-down list.

As with the desktop version of Outlook, when you choose Accept or Tentative, Outlook on the web adds the meeting to your calendar.

LT Leslie Taylor
Required: Leslie Taylor; Leigh Avaire;

When: Mon 10/15/2018 3:00p - 3:30p
Where: Meeting Room B

✓ Accept   ? Tentative   ✗ Decline   🕐 Propose new time

No conflicts.

Outlook on the web automatically checks your calendar and notifies you if a conflict does or does not exist.

Updating and Canceling a Meeting

Quick Steps

Update a Meeting
1. Select meeting or open Meeting window.
2. Change attendees or otherwise edit meeting details.
3. Click Send Update.

 Cancel Meeting

TIP Canceled meeting messages are sent as *High Importance* items.

Periodically, meetings need to be rescheduled or canceled or the list of individuals attending a meeting needs to be revised. Only the organizer of the meeting request can update or cancel a meeting.

Select the meeting in your calendar and use the buttons on the Calendar Tools Meeting tab to make the required changes. You can also open the meeting window to make the required changes and then click the Send Update button when finished to send an email message with the changes to each attendee. Each attendee can then choose to accept or decline the revised meeting request.

To cancel a meeting, use the Cancel Meeting button in the Actions group on the Calendar Tools Meeting tab or within the meeting window. Click the Send Cancellation button to instruct Outlook to send each attendee an email message with the word *Canceled* in the subject line. Each attendee can open the message and remove the meeting from his or her calendar using the Remove from Calendar button in the Respond group on the Meeting tab.

If you are an attendee to a previously accepted meeting and you delete the meeting from your calendar, Outlook prompts you to send a message to the meeting organizer.

Exercise 10 Scheduling and Updating a Meeting

1. With Calendar active and *October 15, 2018* displayed in the Appointment area, click *October 17, 2018* in the Date Navigator.
2. Schedule a new meeting by completing the following steps:
   a. Click next to *1:00 PM* in the Appointment area.
   b. Click the New Meeting button in the New group on the Home tab.
   c. Type the email address for the person you are inviting to the meeting in the *To* text box.
   d. Type Conference volunteer planning meeting in the *Subject* text box.
   e. Type Meeting Room B in the *Location* text box.
   f. Change the *End time* to *2:00 PM (1 hour)*.
   g. Click the High Importance button in the Tags group on the Meeting tab.
   h. Click in the white text box below the *End time* option boxes and then type Please bring the names of volunteers you have confirmed to the meeting.
   i. Click Send.

3. Update the meeting request sent in Step 2 to change the duration of the meeting by completing the following steps:
   a. Double-click the *Conference volunteer planning meeting* meeting box.
   b. Change the *End time* to *3:00 PM (2 hours)*.
   c. Click the Send Update button. Outlook updates the meeting specifications via email message to the attendee(s) and adjusts the appointment within your calendar.

4. Read the updated meeting request by completing the following steps:
   a. Click the Mail text label or icon on the Navigation bar. If necessary, click the Send/ Receive All Folders button on the Quick Access Toolbar. If you are using a secondary email address for yourself, make sure you have signed in to the other account.
   b. With Inbox active, click the message header for the updated meeting request sent from Step 3. Notice in the Reading pane that the updated meeting time displays in color with the original meeting time shown in dimmed text with a line drawn through the text. If you signed in to a secondary email account, sign out and return to the account you normally use for this textbook.

5. Click the Calendar text label or icon on the Navigation bar and display *October 17, 2018* in the Appointment area.

6. Click the File tab and then click *Print*. At the Print backstage area, click *Weekly Calendar Style* in the *Settings* section, and then click the Print button. **Note:** *You will have two meetings scheduled for 1:00 p.m. on October 17 if you sent a meeting request and received a meeting request from another student for this exercise. You are the meeting organizer for one and a meeting attendee for the other meeting.*

Check Your Work

Updating Meeting Attendees and Manually Tracking Responses

Exchange Server

Outlook tracks and updates meeting responses automatically when all attendees are connected to a Microsoft Exchange server.

If after you send a meeting request a new attendee is to be invited to the meeting, open the Meeting window and type the email address of the new attendee in the *To* text box. You can also click the Scheduling Assistant or Tracking button, click over *Click here to add a name* in the attendee list, and then type the name or email address of the person being added to the meeting. To remove an attendee from the meeting, right-click the attendee's name in the *To* text box and then click *Cut* at the shortcut menu. The meeting organizer can choose to send an update message only to the individuals who have been added or deleted or to all the meeting participants.

Outlook tracks the responses received from attendees when they open the message and choose one of the Respond buttons. The replies can be viewed by the meeting organizer in the *Response* column on the Tracking page. If, however, an attendee contacts the meeting organizer by telephone or a subsequent email with a change in his or her status, the meeting organizer can manually change the response status. To do this, open the Meeting window and click the Tracking

TIP The Meeting
Notes feature
integrates Outlook
with OneNote.
Microsoft OneNote
is used to store
notes related to a
meeting. The meeting
organizer can opt
to share the notes
with the attendees,
by distributing the
notes via a link to the
OneNote workbook.
To store notes, open
the Meeting window,
then click the Meeting
Notes button on the
Meeting tab.

button. Click in the *Response* column next to the attendee's name and a drop-down list opens. Click the new status for the attendee, as shown in Figure 3.9.

Figure 3.9 Tracking Response Options on the Tracking Page

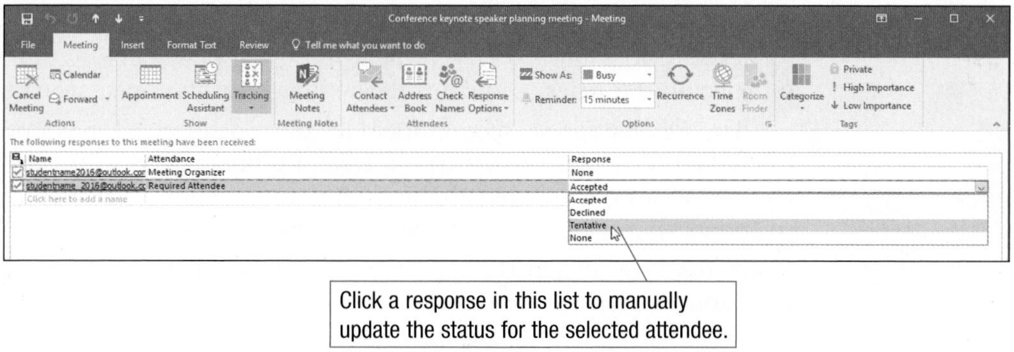

Click a response in this list to manually update the status for the selected attendee.

Changing Calendar Options

Quick Steps

Change Calendar Options
1. Click Calendar Options dialog box launcher in Arrange group on Home tab.
2. Change options as desired.
3. Click OK.
OR
1. Click File tab.
2. Click *Options*.
3. Click *Calendar*.
4. Change options as desired.
5. Click OK.

Calendar Options dialog box launcher

You can customize Calendar in Outlook by changing options in the Outlook Options dialog box. For example, if you work a nonstandard work week, select the days that apply to you in the *Work time* section in the Outlook Options dialog box with Calendar active. Click the Calendar Options dialog box launcher at the bottom right of the Arrange group on the Home tab, or click the File tab and then click *Options* to open the Outlook Options dialog box. With *Calendar* selected in the left pane, the Outlook Options dialog box appears as shown in Figure 3.10.

Change the way the calendar displays in the Date Navigator with options in the *Work time* section. For example, if you change the *First day of week* entry from

Figure 3.10 Calendar Options Dialog Box

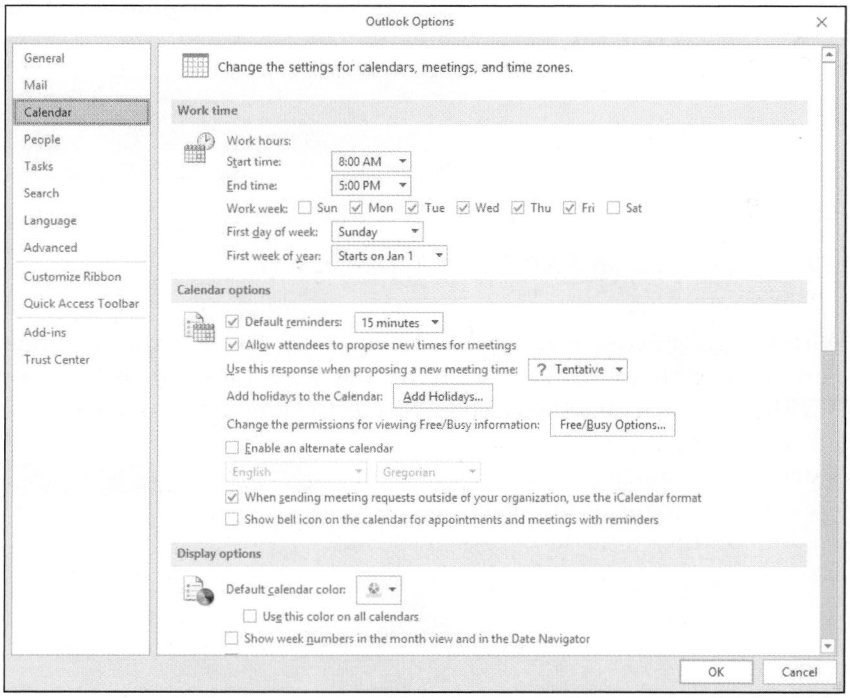

Sunday to *Saturday*, the Date Navigator displays with the first day in each week as *Saturday*. The columns are labeled *S S M T W T F*. Changing the *Start time* and *End time* entries makes the Appointment area background color for work day hours to shorten or lengthen to reflect the length of the new work day.

Buttons or check boxes in the *Calendar options* section set default times for reminders, allow attendees to propose alternative meeting times to your meeting requests, set default responses when proposing new meeting times, add holidays for specific countries, and control calendar information sent via the Internet.

The *Display options* section includes buttons or check box options to change the default calendar color, turn on week numbers in Month view and in the Date Navigator, show free appointments in Schedule view, and set the number of calendars that, when opened, cause the layout to adjust in Schedule view.

Add a text label at the top of the Time bar in the Appointment area for your time zone by typing the label in the *Time zone* section. Add a second time zone to the Time bar by inserting a check mark in the *Show a second time zone* check box. Type a label for the additional time zone and choose the time zone in the *Time zone* list box. Outlook adds a second column to the Time bar in the Appointment area to show appointments at the correct time for each time zone as shown in Figure 3.11.

Use options in the *Scheduling assistant* and *Automatic accept or decline* sections to specify how to show calendar details in meeting requests or turn on automatic replies to requests. Turn off the display of the weather in the Appointment area or change the temperature display from Fahrenheit to Celsius in the *Weather* section.

Figure 3.11 Appointment Area with Two Time Zones on Time Bar

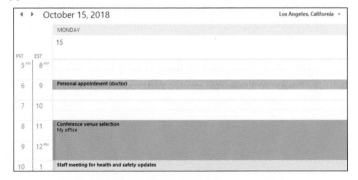

Exercise 11 Customizing the Calendar Appearance

1. With Calendar active and *October 17, 2018* displayed in the Appointment area, change the start and end times for the work day, show week numbers in Month view and in the Date Navigator, and change the calendar's color scheme by completing the following steps:
   a. Click the Calendar Options dialog box launcher located at the bottom right of the Arrange group on the Home tab.

b. Click the *Start time* option box arrow in the *Work time* section and then click *9:00 AM* at the drop-down list.

c. Click the *End time* option box arrow in the *Work time* section, scroll down, and then click *6:00 PM* at the drop-down list.

d. Click the Default calendar color button in the *Display options* section and then click the second color option in the first row (*Green*) at the drop-down color palette.

e. Click to insert a check mark in the *Show week numbers in the month view and in the Date Navigator* check box in the *Display options* section.

f. Click OK to close the Outlook Options dialog box.

2. Review the appearance of the calendar with the new options applied. The Appointment area is shaded white for the new work day times between 9:00 a.m. and 6:00 p.m. Week numbers are added to the months displayed in the Date Navigator, and the color scheme is green.

3. Click the Month button in the Arrange group and review the options shown in this view. Notice the week numbers along the left edge of the calendar.

4. Click the Day button in the Arrange group and then print the calendar with *Daily Style* selected in the *Settings* section of the Print backstage area.

Check Your Work

To customize the calendar, click the Settings button (gear icon near your name) and then click *Calendar* at the drop-down list. Click *Calendar appearance* in the Options pane at the left to display the Calendar appearance options in a panel at the right of the Options pane. Many of the options that can be changed such as the work week days, working hours, and showing week numbers in month view are similar to the options in the desktop version of Outlook. Click the Back button when finished.

Customize the calendar by clicking the Settings button (gear icon near your name at top right of screen) and then clicking *Options* at the drop-down list. Click *Calendar appearance* in the Options pane to change work week, working hours, time zone, and other appearance options in the Calendar appearance panel at the right of the Options pane. Click the Back button at the top of the Options pane when finished.

Quick Steps

Create a New Calendar Folder
1. Right-click *Calendar* in Folder pane.
2. Click *New Calendar*.
3. Type new folder name.
4. Click OK.

Working with More than One Calendar

You can view more than one calendar at the same time. Outlook displays multiple calendars side by side in the Appointment area and all the calendars are synchronized to the same day or time period. For example, you may want to maintain a separate calendar for a special project that you are working on to keep the project activities separate from those of your main job. Another example might be that you want to maintain personal appointments separate from your business appointments.

To add a new calendar, create a new folder in which to store the new calendar items. Outlook adds the name of the new calendar in the *My Calendars* section of the Folder pane. Click to insert a check mark in the check box next to the calendar name in the *My Calendars* section of the Folder pane to display the new calendar beside the existing calendar.

You can lay one calendar over another to better see conflicts in scheduling. To do this, right-click one of the calendars in the Folder pane and then click *Overlay* at the shortcut menu. You can also click the left-pointing arrow next to the calendar name in the Calendar tab in the Appointment area to turn on Overlay mode.

Some Microsoft email accounts are created as an Exchange ActiveSync account. Exchange ActiveSync account types cannot create a new calendar, contact, or task folder in the desktop edition of Outlook. Check the account type by clicking the File tab and then looking in the account information box at the top of the Account Information backstage area. The account type is shown below your email address. If you have multiple accounts, click the list box arrow to view other email account types. If the type is Exchange ActiveSync, you will not be able to add a second calendar.

Exercise 12 Displaying and Working With Two Calendars

Note: If you are connected to Outlook using a Microsoft account that is an Exchange ActiveSync account, you will not be able to complete this exercise. Check your account type by clicking the File tab and then looking in the account information box at the top of the Account Information backstage area. The account type is listed below the email address.

1. With Calendar active and *October 17, 2018* displayed in the Appointment area, create a new calendar folder by completing the following steps:
   a. Right-click *Calendar* below *My Calendars* in the Folder pane and then click *New Calendar* at the shortcut menu.
   b. At the Create New Folder dialog box with the insertion point positioned in the *Name* text box, type Volunteer Schedule.
   c. With *Calendar Items* selected in the *Folder contains* list box and *Calendar* selected in the *Select where to place the folder* list box, click OK.

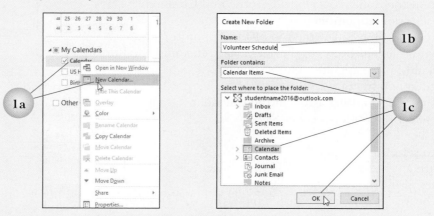

d. If you receive a message saying Outlook cannot create the folder in an Exchange ActiveSync account, click OK, and then close the Create Folder dialog box. You will not be able to complete the remainder of this exercise. Proceed to the next section in the textbook.

2. Click to insert a check mark in the *Volunteer Schedule* check box in the *My Calendars* section in the Folder pane. Outlook displays each calendar in a tab with the calendar folder name in the tab. Each calendar displays appointments for the same day and time, as shown below.

This Volunteer Schedule calendar was added to the Appointment area in Step 2.

3. Click *October 15, 2018* in the Date Navigator. Notice that both calendars display the same day simultaneously.
4. Schedule an appointment in the Volunteer Schedule calendar by completing the following steps:
   a. With *October 15, 2018* the active date, click next to *10:00 AM* within the Volunteer Schedule tab.
   b. Type Ronald McDonald House and then press Enter.
   c. Double-click to open the Appointment window, change the *End time* to *12:00 PM (2 hours)*, and then click the Save & Close button.
5. Click the left-pointing arrow on the Volunteer Schedule tab to select the option *View in Overlay Mode*. Overlay mode displays the two calendars with one on top of the other. The main calendar's appointments are shown in the Volunteer Schedule calendar as dimmed appointments. Overlay mode lets you spot scheduling conflicts easily, such as the one-hour overlap in the Ronald McDonald House and Conference venue selection appointments.
6. Click the Calendar tab at the top of the Appointment area. The main calendar becomes the active calendar, and the Ronald McDonald House appointment is shown as a dimmed appointment.
7. Click the right-pointing arrow in the Calendar tab to select the option *View in Side-By-Side Mode*.
8. Click to select the Ronald McDonald House appointment box within the Volunteer Schedule tab and then print the calendar in Daily style.
9. Click the *Volunteer Schedule* check box in the *My Calendars* section in the Folder pane to clear the check box. Only the main calendar displays in the Appointment area.

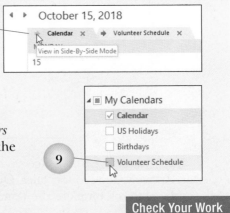

Check Your Work

Sharing a Calendar

Share your calendar with someone outside your network by emailing him or her your calendar. The person can view the details within the email message or import the attached iCalendar file (*.ics* file) into his or her scheduling software. Click the E-mail Calendar button in the Share group on the Home tab. At the Send a Calendar via Email dialog box, choose the calendar and date range and then click the OK button to open a message window with the iCalendar file attached and the calendar entries embedded in the message. Type the person's email address in the *To* text box, type a brief message above the embedded calendar, and then click Send.

Use the Publish Online button in the Share group to publish your calendar as a web page. To do this, you need access to a web server that supports the WebDAV protocol (World Wide Web Distributed Authoring and Versioning protocol). Click the Publish Online button and then click *Publish to WebDAV Server*. Type the URL in the Publish Calendar to Custom Server dialog box, change other options as required, and then click OK.

Deleting a Calendar

Outlook does not let you delete the primary calendar for your account. Any other calendar that you have created can be deleted by right-clicking the name of the calendar you want to remove in the Folder pane, and then clicking *Delete Calendar* at the shortcut menu. Click Yes at the message box that asks if you want to move the calendar to your Deleted Items folder.

Chapter Summary

- Calendar is used to schedule appointments, events, and meetings.
- Create a new appointment using the click-and-type method or with the New Appointment button in the New group on the Home tab.
- An appointment that occurs on an ongoing basis can be set up as a recurring appointment.
- An event is an activity that lasts an entire day or longer.
- Edit or delete an appointment by double-clicking the appointment box to open the Appointment window, or select the appointment box and use the buttons on the Calendar Tools Appointment tab.
- Change the calendar view using the Day, Work Week, Week, and Month buttons in the Arrange group on the Home tab.
- Display appointments in a table format using the *List* or *Active* option at the Change View button drop-down list in the Current View group on the View tab.
- Display the Reading pane to view appointment details at the right or bottom of the screen.
- Assign color categories to appointments to group related items.
- View appointments displayed in a table format grouped by color categories using the Categories button in the Arrangement group option box on the View tab.

- Outlook can automatically apply color formatting to appointments based on criteria specified in a rule at the Conditional Formatting dialog box.

- Scheduling a meeting in Outlook is similar to setting up an appointment, except that you invite people to the meeting by sending a meeting request email.

- The invitee responds to the meeting organizer using the Accept, Tentative, Decline, or Propose New Time button in the meeting request message.

- Responses to the organizer's meeting request are automatically tracked by Outlook for users connected to a Microsoft Exchange server.

- Open the Meeting window to edit the details or change attendees. Click the Send Update button to send an email to meeting participants with details about the changes made to the day, time, location, or attendee list.

- Cancel a meeting with the Cancel Meeting button in the Actions group on the Meeting tab.

- Use the Tracking page in the Meeting window to manually change a response.

- Customize Calendar by changing options in the Outlook Options dialog box.

- Create a new calendar to store items separately from the main calendar.

- Click the check boxes for the calendars you want to display in the *My Calendars* section in the Folder pane. Outlook displays the same day and time in each open calendar.

- Display calendars in Overlay mode to view two calendars with one on top of the other; this allows you to see scheduling conflicts easily.

- Share your calendar information with someone outside your internal network by emailing the calendar or by publishing the calendar online.

- The primary calendar cannot be deleted; however, any calendar you have created can be deleted by right-clicking the calendar name in the Folder pane and choosing *Delete Calendar* at the shortcut menu.

Commands Review

FEATURE	BUTTON	RIBBON TAB AND GROUP, OR OTHER METHOD	SHORTCUT
Apply conditional formatting		View, Current View	
Assign color category		Appointment, Event, OR Meeting, Tags	
Cancel meeting		Meeting, Actions	
Change calendar options		Home, Arrange, OR File, *Options*, *Calendar*	
Change current view		Home, Arrange OR View, Current View	
Create appointment		Home, New	Ctrl + N OR Ctrl + Shift + A
Create event		Home, New OR double-click in white text box below day of week colored bar at top of Appointment area	
Create meeting request		Home, New	Ctrl + Shift + Q
Create new calendar folder		Right-click Calendar folder, New Calendar	Ctrl + Shift + E
Create recurring appointment		Appointment, Event OR Meeting, Options	
Delete appointment or event		Appointment OR Event, Actions	Ctrl + D
Display Reading pane		View, Layout	
Email calendar		Home, Share	
Go to date		Home, Go To	Ctrl + G

Managing Contacts

Performance Objectives

Precheck

Check your current skills to help focus your study.

Upon successful completion of Chapter 4, you will be able to:

1 Add, edit, and delete contacts

2 Add a new contact from an existing contact

3 Add a picture of a contact to the Contact window

4 Flag contacts for follow-up

5 Sort and filter contacts

6 Apply color categories to contacts

7 Find contacts using search tools

8 Customize the current view

9 Change contact names and filing options

10 Send email messages from the Contacts module

11 Schedule meetings from the Contacts module

12 Create and use a contact group

In Outlook, the Contacts module displays when you click People on the Navigation bar. The Contacts module is used to maintain all the information you need about the individuals or companies with whom you regularly communicate. The information you store about an individual can include details such as manager's name, assistant's name, spouse's name, children's names, birthday, and anniversary. You can also store the contact's photograph with the contact form so that you can see the individual while looking at his or her name, address, and phone numbers. Outlook provides several methods for viewing contacts by sorting, filtering, and grouping related records.

Data Files

Six student data files are required for this chapter. Before beginning the chapter exercises and assessments, download the files by going to the Ancillary Links menu on this page in your ebook, clicking the Student Data Files link, and saving the files to your storage medium (such as a USB flash drive).

SNAP

If you are a SNAP user, launch the Precheck and the Tutorial from your Assignments page.

Adding Contacts

Quick Steps

Add a Contact
1. Click New Contact button in New group on Home tab.
2. Type data in required fields.
3. Click Save & Close.

Data saved in the Contacts module is like an electronic address book with the names, addresses, telephone numbers, email addresses, and other information for individuals that you want to call, text, or email. The Contacts folder is like a database, with each contact occupying a *record* in the folder. Each unit of information about an individual within the record, such as a telephone number, is referred to as a *field*. Approximately 140 fields are available for storing information about a contact, including three addresses, three email addresses, and up to 19 telephone numbers. This information can be viewed or printed in a variety of formats and orders.

A new contact record is stored in the Contacts folder, which is automatically displayed when you activate the People module. The Contacts folder displays in the Folder pane below *My Contacts*. More than one contacts folder may display in the Folder pane. For example, a folder for LinkedIn will display below the Contacts folder if you have your account connected to that social network.

The default view for the Contacts folder is People view, as shown in Figure 4.1. The first contact you will add to the Contacts folder in Exercise 1 is shown in Figure 4.1, with the Reading pane displaying the People card for the selected contact (Ms. Kayla McAllister).

New Contact

To open the Contact window with the General page displayed (see Figure 4.2 on page 111), click the New Contact button in the New group on the Home tab. The General page displays the most frequently used fields, such as job title, company name, business address, and telephone numbers, as well as email, web, and instant messaging addresses.

Use the *Notes* text box at the right side of the window to type information about the contact that you want to remember. For example, type the person's favorite color, a memorable vacation the person has mentioned, or a reminder about how you know the person.

Figure 4.1 People View for Contacts

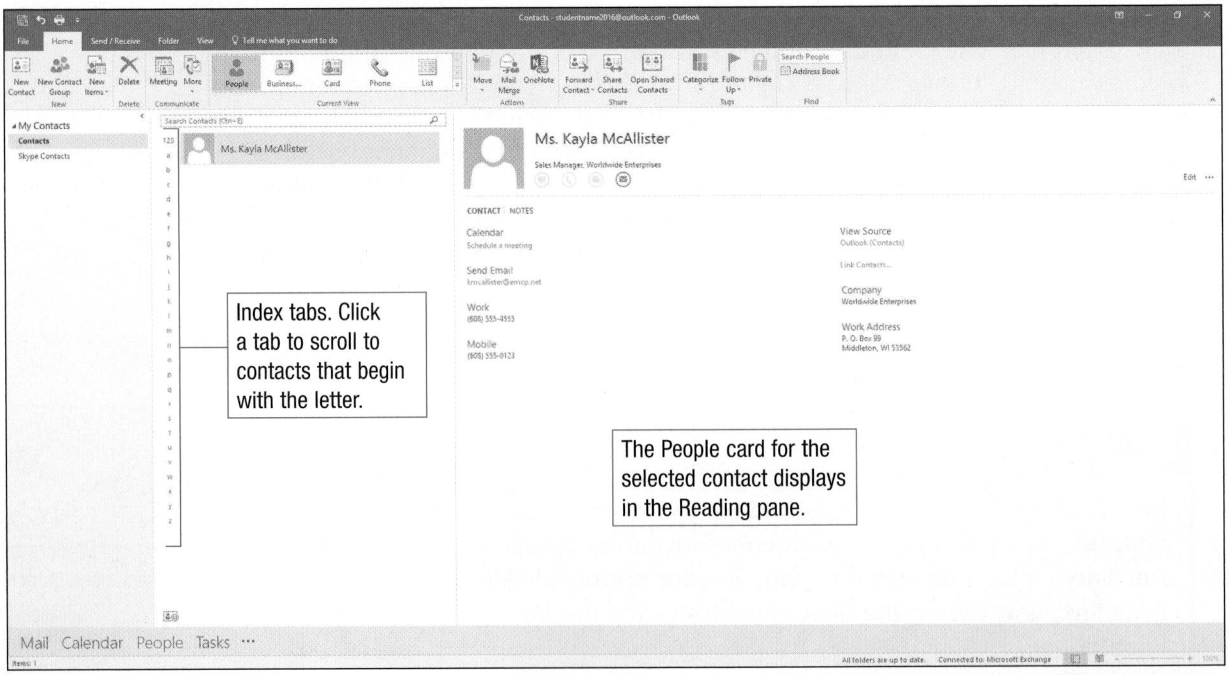

Index tabs. Click a tab to scroll to contacts that begin with the letter.

The People card for the selected contact displays in the Reading pane.

Figure 4.2 New Contact Window with General Page Displayed

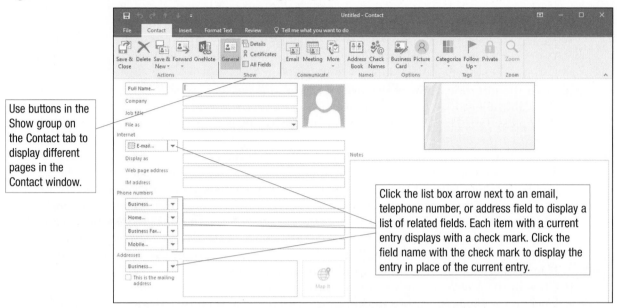

Use buttons in the Show group on the Contact tab to display different pages in the Contact window.

Click the list box arrow next to an email, telephone number, or address field to display a list of related fields. Each item with a current entry displays with a check mark. Click the field name with the check mark to display the entry in place of the current entry.

Buttons in the Show group on the Contact tab display pages with additional fields for the contact. At the Details page, you can enter details about the contact's business in the following fields: *Department, Office, Profession, Manager's name,* and *Assistant's name.* If you would like to keep track of personal information about the contact, type entries in the *Nickname, Title, Suffix, Spouse/Partner, Birthday,* or *Anniversary* fields. If the contact will be sharing calendar information, enter his or her web address in the *Internet Free-Busy* field.

At the Certificates page, import or export digital IDs that can be used to encrypt mail sent to the contact. Additional fields not shown at the previous pages can be viewed at the All Fields page by selecting a category of fields from the *Select from* drop-down list. The *All Contact fields* option at the *Select from* drop-down list shows all the fields for the active contact in one window.

Consider using the All Fields page to view a subset of related fields. For example, if you have a contact with several phone numbers stored in the contact record, you can view all the telephone numbers on one page by selecting *Phone number fields* from the *Select from* drop-down list.

Click the Save & Close button in the Actions group on the Contact tab when you are finished typing information into the contact fields for a new contact. If you are going to add another new contact immediately after saving the current contact, click the Save & New button in the Actions group.

Exercise 1 Adding New Contacts

1. With Outlook open, click the People text label or icon on the Navigation bar.
2. Add a new record to the Contacts module by completing the following steps:
   a. Click the New Contact button in the New group on the Home tab.

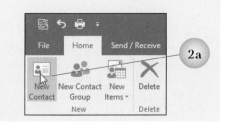

b. With the insertion point positioned in the *Full Name* text box, type Ms. Kayla McAllister and then press Tab. The *File as* text box automatically displays the name (with the last name first for sorting purposes) when you move to the next field.

c. With the insertion point positioned in the *Company* text box, type Worldwide Enterprises and then press Tab.

d. With the insertion point positioned in the *Job title* text box, type Sales Manager.

e. Click in the *Email* text box in the *Internet* section, type kmcallister@emcp.net, and then press Tab. The *Display as* text box automatically converts the email entry to *Kayla McAllister (kmcallister@emcp.net)*.

f. Click in the *Business* text box in the *Phone numbers* section, type 6085554555, and then press Tab. Outlook converts the telephone number to *(608) 555-4555*. You can type telephone numbers with or without spaces or hyphens between sections. ***Note:*** *A Location Information (or Enter Location) dialog box may appear if Windows does not currently have a country and area code set up for the computer you are using. This dialog box stores information related to where you reside and is required for Outlook's telephone features to function correctly. Enter the required location information and then click OK. Click OK if the Phone and Modem dialog box appears, showing your area code.*

g. If necessary, resize the Contact window to view all the fields.

h. Click in the *Mobile* text box in the *Phone numbers* section and then type 6085550123.

i. Click in the *Business* text box in the *Addresses* section and then type the following street address, city, state, and zip code as shown:

    P. O. Box 99
    Middleton, WI 53562

j. Click the Save & Close button in the Actions group on the Contact tab.

3. Examine the contact record added to the Content pane and the People card displayed in the Reading pane by comparing your screen with the one shown in Figure 4.1 on page 110.

4. Add a second record to the Contacts module using the Check Full Name and Check Address dialog boxes by completing the following steps:

a. Double-click in a blank area in the Content pane below the selected contact record for Ms. Kayla McAllister. This action opens a new Contact window.

b. With the insertion point positioned in the *Full Name* text box, click the Full Name button to open the Check Full Name dialog box.

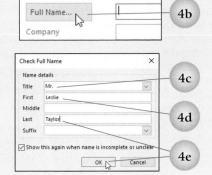

c. With the insertion point positioned in the *Title* text box in the *Name details* section, type Mr. and then press Tab or click in the *First* text box.

d. Type Leslie in the *First* text box and then press Tab two times or click in the *Last* text box.

e. Type Taylor in the *Last* text box and then press Enter or click OK.

f. Click in the *Company* text box and then type Globalware Distributors.

g. Click in the *Job title* text box and then type Sales Representative.

h. Click in the *Email* text box and then type ltaylor@emcp.net.

i. Type the following telephone numbers in the appropriate fields in the *Phone numbers* section:

   Business   6085552199
   Mobile   6085554975

j. Click the Business button in the *Addresses* section to open the Check Address dialog box.

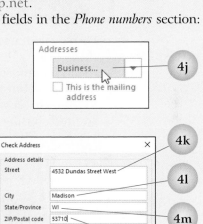

k. With the insertion point positioned in the *Street* text box in the *Address details* section, type 4532 Dundas Street West, and then press Tab or click in the *City* text box.

l. Type Madison and then press Tab or click in the *State/Province* text box.

m. Type WI and then press Tab or click in the *ZIP/Postal code* text box.

n. Type 53710 and then press Enter or click OK.

o. Click the Save & Close button in the Actions group on the Contact tab.

5. Click the Card button in the Current View group on the Home tab.

6. Increase the width of the first column of contacts in the Content pane by pointing to the gray vertical line at the right of the first column of contact names until the pointer displays with a left-and-right-pointing arrow and then dragging right until all data is visible.

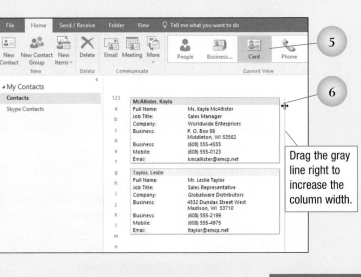

Drag the gray line right to increase the column width.

7. Click the File tab and then click *Print*. At the Print backstage area with *Card Style* selected in the *Settings* section, click the Print button.

Check Your Work

TIP The Check Address dialog box often appears for international addresses due to differences in zip/postal codes. To save time, type these addresses directly into the Check Address dialog box.

In Exercise 1, Step 2, you typed text directly into the *Full Name* and *Business* text boxes, but in Step 4, you typed text into the individual fields for the name and address using the Check Full Name and Check Address dialog boxes. Outlook separates input into the individual fields based on the text that you type unless the entry is not recognized. If the entry is not recognized, the Check Full Name or Check Address dialog box opens automatically so that you can edit the entries. Insert and delete text as required to correct the text in the fields, or click OK to accept the entries.

Outlook automatically recognizes the titles *Dr., Miss, Mr., Mrs., Ms.,* and *Prof.* The Check Address dialog box automatically opens when an address has been typed that Outlook does not recognize as containing a valid street, city, state or province, and zip or postal code.

Adding Contacts in Outlook on the web

Display contacts by clicking the Microsoft Apps button (waffle icon), and then clicking the People tile. Click the New button on the Menu bar and then type information in the fields on the Add contact page. Click the Expand button next to a section title to display more fields for the section. Expand the *Work* section to locate the *Job title* and *Company* fields when adding a business contact. Click the Save button when finished.

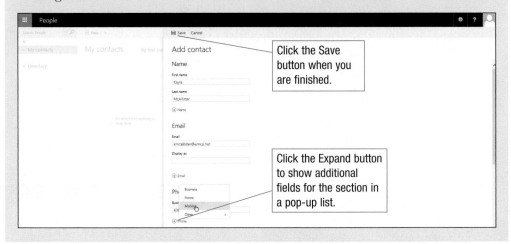

Click the Save button when you are finished.

Click the Expand button to show additional fields for the section in a pop-up list.

Adding Contacts at Outlook.com

Click the Microsoft Apps button (waffle icon) and then click the People tile at the drop-down Navigation bar to display contacts.

Click the New button on the Menu bar to add a new contact. Type information in the fields at the Add contact page. Click the Save button when finished.

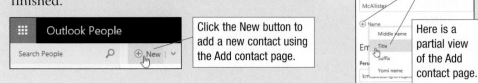

Click the New button to add a new contact using the Add contact page.

The Expand button shows more fields related to the section.

Here is a partial view of the Add contact page.

Editing and Deleting Contacts

Quick Steps

Edit a Contact
1. Display contacts in People view.
2. Click to select name in Content pane.
3. Click Edit Contact button in Reading pane.
4. Edit fields as required.
5. Click Save button.

Delete a Contact
1. Click to select name in Content pane.
2. Click Delete button in Delete group on Home tab.

 Delete

Maintaining contact records involves activities such as changing addresses, telephone numbers, and email addresses as individuals move or change companies. It also involves adding information to fields not previously completed and deleting contacts for which you no longer require records in the Contacts folder.

To edit a contact, display the contacts in People view, select the desired name in the Content pane, and then click the Edit Contact button near the top right of the Reading pane. Edit the data in the fields as required. Use the Expand button (plus symbol inside circle) at the top of a section to show more fields in the People card. For example, click the Expand button in the *Email* section to add a second email address for the contact. Click the Save button when you are finished editing the contact record.

You can also edit a contact by clicking the link below *View Source* in the Reading pane. This action opens the Contact window that you used to add the person to the contacts list. Make the desired changes and then click Save & Close in the Actions group on the Contact tab when finished.

To delete a contact, click to select the name in the Content pane for the contact that you want to remove and then press Delete. You can also click the Delete button in the Delete group on the Home tab.

Exercise 2 Adding and Editing Contacts

1. With Outlook open and the contacts list active in Card view, add a new contact by completing the following steps:
   a. Right-click in a blank area in the Content pane and then click *New Contact* at the shortcut menu.
   b. With the insertion point positioned in the *Full Name* text box, type Celia D'Allario.
   c. Click in the *Email* text box and then type cdallario@emcp.net.
   d. Type the following telephone numbers in the appropriate text boxes:
Home	6085554968
Mobile	6085553795
   e. Click the Business button arrow in the *Addresses* section and then click *Home* at the drop-down list.
   f. With the insertion point positioned in the *Home* text box in the *Addresses* section, type the following text:
      44 Queen Street
      Madison, WI 53562
   g. Click the Private button in the Tags group on the Contact tab.
   h. Click Save & Close in the Actions group on the Contact tab.

1b-1f

1g

2. Edit the telephone numbers for Leslie Taylor in the Reading pane in People view by completing the following steps:

   a. Click the People button in the Current View group on the Home tab.

   b. Click to select *Mr. Leslie Taylor* in the Content pane.

   c. If necessary, turn on the Reading pane. Click the Edit Contact button near the top right of the Reading pane (displays as *Edit*).

   d. Click to place the insertion point in the *Work* text box in the *Phone* section and then insert and delete text as required to change the telephone number from *(608) 555-2199* to *(608) 555-2267*.

   e. Change the mobile telephone number from *(608) 555-4975* to *(608) 555-3311* by completing a step similar to Step 2d.

   f. Click the Save button near the bottom right of the Reading pane.

3. Change the street address for Kayla McAllister from *P. O. Box 99* to *18 Forsythia Avenue* by completing steps similar to Steps 2b through 2f. Click OK at the Check Address dialog box if it appears after you save the changes.

4. Click the File tab and then click *Print*. With *Card Style* selected in the *Settings* section of the Print backstage area, click the Print button.

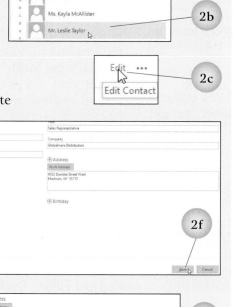

Check Your Work

Editing Contacts in Outlook on the web

Edit a contact in Outlook on the web by selecting the contact in the contact list, clicking the More commands button and then clicking the Edit button. Make the desired changes at the Edit contact page and then click the Save button. Delete a selected contact by clicking the Delete button and then clicking the Delete button in the Delete contact? message box that appears.

Editing Contacts at Outlook.com

Edit a contact at Outlook.com by selecting the contact in the contact list and then clicking the Edit button on the Menu bar. Make the desired changes at the Edit contact page and then click the Save button. Delete a selected contact by clicking the Delete button on the Menu bar and then clicking the Delete button in the Delete contact? message box that appears.

Quick Steps

Add a New Contact from an Existing Contact

1. Select existing contact in Content pane.
2. Click New Items button in New group on Home tab.
3. Click *Contact from the Same Company*.
4. Type data as required.
5. Click Save & Close.

New Items

Adding New Contacts from Existing Contacts

When you communicate with more than one person from the same company, you can quickly add the second and subsequent records by basing them on the first record. Outlook inserts the company name, company address, and business telephone number in the Contact window so that you do not have to retype the information. Basing a new record on an existing one not only avoids duplication of effort but also ensures that records are consistent and that typing errors are minimized.

Once one of the contacts has been created for the company, the remaining contacts for the same company can be added by selecting the contact record in the Contact pane, clicking the New Items button in the New group on the Home tab, and then clicking *Contact from the Same Company* at the drop-down list. Enter the name, job title, email address, and other unique information for the contact and then click the Save & Close button.

Exercise 3 Adding a New Contact from an Existing Contact

1. With Outlook open and the contacts list active in People view, add a new contact based on the record of an existing contact by completing the following steps:
   a. If necessary, click to select *Ms. Kayla McAllister* in the Content pane.
   b. Click the New Items button in the New group on the Home tab and then click *Contact from the Same Company* at the drop-down list.
   c. With the insertion point positioned in the *Full Name* text box, type Mr. Henry Miele.
   d. Click in the *Job title* text box and then type Sales Manager, EuropeanDivision.
   e. Click in the *Email* text box and then type hmiele@emcp.net.
   f. Click in the *Mobile* text box and then type 6085551884.
   g. Click Save & Close.
2. Print the contacts in Card style.

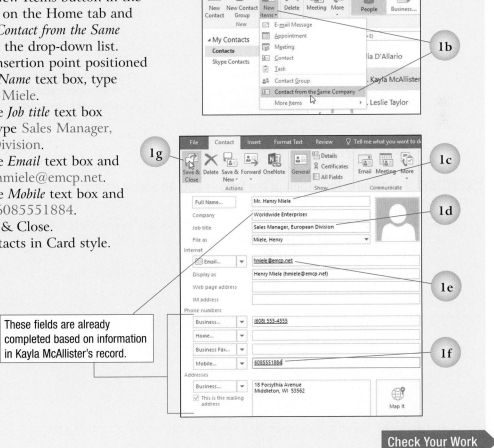

These fields are already completed based on information in Kayla McAllister's record.

Check Your Work

Using the Details and All Fields Pages

Details

All Fields

Approximately 140 fields are available for storing information about a contact, including four user-defined fields. The Details page in the Contact window, which is shown in Figure 4.3, groups fields related to the contact's business and personal relationships. The All Fields page provides the ability to view subsets of related fields or all the contact fields in a table format. Click the Details or All Fields button in the Show group on the Contact tab to change the page displayed in the Contact window.

Figure 4.3 Contact Window with Details Page Displayed

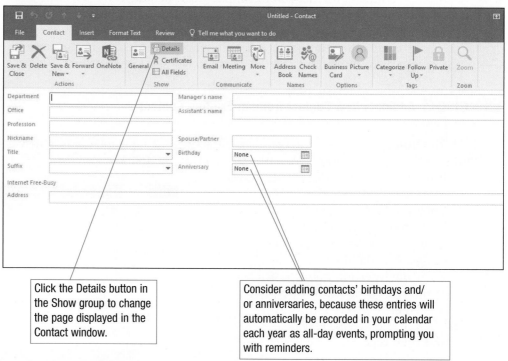

Click the Details button in the Show group to change the page displayed in the Contact window.

Consider adding contacts' birthdays and/or anniversaries, because these entries will automatically be recorded in your calendar each year as all-day events, prompting you with reminders.

Exercise 4 Adding Information in the Details and All Fields Pages

1. With Outlook open and the contacts list active in People view, add a new contact with information at the Details page by completing the following steps:
   a. Click the New Contact button in the New group on the Home tab.
   b. Type the following information in the appropriate text boxes at the General page:

Full Name	Dr. Tory Nguyen
Company	Globe Products
Job title	Director, Marketing and Sales
Email	tnguyen@emcp.net
Business	6085552689
Mobile	6085551598
Business	393 Brentwood Road Madison, WI 53562

   c. Click the Details button in the Show group on the Contact tab.

d. With the insertion point positioned in the *Department* text box, type Marketing.

e. Click in the *Manager's name* text box and then type Kyle Winston.

f. Click in the *Assistant's name* text box and then type Dana Gauthier.

g. Click in the *Spouse/Partner* text box and then type Chris Greenbaum.

2. View all the contact fields and add the names of the children for the contact by completing the following steps:

a. Click the All Fields button in the Show group on the Contact tab.

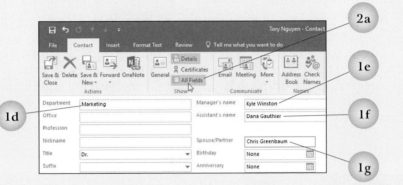

b. Click the *Select from* list box arrow, scroll down the list box, and then click *All Contact fields*.

c. Scroll down to the bottom of the list box and examine all the fields that are available for storing information about contacts.

d. Scroll up the list box until you see the field *Children*. **Note:** *The field names are in alphabetical order*.

e. Click in the column labeled *Value* beside the field *Children* to select the field and position the insertion point inside the dotted text box.

f. Type Brooke, Justin, Jamie.

g. Click the File tab inside the Contact window and then click *Print*. With *Memo Style* selected in the *Settings* section of the Print backstage area, click the Print button.

h. Click Save & Close.

3. Add the birthday information for an existing contact by completing the following steps:

a. If necessary, click to select *Ms. Kayla McAllister* in the Content pane and then click the Edit Contact button in the Reading pane.

b. Click the Expand button next to *Birthday*.

c. Click in the *Birthday* text box and then type 10/15/1960.

d. Click the Save button. A reminder will now automatically occur in the calendar each year on Kayla's birthday.

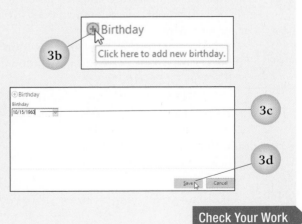

Check Your Work

Adding Pictures to Contacts

Quick Steps

Add a Picture to a Contact Record
1. Open Contact window.
2. Click *Add Contact Picture* box.
3. Navigate to drive and/or folder.
4. Double-click image file name.
5. Click Save & Close.

Add Contact Picture

TIP Picture images show next to contact names in the Content pane in People view, in Business Card view, and within a Contact window. Other views do not display the photos.

Click the *Add Contact Picture* box located within the Contact window to add a photograph of the individual to the contact record. You can also click the Picture button in the Options group on the Contact tab and then click *Add Picture* at the drop-down list. At the Add Contact Picture dialog box, navigate to the drive and/or folder where the image file is stored and then double-click the file name. Outlook recognizes standard graphics file formats, such as GIF, JPEG, and PNG and their corresponding file extensions *.gif*, *.jpg*, and *.png*. It also resizes the image to fit within the picture box, maintaining the aspect ratio so the image does not become distorted.

Figure 4.4 shows Kayla McAllister's Contact window with a picture of her in the *Add Contact Picture* box. (You will add this picture in Exercise 5.) If you need to change or remove a picture, open the Contact window for the individual, click the Picture button in the Options group on the Contact tab, and then click *Change Picture* or *Remove Picture* at the Picture button drop-down list.

Figure 4.4 Picture Added to Contact Window

The photo appears in the *Add Contact Picture* box.
You will add Kayla McAllister's picture here in Exercise 5.

Exercise 5 Adding Pictures to Contacts

Note: Make sure you have copied the student data files for this chapter to your storage medium before completing this exercise.

1. With Outlook open and the contacts list active in People view, add a picture to Kayla McAllister's contact record by completing the following steps:
   a. If necessary, click to select *Ms. Kayla McAllister* in the Content pane.
   b. Click the link in the *View Source* section of the Reading pane. This action opens the Contact window for the active contact.
   c. Click the *Add Contact Picture* box.
   d. At the Add Contact Picture dialog box, navigate to the drive and/or folder containing the student data files.
   e. Double-click *K_McAllister.jpg*.
   f. Click Save & Close.

2. Add the following pictures to the contacts noted by completing steps similar to Steps 1a through 1f:

Celia D'Allario	*C_DAllario.jpg*
Mr. Henry Miele	*H_Miele.jpg*
Dr. Tory Nguyen	*T_Nguyen.jpg*
Mr. Leslie Taylor	*L_Taylor.jpg*

3. Click the Business Card button in the Current View group on the Home tab. In Business Card view, pictures are displayed in miniature business cards for those contacts that have a picture attached to the record.

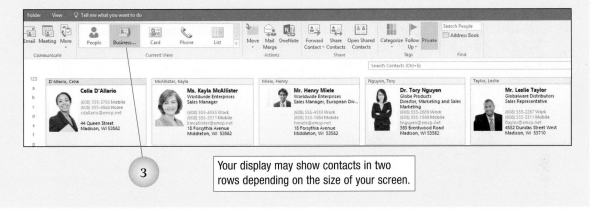

Your display may show contacts in two rows depending on the size of your screen.

Flagging a Contact for Follow-up

You can set a reminder to follow up on an outstanding issue with a contact by flagging the contact's record. To do this, select the contact record that you want to mark with a flag, click the Follow Up button in the Tags group on the Home tab, and then click the desired follow-up option at the drop-down list. Figure 4.5 displays the predefined follow-up flags.

If none of these flags suits your needs, click *Custom* to open the Custom dialog box. Click the *Flag to* option box arrow in the dialog box and then click the type of flag that you want to set. To enter a Start date or a Due date, type the date in the required text box or click the option box arrow to select a date from a drop-down calendar. Reminders for flags can also be set at the Custom dialog box. Click OK when you have finished defining the criteria for the custom flag.

Figure 4.5 Follow-up Flags

This is the Follow Up flag list for an account *not* set up as a POP3 or Microsoft Exchange account.

This is the Follow Up flag list for POP3 and Microsoft Exchange Server accounts. Notice that these accounts have an additional option, *Mark Complete*.

Exercise 6 Flagging Contacts for Follow-up

1. With Outlook open and the contacts list active in Business Card view, complete the following steps to attach a follow-up flag to a contact record that will remind you to schedule a meeting.
   a. Click to select the business card for Ms. Kayla McAllister.
   b. Click the Follow Up button in the Tags group on the Home tab and then click *Custom* at the drop-down list.
   c. At the Custom dialog box, click the *Flag to* option box arrow and then click *Arrange Meeting*.
   d. Select the current date in the *Due date* text box, type one week from today, and then press Enter or click OK. Outlook allows all dates to be entered using natural language phrases. The *Due date* will be set to one week from the current date.

The start date in your Custom dialog box will vary depending on your current date.

2. Click the Card button in the Current View group on the Home tab. Look at the Follow Up Flag information that appears in the card below the name banner for Kayla McAllister. Outlook also adds an item to the task list in the Tasks folder.

McAllister, Kayla	
Follow Up Flag:	Arrange Meeting
Full Name:	Ms. Kayla McAllister
Job Title:	Sales Manager
Company:	Worldwide Enterprises
Business:	18 Forsythia Avenue Middleton, WI 53562
Business:	(608) 555-4555
Mobile:	(608) 555-3311
Email:	kmcallister@emcp.net

3. Click the People button in the Current View group, click to select *Ms. Kayla McAllister*, click the link in the *View Source* section of the Reading pane, and then view the Follow Up message inside the Contact window.

Arrange Meeting. Start by Monday, July 23, 2018. Due by Monday, July 30, 2018.

Full Name...	Ms. Kayla McAllister
Company	Worldwide Enterprises
Job title	Sales Manager
File as	McAllister, Kayla

The Follow Up message appears at the top of the Contact window. The dates in your message will vary depending on your current date.

4. Close the Contact window.
5. Add a follow-up flag to the contact record for Dr. Tory Nguyen by completing the following steps:
   a. Right-click *Dr. Tory Nguyen* in the Content pane.
   b. Point to *Follow Up* and then click *No Date* at the shortcut menu.
6. Change the current view to Card view and then print the contacts in Card style.

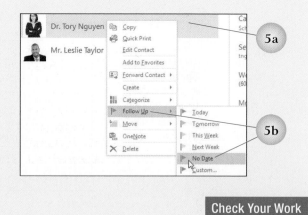

Check Your Work

TIP In Card view, the data for a contact in which a follow-up flag due date has passed without the flag being cleared or marked complete displays in red.

Once the follow-up activity has been completed, remove the flag by selecting the contact in the Content pane, clicking the Follow Up button, and then clicking *Clear Flag* at the drop-down list. Exchange Server users and users that have Outlook set up with a POP3 account can choose the *Mark Complete* option at the Follow Up drop-down list as an alternative method to note the activity has been finished. By choosing *Mark Complete*, you leave the follow-up flag in place in the contact record along with the date the follow-up activity was marked complete. Use this method if retaining the activity details is important to you.

Sorting Contacts

Quick Steps

Sort Contacts
1. Click View tab.
2. Click View Settings button in Current View group.
3. Click Sort button.
4. Define sort fields.
5. Click OK two times.

 View Settings

Contacts are displayed in the Content pane alphabetically in ascending order by the *File As* field, which defaults to the contact's last name followed by his or her first name. In the Sort dialog box, shown in Figure 4.6, you can specify up to four fields by which to sort the contacts list.

The drop-down list of fields for *Sort items by* and *Then by* defaults to *Frequently-used fields*. Click the *Select available fields from* list box arrow to change to any of the subsets of related fields or all the contact fields.

To begin a sort, click the View tab, click the View Settings button in the Current View group, and then click the Sort button in the Advanced View Settings dialog box. The Sort dialog box opens, which is where you define the sort criteria. Click OK two times after defining the sort field(s), and the contact list reorders to the new sort settings.

Figure 4.6 Sort Dialog Box

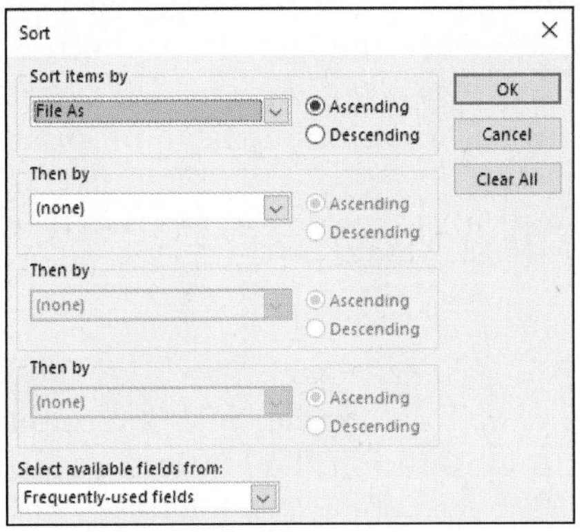

Exercise 7 Sorting Contacts

1. With Outlook open and the contacts list active in Card view, sort the contacts list by company name and then by last name within each company by completing the following steps:
   a. Click the View tab and then click the View Settings button in the Current View group.
   b. Click the Sort button in the Advanced View Settings dialog box.

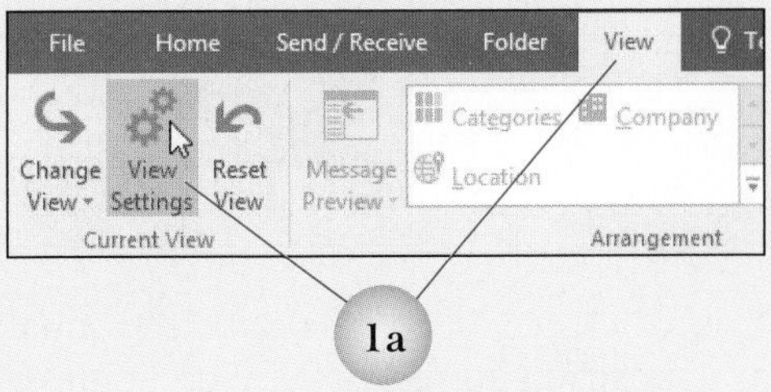

c. Click the *Sort items by* list box arrow, scroll up the list box, and then click *Company*. The default sort order is *Ascending*.

d. Click the first *Then by* list box arrow, scroll down the list box, and then click *Last Name*. The default sort order is *Ascending*.

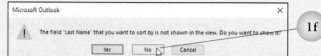
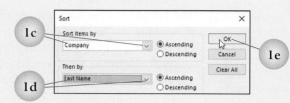

e. Click OK to close the Sort dialog box.

f. At the Microsoft Outlook message box informing you that the field *Last Name* is not shown in the view and asking if you want to show it, click No. You do not need to display the *Last Name* field because the banner for each card displays the *File As* field, which includes the last name.

g. With the current sort settings displayed next to the Sort button in the Advanced View Settings dialog box, click OK.

h. Examine the order of the records in the Content pane. If necessary, scroll in the Content pane to view all the contact records.

2. Add a new contact that is based on an existing contact by completing the following steps:

a. Click to select the card for Dr. Tory Nguyen.

b. Click the Home tab, click the New Items button in the New group, and then click *Contact from the Same Company*.

c. Type the following information in the appropriate text boxes:

Full Name	Mr. Luis Phillips
Job title	Sales Manager
E-mail	lphillips@emcp.net
Mobile	6085553884

d. Replace the picture of Tory Nguyen with the correct image by completing the following steps:
   1) Click the Picture button in the Options group on the Contact tab.
   2) Click *Change Picture* at the drop-down list.
   3) If necessary, navigate to the student data files.
   4) Double-click *L_Phillips.jpg*.

Mr. Luis Phillips
Globe Products
Sales Manager

(608) 555-2689 Work
(608) 555-3884 Mobile
lphillips@emcp.net
393 Brentwood Road
Madison, WI 53562

This is the business card for the new contact added in Step 2 from inside the Contact window.

e. Click Save & Close. Notice that the new record is arranged in the list at the correct position sorted first by company and then by the last name within each company.

3. Print the contacts in Card style.
4. Restore the sort order to the default settings by completing the following steps:
   a. Click the View tab.
   b. Click the Reset View button in the Current View group.
   c. Click Yes at the Microsoft Outlook message asking if you want to reset the Card view to the original settings.

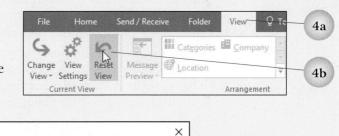

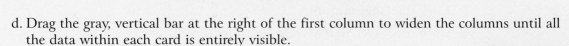

   d. Drag the gray, vertical bar at the right of the first column to widen the columns until all the data within each card is entirely visible.

Check Your Work

Sorting Contacts in Outlook on the web

Contacts are initially arranged in the Content pane sorted by first name in ascending order. Click the *By first name* arrow at the top of the contacts list in the Content pane to change the sort order to *Last name*. Change the order in which names are displayed (e.g., first then last) using the options in the *Display order* section of the drop-down list.

The title *By first name* at the top of the contacts list in the Content pane changes to reflect the current sort order.

Sorting Contacts at Outlook.com

Contacts are sorted by first name and display the contact's first name followed by his or her last name. To change the sort order to last name, click the *By first name* arrow at the top of the contacts list, and then click *Last name* in the *Sort order* section of the drop-down list. If desired, you can also change the order names are displayed in the list from First last to Last first in the *Display order* section.

Filtering Contacts

Quick Steps

Filter Contacts
1. Click View tab.
2. Click View Settings button in Current View group.
3. Click Filter button.
4. Define filter criterion.
5. Click OK two times.

A filtered contacts list is a subset of contact records that has been selected based on a criterion specified in the Filter dialog box. Records that do not meet the condition are temporarily removed from the contacts list. The message *Filter applied* appears in the Status bar next to the total number of records (labeled *Items*) to indicate that not all records are currently displayed.

To specify the condition upon which to display records, click the View tab and then click the View Settings button in the Current View group. Click the Filter button in the Advanced View Settings dialog box and then specify which records to display in the Filter dialog box with the Contacts tab selected (shown in Figure 4.7).

View and print the filtered list as necessary. When you are done, restore all records by completing the following steps:

1. Click the View tab.
2. Click the View Settings button.
3. Click the Filter button.
4. Click the Clear All button in the Filter dialog box.
5. Click OK two times.

Figure 4.7 Filter Dialog Box with Contacts Tab Selected

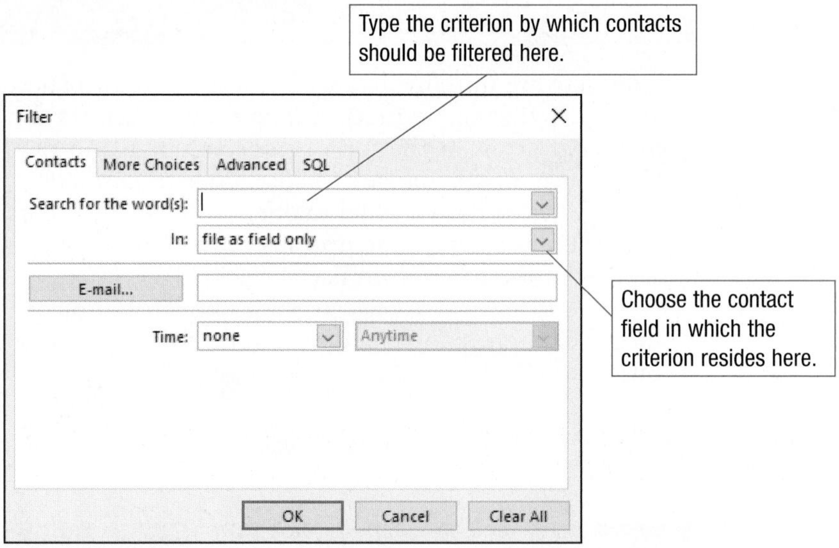

Type the criterion by which contacts should be filtered here.

Choose the contact field in which the criterion resides here.

Exercise 8 Filtering Contacts

1. With Outlook open and the contacts list active in Card view, filter the contacts list to display only those records for Globe Products by completing the following steps:
   a. Click the View Settings button in the Current View group on the View tab.
   b. Click the Filter button in the Advanced View Settings dialog box.

c. At the Filter dialog box with the Contacts tab selected and the insertion point positioned in the *Search for the word(s)* text box, type Globe Products.

d. Click the *In* list box arrow and then click *company field only* at the drop-down list.

e. Click OK to close the Filter dialog box.

f. With the current filter settings displayed next to the Filter button in the Advanced View Settings dialog box, click OK. Only two records are displayed in the Content pane and the message *Filter applied* displays at the left edge of the Status bar.

2. Print the filtered list in Phone Directory style by completing the following steps:
   a. Click the File tab and then click *Print*.
   b. Click *Phone Directory Style* in the *Settings* section of the Print backstage area.
   c. Click the Print button.

3. Restore the Content pane to display all contacts by completing the following steps:
   a. Click the View Settings button.
   b. Click the Filter button in the Advanced View Settings dialog box.
   c. Click the Clear All button in the Filter dialog box.
   d. Click OK two times.

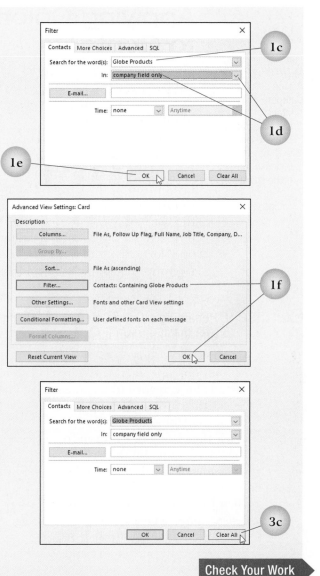

Check Your Work

Filtering Contacts at Outlook.com

Contacts from connected social media accounts, such as Twitter and LinkedIn, are automatically added to the people list at Outlook.com. You can filter the people list to show contacts by social media account. To do this, click the *Your contacts* arrow in the left pane of the browser window, and then click the list you want to view in the Content pane. For example, click *LinkedIn Contacts* to view only those people to whom you are connected via LinkedIn. Click *Connect to social networks* if you have not set up your social network accounts and wish to connect them to your Outlook.com account. Click *Contacts* to remove the filter and view all records for all connected accounts in the people list.

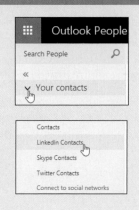

Applying Color Categories to Contacts

Quick Steps

Assign a Color Category to a Contact
1. Select contact in Content pane.
2. Click Categorize button in Tags group on Home tab.
3. Click desired color category.

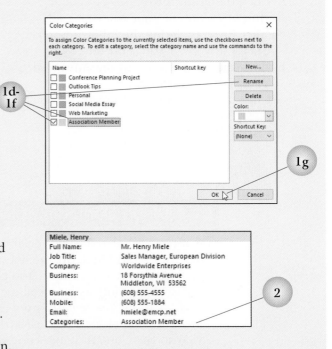 Categorize

The same six color categories that can be applied to messages and appointments can be applied to contacts. The various methods you learned to apply a color category and rename a color category for messages and appointments can be used to categorize contacts.

In Card view, the category applied to a contact displays at the bottom of the address card. You can also display the contacts list in table format using the *List* option and then group the contacts by color category. To do this, click the List button in the Current View group on the Home tab. You can also change to List view using the *List* option at the Change View button drop-down list in the Current View group on the View tab. List view displays the contacts in table format with the column headings *FULL NAME, JOB TITLE, COMPANY*, and so on. Next, click the Categories button in the Arrangement group on the View tab to group the contacts by color categories.

Exercise 9 Renaming a Color Category, Applying Color Categories to Contacts, and Viewing Contacts by Category

1. With Outlook open and the contacts list active in Card view, rename a color category and apply a color category to a contact by completing the following steps:
   a. Select the card for Henry Miele.
   b. Click the Home tab.
   c. Click the Categorize button in the Tags group and then click *All Categories* at the drop-down list.
   d. At the Color Categories dialog box, click to insert a check mark in the *Yellow Category* check box.
   e. Click the Rename button.
   f. Type Association Member and then press Enter.
   g. Click OK.
2. Look at the bottom of the card for Henry Miele. Notice that Outlook added a new line to the bottom of the card with the category name you created in Step 1.
3. Right-click the card for Luis Phillips, point to *Categorize*, and then click *Association Member* at the shortcut menu.
4. Assign the Association Member color category to the card for Dr. Tory Nguyen.
5. Display the contacts grouped by color category in table format by completing the following steps:
   a. Click the View tab, click the Change View button in the Current View group, and then click *List* at the drop-down list. This view displays the contacts in table format grouped by company name.

b. Click the Categories button in the Arrangement group option box on the View tab. The contacts are grouped according to the categories to which they were assigned in an expanded list.

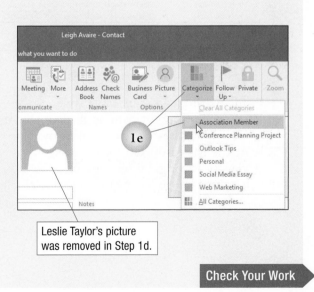

6. Print the contacts in Table style.

Check Your Work

Exercise 10 Applying a Color Category While Creating a Contact

1. With Outlook open and the contacts list active in List view, apply a color category while adding a new contact by completing the following steps:

   a. Click to select the miniaturized business card in the first column of the table next to *Mr. Leslie Taylor*. This action selects the record.

   b. Click the Home tab, click the New Items button in the New group, and then click *Contact from the Same Company*.

   c. Type the following information in the appropriate text boxes:

Full Name	Ms. Leigh Avaire
Job title	District Sales Manager
E-mail	lavaire@emcp.net
Mobile	6085551158

   d. Click the Picture button in the Options group on the Contact tab and then click *Remove Picture* at the drop-down list.

   e. Click the Categorize button in the Tags group on the Contact tab and then click *Association Member* at the drop-down list. Notice that Outlook displays the color category assigned to the contact in the information bar along the top of the Contact window below the ribbon.

   f. Click Save & Close. Notice that Outlook automatically adds the new contact to the bottom of the *Association Member* color category in the table.

2. Print the contacts in Table style.

Leslie Taylor's picture was removed in Step 1d.

Check Your Work

Exercise 11 Filtering a Contact List by Category

1. With Outlook open and the contacts list active in List view, filter the contacts list to produce a list of only those contacts in the *Association Member* category by completing the following steps:
   a. Click the View tab and then click the View Settings button in the Current View group.
   b. Click the Filter button in the Advanced View Settings dialog box.
   c. Click the More Choices tab in the Filter dialog box.
   d. Click the Categories button.
   e. At the Color Categories dialog box, click to insert a check mark in the *Association Member* check box and then click OK.
   f. Click OK to close the Filter dialog box and then click OK to close the Advanced View Settings dialog box. Only four records are displayed in the Content pane. The message *Filter applied* appears at the left end of the Status bar.

1c

Filter ✕

Contacts **More Choices** Advanced SQL

Categories... | Association Member   ∨ |

☐ Only items that are: | unread   ∨ |

1d-1e

☐ Only items with: | one or more attachments   ∨ |

☐ Whose importance is: | normal   ∨ |

☐ Only items which: | are flagged by me   ∨ |

☐ Match case

Size (kilobytes)
| doesn't matter   ∨ | | 0 | and | 0 |

[OK] [Cancel] [Clear All]

1f

	FULL NAME	JOB TITLE	COMPANY	FILE AS	COUNTRY/REGION	DEPARTMENT	BUSINESS PHONE
	Click here to add a new ...						
▲	Categories: Association Member: 4 item(s)						
	Mr. Henry Miele	Sales Manag...	Worldwide Enter...	Miele, Henry	United States of Am...		(608) 555-4555
	Dr. Tory Nguyen	Director, Mar...	Globe Products	Nguyen, Tory	United States of Am...	Marketing	(608) 555-2689
	Mr. Luis Phillips	Sales Manager	Globe Products	Phillips, Luis	United States of Am...		(608) 555-2689
	Ms. Leigh Avaire	District Sales...	Globalware Distr...	Avaire, Leigh			(608) 555-2267

Contacts are filtered by *Association Member* color category in Step 1.

2. Print the filtered list in Table style.
3. Restore the Content pane to display all contacts by completing the following steps:
   a. Click the Reset View button in the Current View group on the View tab.
   b. At the Microsoft Outlook message box asking if you are sure you want to reset the List view to its original settings, click Yes.
4. Click the Change View button and then click *Card* at the drop-down list.

Check Your Work

Finding a Contact

When a Contacts folder contains a lot of records, browsing through the folder to find a contact record can be time consuming. Outlook provides three tools to assist with locating a record quickly:

- The *Search People* box in the Find group on the Home tab
- The *Search Contacts* box at the top of the Content pane
- The Advanced Find dialog box

In addition to the three tools listed above, the letter tabs (called the *alphabet index*) along the left side of the Content pane in the Card, Business Card, and People views can be used to move to the first record that begins with the letter. For example, to move the selected record to the first contact whose last name begins with *w*, click the *w* letter tab in the alphabet index.

Using the *Search People* Box

Quick Steps

Find a Contact Using the *Search People* Box
1. Click in *Search People* box.
2. Type name or partial name.

To find a contact record quickly, click in the *Search People* box in the Find group on the Home tab (currently displays *Search People*), type the name of the individual whose record you want to see, and then press Enter. Outlook can locate records based on a partial entry (e.g., *Joe Sm*), a first name only, a last name only, an email alias, or a company name. The *Search People* box cannot be used to find people based on a telephone number or address. For these types of searches, use the *Search Contacts* box, which is described in the next section.

Exercise 12 Locating Contacts Using Letter Tabs and the *Search People* Box

1. With Outlook open and the contacts list active in Card view, locate and select records using the alphabet index tabs by completing the following steps:
   a. Click the *t* letter tab along the left edge of the Content pane. ***Note:*** *Depending on your screen size and resolution setting, your letter tabs may display with two letters per tab.*
      The screen scrolls if necessary and the card for Leslie Taylor is selected.
   b. Click the *a* letter tab. The screen scrolls if necessary and the card for Leigh Avaire is selected.
   c. Click the *m* letter tab. The card for Kayla McAllister is selected.
2. Locate and view records using the *Search People* box by completing the following steps:
   a. Click the Home tab.
   b. Click inside the *Search People* box in the Find group and then type leslie. Outlook displays the search results immediately as it begins locating records that match your search text.
   c. Click *Mr. Leslie Taylor* in the search results drop-down list. Review the information in the Contact window that opens and then close the window by clicking the Close button (displays as ×) at the top right corner of the window.

d. Click inside the *Search People* box and then type worldwide. You can locate contacts by a person's name or by a company name.

e. Click *Ms. Kayla McAllister* in the search results list to open her Contact window.

f. Review the information in the Contact window for Kayla McAllister and then close the Contact window.

Using the *Search Contacts* Box

Quick Steps

Find a Contact Using the *Search Contacts* Box
1. Click in *Search Contacts* box.
2. Type name, partial name, or other search text.
3. Refine search as needed.
4. Click Close Search button.

 Recent Searches

The *Search Contacts* box, with the text *Search Contacts*, is at the top of the Content pane. To find a contact in the current Contacts folder, click in the box and start typing the name by which you want to search the folder. As soon as you begin typing, Outlook begins filtering the Content pane to include only those records that match your search text. Continue typing the name until the list is filtered to the contact(s) for whom you are looking.

The Search Tools Search tab, shown in Figure 4.8, displays when you type an entry in the *Search Contacts* box. Use buttons in the Scope group to change the target folders for the search. Notice that the current folder is automatically the target for the current search word. Use buttons in the Refine group to narrow the search results to a specific color category, telephone number, address, or other contact field property.

The Recent Searches button in the Options group displays a history of your recent search requests. To repeat a search, click the search word or phrase in the Recent Searches button drop-down list. Click the Search Tools button in the Options group to display the indexing status of your Outlook items, to change the location in which to search (that is, to search in a different email account), to open the Advanced Find dialog box, or to modify search options at the Outlook Options dialog box.

Figure 4.8 Search Tools Search Tab for Contacts

Exercise 13 Locating Contacts Using the *Search Contacts* Box

1. With Outlook open and the contacts list active in Card view, locate records for contacts from Globe Products using the *Search Contacts* box by completing the following steps:
   a. Click in the *Search Contacts* box that displays *Search Contacts*, at the top of the Content pane, and then type globe.
   b. Outlook displays the records for the two contacts that meet the search criterion—Tory Nguyen and Luis Phillips.
2. Click the Close Search button in the Close group on the Search Tools Search tab or at the right of the *Search Contacts* box. All contact records are restored to the Content pane.

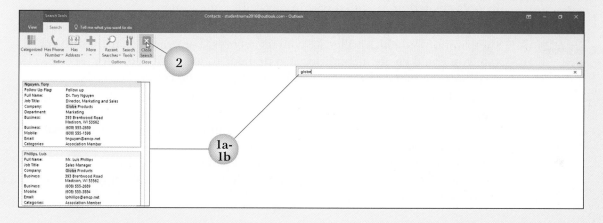

3. Conduct another search to locate the records of sales manager contacts that are association members by completing the following steps:
   a. Click in the *Search Contacts* box and then type sales manager. Outlook filters the Content pane to show four contacts that have *Sales Manager* in the *Job Title* field.
   b. Click the Categorized button in the Refine group on the Search Tools Search tab and then click *Association Member* at the drop-down list. Notice that the contacts are filtered again and that three contacts remain.

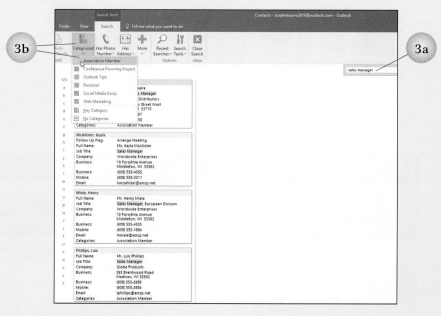

4. Click the Close Search button.

Using the Advanced Find Dialog Box

Quick Steps

Locate a Contact Using the Advanced Find Dialog Box
1. Click in or type search word in *Search Contacts* box.
2. Click Search Tools button in Options group on Search Tools Search tab.
3. Click *Advanced Find*.
4. Enter search criterion.
5. Click Find Now button.
6. Close dialog box when finished.
7. If necessary, click Close Search button.

If you cannot locate a record using the *Search People* or *Search Contacts* box, consider opening the Advanced Find dialog box, shown in Figure 4.9. Click in or type a search word in the *Search Contacts* box to begin a search using the Advanced Find feature. When the contacts are filtered in the Content pane, click the Search Tools button in the Options group on the Search Tools Search tab and then click *Advanced Find* at the drop-down list. The Contacts tab that is active when the dialog box opens contains options to locate records by typing a word that exists within the record, such as a name, telephone number, or email address; to search within a set of related fields, such as address fields; and to restrict the search to records created or modified within a specific timeframe.

Click the Advanced tab to enter a conditional statement for a field to use as the criterion on which to locate contact records. For example, at the Advanced tab, you could create a conditional statement to locate a record for a contact based on the manager's name you know exists in the contact record.

Click the Find Now button to begin the search using the Advanced Find parameters. Outlook displays contacts that meet the search specifications at the bottom of the dialog box. Double-click the contact name in the search results list to open the contact record. Click the Close button in the Advanced Find dialog box title bar when you are finished searching and viewing contacts. If necessary, click the Close Search button on the Search Tools Search tab to restore the full list of contacts.

Figure 4.9 Advanced Find Dialog Box

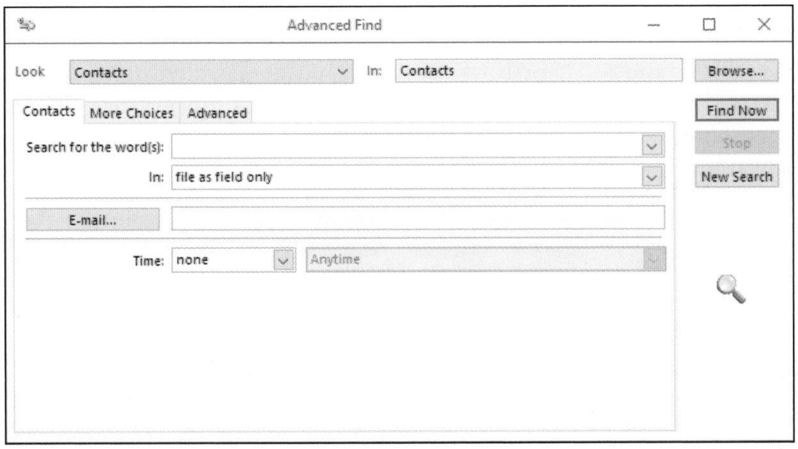

Finding a Contact in Outlook on the web

Click in the search box that contains the text *Search People* at the top of the Folder pane, type the name of a contact you want to find, and then press Enter or click the search button (displays as a magnifying glass). When you have finished the search, click *Exit search* to restore the full contacts list.

A search box (displays with the text *Search People*) is at the top of the left pane in the browser window. Click in the box, type the name of the contact whose record you want to view and then press Enter or click the search button (magnifying glass). Click a contact in the search results list to view the contact record. Click *Exit search* in the left pane to restore the full list of contacts.

Type the name of the contact to find here.

Tutorial

Adding and Removing Fields in the Current View

Customizing the Current View

You can change the current view using a button in the Current View group on the Home tab or by choosing a view at the drop-down list from the Change View button in the Current View group on the View tab. For each view, Outlook displays contact information using predefined view settings. You can customize each view to suit your own preferences by adding and/or removing contact fields.

With contacts displayed in a table format, as in List view or Phone view, you can customize the view by adding or removing columns. Add a contact field to the view by right-clicking a column heading and then clicking *Field Chooser* to display the Field Chooser dialog box containing a list of contact fields. Drag a field name from the *Field Chooser* list box to the column headings row in the Content pane, releasing the mouse button with the new field positioned at the desired location. Red arrows display above and below the field button as you drag the field in the headings row, to assist you with placing the field.

Remove a column by right-clicking the column heading in the Content pane and then clicking *Remove This Column* at the shortcut menu.

Exercise 14 Adding and Removing Fields in the Current View

1. With Outlook open and the contacts list active in Card view, change the current view to Phone view and then delete columns from the view by completing the following steps:
   a. Click the Phone button in the Current View group on the Home tab.
   b. Notice that the *BUSINESS FAX* column in the view contains no information. If necessary, scroll right to view the column in the Content pane.
   c. Right-click the *BUSINESS FAX* column heading and then click *Remove This Column* at the shortcut menu.
   d. Remove the following columns from the current view by completing a step similar to Step 1c:
      FILE AS
      COUNTRY/REGION
      JOURNAL
      CATEGORIES

2. Double-click the right column boundary for the *COMPANY* column to expand the width of the column to the length of the longest entry.

3. Add a field to the current view by completing the following steps:
   a. Right-click any column heading to display the shortcut menu and then click *Field Chooser*. The Field Chooser dialog box appears with the field set *Frequently-used fields* displaying in the *Field Chooser* list box.
   b. Scroll down the *Field Chooser* list box until you see the field *Job Title* and then drag the field button from the list box to the column headings row between *COMPANY* and *BUSINESS PHONE*. A red arrow appears above and below the column headings, indicating where the new field will be placed.
   c. Click the Close button on the Field Chooser dialog box.

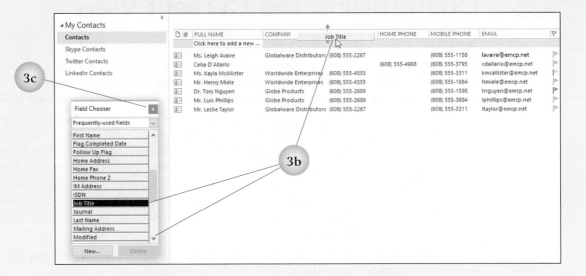

   d. Double-click the right column boundary for the *JOB TITLE* column to expand the column width to the length of the longest entry.
4. Print the contacts in Table style.
5. Change the current view to Card view.

Check Your Work

You can also customize Card view by adding and/or removing fields shown for each contact in the Content pane. Click the View tab and then click the View Settings button. At the Advanced View Settings dialog box, click the Columns button to open the Show Columns dialog box, shown in Figure 4.10 on page 137.

Click a field name in the *Available columns* list box and then click the Add button to add a field to the current view. To remove a field, click to select the field name in the *Show these columns in this order* list box and then click the Remove button. To change the order in which the fields appear, click to select the field name you want to reorder in the *Show these columns in this order* list box and then click the Move Up or Move Down button below the list box as needed. Click OK when you are finished customizing the view and then click OK to close the Advanced View Settings dialog box.

Figure 4.10 Show Columns Dialog Box

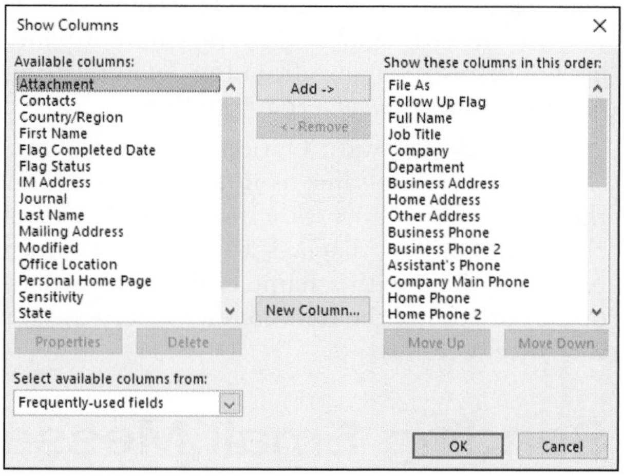

Changing Contact Names and Filing Options

Quick Steps

Change Contact Options
1. Click File tab.
2. Click *Options*.
3. Click *People* in left pane.
4. Change settings as required.
5. Click OK.

Open the Outlook Options dialog box with the People pane active, as shown in Figure 4.11, to change options for working with contacts by clicking the File tab, clicking *Options*, and then clicking *People* in the left pane of the Outlook Options dialog box. The default order that Outlook uses to interpret the name that is being typed in the *Full Name* text box is first name followed by middle name and then last name. Click the *Default "Full Name" order* list box arrow to change this option to *Last First* or *First Last1 Last2*.

Figure 4.11 Outlook Options Dialog Box with *People* Selected

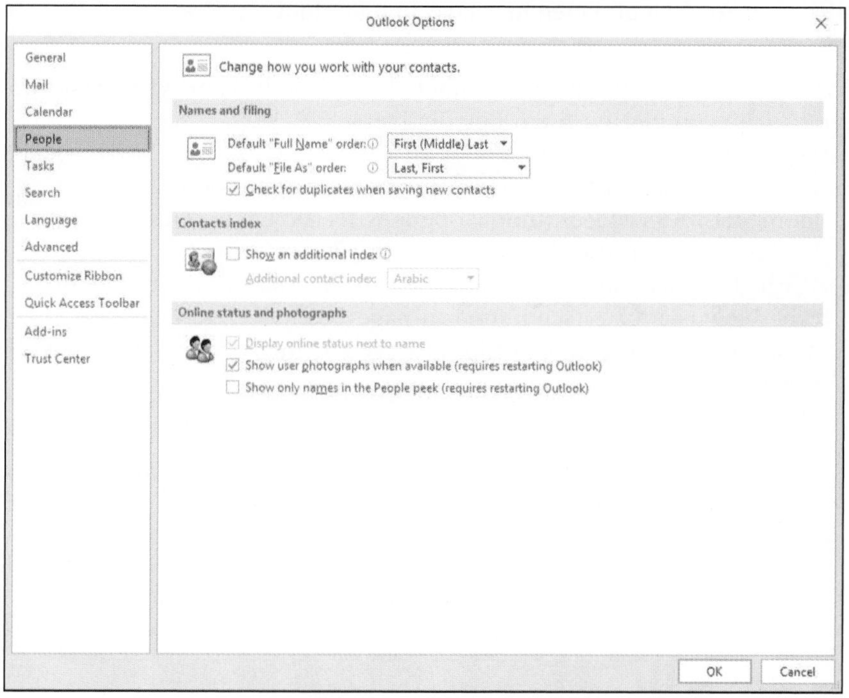

The *Default "File As" order* list box allows you to choose the field(s) that Outlook uses to organize contact records. The *File As* setting is the default sort order for records displayed in the Content pane. Click the *Default "File As" order* list box arrow to change from the default setting to *First Last*; *Company*; *Last, First, (Company)*; or, *Company (Last, First)*.

If you do not want Outlook to prompt you when adding a new record with a name that is the same as in a record that already exists in the folder, clear the *Check for duplicates when saving new contacts* check box. When this option is checked, Outlook displays a Duplicate Contact Detected dialog box when a record is added with a name that already exists in another record. You have the option of adding the new contact record anyway or updating the information in the current record.

Sending Email Messages to Contacts

You can create an email message to a contact without leaving the Contacts folder and displaying the Inbox. To do this, first select the contact record for the person to whom you want to send an email and then perform one of the following actions:

- Click the Email button in the Reading pane (People view) or in the Communicate group on the Home tab (Card or Business Card view).
- Right-click the card for the desired contact, point to *Create*, and then click *Email*.
- Open the Contact window for the individual and then click the Email button in the Communicate group on the Contact tab.

Exercise 15 Sending an Email Message to a Contact

1. With Outlook open and the contacts list active in Card view, send an email message to a contact by completing the following steps:
   a. Select the card for Leslie Taylor.
   b. Click the Email button in the Communicate group on the Home tab. A message window opens with the email address for Leslie Taylor already entered in the *To* text box.

   c. With the insertion point positioned in the *Subject* text box, type New products (see figure on page 139).
   d. Type the following text in the message editing window and then add your name a double space below the closing.

   Leslie,

   I would like to arrange a meeting with you sometime next week to review the new products. Please let me know a day and time that work best for you.

   Regards,

   e. Click Send.

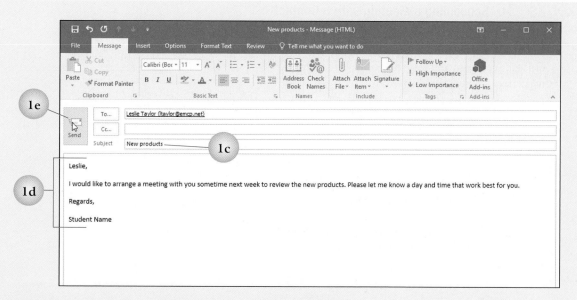

2. View and print the message by completing the following steps:
   a. Switch to the Mail module and display the Sent Items folder in the Content pane.
   b. Double-click the message header for the message created in Step 1.
   c. Print the message and then close the message window.
3. Switch back to the People module and the contacts list in Card view. **Note:** *You will eventually receive a message in your Inbox stating that the message was not delivered because the email address for Leslie Taylor is fictitious.*

Check Your Work

Sending Email Messages to Contacts at Outlook.com

Select a contact in the contacts list and then click the email address in the Reading pane. Outlook.com opens a message window addressed to the contact. Type the subject and message text and then click Send.

> Send email
>
> Personal: ltaylor@emcp.net

Quick Steps

Schedule a Meeting with a Contact
1. Select contact or open Contact window.
2. Click Meeting button in Communicate group on Home tab or Contact tab.
3. Enter meeting details.
4. Click Send.

 Meeting

Scheduling Meetings with Contacts

You can schedule a meeting with a contact without leaving the Contacts folder. If you already know that you are available on the required day and time, you do not need to display your calendar to complete the scheduling. Select the contact and complete one of the following actions:

- Click the Meeting button in the Communicate group on the Home tab.
- Right-click the contact's card, point to *Create*, and then click *Meeting*.
- Open the Contact window for the individual and then click the Meeting button in the Communicate group on the Contact tab.

Enter the subject, location, start day and time, and end day and time, and then click the Send button.

Exercise 16 Scheduling a Meeting with a Contact

1. With Outlook open and the contacts list active in Card view, schedule a meeting with a contact by completing the following steps:
   a. If necessary, select the card for Leslie Taylor.
   b. Click the Meeting button in the Communicate group on the Home tab. A meeting window opens with the contact's name automatically entered in the *To* text box.

   c. With the insertion point positioned in the *Subject* text box, type New products review meeting.
   d. Click in the *Location* text box and then type Globalware Distributor's office.
   e. Select the current date in the *Start time* day text box and then type one week from today.
   f. Select the current time in the *Start time* time text box and then type noon.
   g. Change the *End time* time to *1:30 PM*.
   h. Click Send.

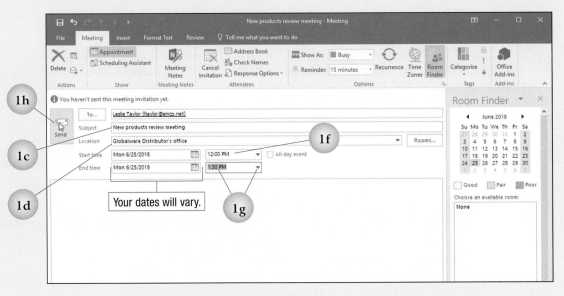

2. Switch to the Mail module and display the Sent Items folder in the Content pane. Double-click the message header for the meeting invitation message sent to Leslie Taylor in Step 1, print the message, and then close the message window.

3. Switch back to the People module and the contacts list in Card view. **Note:** *You will eventually receive a message stating that the message was not delivered.*

Check Your Work

Scheduling a Meeting with a Contact at Outlook.com

Select a contact in the contact list and then click the *Schedule a meeting* link in the Reading pane. An appointment window opens with the contact added to the Attendees list. Enter the meeting details and then click Send.

Calendar
Schedule a meeting

Creating a Contact Group

Quick Steps

Create a Contact Group from Contacts
1. Click New Contact Group button in New group on Home tab.
2. Type name in *Name* text box.
3. Click Add Members button.
4. Click *From Outlook Contacts.*
5. Double-click names to add to group.
6. Click OK.
7. Click Save & Close.

👥 New Contact Group

Quick Steps

Create a Contact List at Outlook.com
1. Open browser window and navigate to Outlook.com.
2. If necessary, sign in to your account.
3. Navigate to *People.*
4. Click New button arrow.
5. Click *Contact list.*
6. Click in *List name* text box and type name for new contact list.
7. Click in *Add members* text box, and type and select names for members of list.
8. Click Save button.

If you frequently send email messages to the same group of people, consider creating a contact group to enable you to create and send the messages more quickly. This feature is sometimes referred to as a ***distribution list***. A ***contact group*** is a name associated with a group of contact records. For example, if you send a weekly status message to members of a project team, you could create a contact group named *Project Team* that contains the names of all the people working on the project. Whenever you need to send a status message, type *Project Team* in the Message window *To* text box and Outlook sends the message to the email addresses of all the members stored in the contact group. Contact groups can also be used in meeting requests. A contact group displays with the group name in the Content pane.

Click the New Contact Group button in the New group on the Home tab to open the Contact Group window shown in Figure 4.12. Type a name for the group in the *Name* text box. Click the Add Members button in the Members group on the Contact Group tab and then click *From Outlook Contacts, From Address Book,* or *New Email Contact* at the drop-down list to add names to the list. When you are finished adding members to the group, click OK and then click the Save & Close button in the Actions group on the Contact Group tab.

The desktop edition of Outlook does not support the creation and management of contact groups for accounts set up as Exchange ActiveSync accounts. This means that if you are using Outlook with an account type of Exchange ActiveSync, you need to create and manage groups in the browser version of Outlook. See the Quick Steps in the margin area for the steps to create a contact group (called a contact list) at Outlook.com.

Figure 4.12 Contact Group Window

Click here to replace the Members page with the Notes page. Type notes about the contact group that you want to store on the Notes page.

Exercise 17 Creating and Using a Contact Group

Note: If you are connected to Outlook using an account type that is Exchange ActiveSync, you need to create a new contact group from the browser version of Outlook at Outlook.com. In this case, skip Step 1 and begin the exercise at Step 2. Check your account type by clicking the File tab and then looking in the account information box at the top of the Account Information backstage area. The account type is listed below the email address.

1. With Outlook open and the contacts list active in Card view, create a new contact group for the sales managers by completing the following steps:

   a. Click the New Contact Group button in the New group on the Home tab. *Note: If the button is dimmed and not accessible, proceed to Step 2.*
   b. At the Untitled - Contact Group window with the insertion point positioned in the *Name* text box, type Sales Managers.
   c. Click the Add Members button in the Members group on the Contact Group tab and then click *From Outlook Contacts* at the drop-down list.

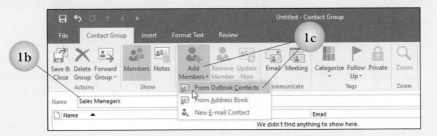

   d. At the Select Members: Contacts dialog box, double-click *Celia D'Allario (cdallario@emcp .net)* to add the email address for Celia D'Allario to the *Members* text box at the bottom of the dialog box.
   e. Double-click the following sales managers' names to add them to the *Members* list:

   > Henry Miele
   >
   > Kayla McAllister
   >
   > Luis Phillips

   f. Click OK to close the Select Members: Contacts dialog box.

g. Click the Notes button in the Show group on the Contact Group tab.

h. Type All the members in this group have accounts on the supplier web portal.

i. Click Save & Close in the Actions group on the Contact Group tab. A contact group entry appears in the Content pane with the name of the group. Proceed to Step 3.

2. Account types that are Exchange ActiveSync create a new contact group (called a *contact list* in Outlook.com) by completing the following steps:

a. Open a browser window and navigate to Outlook.com.

b. If necessary, sign in to Outlook.com with your email address and password.

c. Click the Microsoft Apps button (waffle icon) and then click the People tile at the drop-down Navigation bar.

d. Click the New button arrow on the Menu bar and then click *Contact list* at the drop-down list.

e. With the insertion point positioned in the *List name* text box, type Sales Managers.

f. Click in the *Add members* text box and then type celia. Celia D'Allario's contact entry appears in a drop-down list below the text box. Click to select the contact entry and add Celia D'Allario to the member list.

g. Type henry and then click to select *Henry Miele* and add his contact entry to the member list.

h. Add the following contacts to the member list by completing a step similar to Step 2g:

   Kayla McAllister

   Luis Phillips

i. Click in the *Notes* text box and then type All the members in this list have accounts on the supplier web portal.

j. Click the Save button at the top of the page.

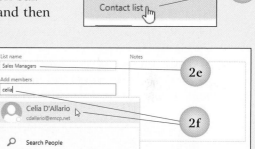

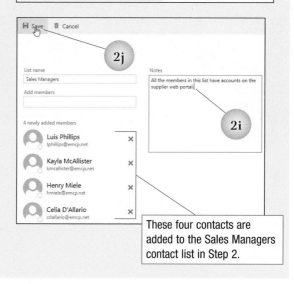

These four contacts are added to the Sales Managers contact list in Step 2.

3. Send an email message to the members of the Sales Managers contact group by completing the following steps:

   a. Click the *Sales Managers* card in the Content pane and then click the Email button in the Communicate group on the Home tab, or click Send email on the Sales Managers contact list page at Outlook.com.

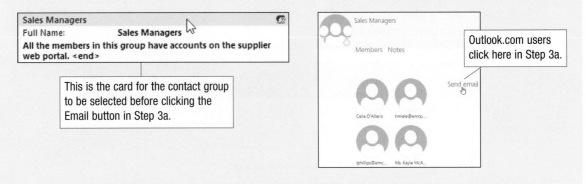

b. Type Supplier Web Portal as the message subject text.

c. Type the following message text and add your name a double space below the closing:

   Dear Valued Supplier,

   A new supplier web portal will be activated the first of next month. Existing accounts are already converted for the new website. We have incorporated many improvements to streamline order entry and provide real-time stock updates. Call or email me if you have any questions.

   Regards,

d. Print the message. Outlook.com users print the message using the web browser's Print command.

e. Send the message. ***Note:*** *Check with your instructor before sending the message. Since the email addresses are fictitious, you will receive a message saying that your message was undeliverable for each member in the group. Your instructor may prefer that you close the message after completing Step 3d.*

4. Change the view to People view. If you are using Outlook.com, sign out of Outlook.com and then close the browser window.

Check Your Work

Maintaining Contact Groups

TIP You can nest contact groups. For example, in a group that is divided into two teams, you can create a group for each team and then add the two team names as members in the main contact group. By nesting the groups, you can send messages to an individual team or use the main contact group to send a message to all team members.

Double-click the group name in the Content pane to open the Contact Group window with the names of the members shown in the Members page, as in Figure 4.13. Use the Add Members button in the Members group on the Contact Group tab to add new members to the group following the process you learned in Exercise 17. To delete a member from the group, click to select the member's name in the list box and then click the Remove Member button in the Members group.

If you change an email address in a contact record, the corresponding entry in the contact group does not automatically update to reflect the same change. Open a contact group window and click the Update Now button in the Members group to update changes to members' email addresses. Click Save & Close when you have finished adding, deleting, or updating group members.

Deleting a Contact Group

Some contact groups are created to facilitate messaging and scheduling for a limited time period, such as the duration of a project. When the project is finished, the contact group is no longer needed. To remove the contact group from the contacts list, select the group name in the Content pane and then click the Delete button in the Delete group on the Home tab.

Expanding the Contact Group in the Message Window

Exchange Server

Share your Contacts folder with other users so that contacts and/or contact groups can be viewed and used to schedule meetings by individuals who communicate with the same people. Select the folder in the Folder pane and then click the Share Contacts button in the Share group on the Home tab. Type the name of the person with whom you want to share the folder in the message window and then send the share invitation message.

If you are creating a message that will be sent to a group and want to view the members' individual names instead of the group name, click the Expand button that displays next to the group name in the *To* text box. Click OK at the Expand List message box, indicating that once the list has been expanded, it cannot be collapsed. The group name is then replaced with the individual names and email addresses of the members.

You can add or delete names in the *To* text box for the current message without affecting the original list. For example, you can expand the group list to remove someone who is on vacation when sending a meeting request message.

Figure 4.13 Contact Group Window with Members Page Shown

Click here to add a new member to the group.

Select a member's name and then click here to remove him or her from the group.

Click here to update email addresses to reflect changes made to contact records.

Chapter Summary

- Add a new contact using the New Contact button in the New group on the Home tab. Type information into the General, Details, and All Fields pages.

- Outlook displays the Check Full Name and Check Address dialog boxes when the entry typed into a name or address field is not recognized.

- To edit a selected contact record in People view, click the Edit Contact button in the Reading pane. Click the Expand button to display more fields.

- Delete a selected contact by pressing Delete or by clicking the Delete button in the Delete group on the Home tab.

- Add a contact from the same company by selecting a contact and choosing *Contact from the Same Company* from the New Items button drop-down list.

- Use the *Add Contact Picture* box in the Contact window to attach a photograph of the person in a contact record. Pictures display in People view and Business Card view.

- Attach a follow-up flag to a contact as a reminder to follow up on an issue.

- Contact records can be sorted by up to four fields at the Sort dialog box.

- Open the Filter dialog box to temporarily remove from the contacts list records that do not meet the specified condition.

- The same six color categories that can be applied to messages and appointments can be applied to contacts.

- Use the letter tabs in the alphabet index along the left side of the Content pane to move to records.

- Find a contact record by typing a name, partial name, or other entry in the *Search People* box in the Find group on the Home tab or the *Search Contacts* box at the top of the Content pane. Use buttons on the Search Tools Search tab to narrow the results.

- Use the Advanced Find dialog box to locate contact records by performing more complex searches based on a conditional statement by which to find records.

- Buttons in the Current View group on the Home tab or View tab can be used to change how contacts are displayed, sorted, filtered, or grouped.

- Customize the current view by adding or removing fields using the *Remove This Column* or *Field Chooser* options at a column heading shortcut menu.

- To change the fields by which records are created, sorted, and displayed, open the Outlook Options dialog box and click *People* in the left pane.

- Create a message to, or schedule a meeting with, a contact from the People module by selecting the contact and using the Email or Meeting button in the Communicate group on the Home tab or Contact tab.

- A contact group is a distribution list of contacts that is stored using a group name, which can be used to send email messages or meeting invitations.

- Add and delete members and update member data by using the Add Members, Remove Member, and Update Now buttons in the Members group on the Contact Group tab.

- You can delete a contact group when the distribution list is no longer needed.

- Expand the group name in a message to show individual member names and email addresses in the *To* text box in place of the group name; additions and removals in the email do not affect the original member list.

Commands Review

FEATURE	BUTTON	RIBBON TAB AND GROUP, OR OTHER METHOD	SHORTCUT
Add contact		Home, New	Ctrl + N
Add contact from existing contact		Home, New	
Add contact group		Home, New	Ctrl + Shift + L
Add, change, or view contact details		Contact, Show	
Add, change, or view contact fields		Contact, Show	
Add contact picture		Contact, Options	
Apply color category		Home, Tags OR Contact, Tags	
Change contact options		File, *Options*, *People*	
Delete contact		Home, Delete OR Contact, Actions	Ctrl + D
Filter contacts		View, Current View	
Find contact using *Search Contacts* box		Click in *Search Contacts* box	Ctrl + E
Find contact using *Search People* box	Search People	Home, Find	
Flag contact for follow-up		Home, Tags OR Contact, Tags	Ctrl + Shift + G
Schedule meeting with contact		Home, Communicate OR Contact, Communicate	Ctrl + Shift + Q
Send email to contact		Home, Communicate OR Contact, Communicate OR Email button in Reading pane (People view)	
Sort contacts		View, Current View	
View history of recent search requests		Search Tools Search, Options	

Workbook

Chapter study tools and assessment activities are available in the *Workbook* pages of the ebook. These resources are designed to help you further develop and demonstrate mastery of the skills learned in this chapter.

Creating Tasks and Notes

Performance Objectives

Upon successful completion of Chapter 5, you will be able to:

1 Create, update, print, and delete tasks

2 Assign a task to someone else

3 Respond to a task request

4 Send task information to other users

5 Change the task view to create task lists

6 Change task options

7 Create, edit, and delete notes

8 Apply a color category to a note

9 Customize the note view

10 Forward a note by email

11 Track activities using journal entries

Precheck

Check your current skills to help focus your study.

Working in Tasks is similar to maintaining a to-do list. Outlook provides the capability to track information about a particular task, such as how much of it has been completed, the priority it has been assigned, and its due date. You can send a task request via email to assign someone else the responsibility for completing the activity. Display the To-Do bar or use the Peek feature to see the list of tasks to be completed.

Use the Notes folder to enter small, unstructured text reminders. For example, you may have an idea for a task or project that you do not want to forget and decide to store a short reminder to yourself. Details related to an activity, such as a telephone discussion or meeting, can be recorded in a journal entry for time keeping or other reporting purposes. Journal entries, which are created to keep track of time spent on a phone call, event, or other activity, are saved in the Journal folder.

Data Files

No student data files are required for this chapter.

SNAP

If you are a SNAP user, launch the Precheck and the Tutorial from your Assignments page.

Creating and Managing Tasks

Quick Steps

Create a Task in the *Type a new task* Text Box
1. Activate the Tasks module.
2. Click in *Type a new task* text box.
3. Type task subject.
4. Press Enter.

Adding activities in Tasks is similar to jotting down jobs in a to-do list on your desk. Tasks are added using the *Type a new task* text box or in the Task window. *Type a new task* may display as *Click here to add a new Task* if Outlook has been customized.

Creating Tasks in the *Type a new task* Text Box and Deleting Tasks

The Tasks folder in To-Do List view is shown in Figure 5.1. Add new tasks by clicking in the *Type a new task* text box located at the top of the To-Do list, typing a short description of the job or activity, and then pressing Enter.

Delete

Delete a task by selecting the task in the task list and then pressing Delete, or by clicking the Delete button in the Delete group on the Home tab.

Figure 5.1 The Tasks Module in To-Do List View

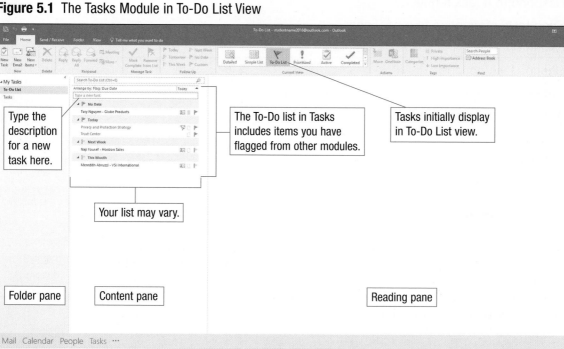

Exercise 1 Deleting Tasks and Creating Tasks Using the *Type a new task* Text Box

1. With Outlook open, access the Peek feature by pointing to the Tasks text label or icon on the Navigation bar. If you are using a touch device, press and hold the Tasks icon or text label on the Navigation bar and then tap *Show the peek*. The Peek feature in Outlook shows a preview of the tasks in the To-Do list. The items that appear in the illustrations for this exercise have been added to the To-Do list as a result of flagging email messages and contacts in exercises and assessments in Chapters 1 and 4.

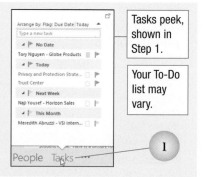

Tasks peek, shown in Step 1.

Your To-Do list may vary.

2. Click the Tasks text label or icon on the Navigation bar to display the Tasks module in the Content pane.

3. Delete the tasks from Chapters 1 and 4 that appear in the To-Do list by completing the following steps:

   a. Press Ctrl + A to select all the items in the To-Do list. *Note: If you have items in your To-Do list in addition to the tasks created in Chapters 1 and 4, do not use the Select All feature. Instead, select only those items created in Chapters 1 and 4 by using the Ctrl key while clicking each item. Touch users need to select and delete these items individually.*

   b. Click the Delete button in the Delete group on the Home tab.

   c. At the Microsoft Outlook message that indicates deleting these items will also delete associated email messages and/or contacts, click OK.

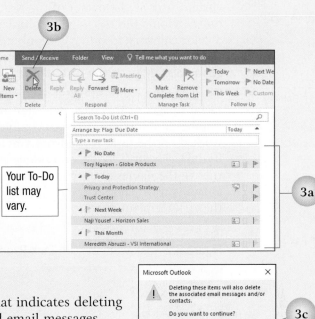

4. Add new tasks to the Tasks folder by completing the following steps:

   a. Click in the text box located at the top of the To-Do list that contains the text *Type a new task*.

   b. Type Assemble research on social media and then press Enter. Outlook adds the item to the To-Do list under a flag with the heading *Today*, and at the same time clears the task entry text box so that it displays the insertion point, indicating another new task can be typed.

   c. Type Upload pictures to Flickr.com in the task entry text box and then press Enter.

   d. Click in a blank area of the Content pane to deactivate the new task entry box.

5. Click the File tab and then click *Print*. With *Table Style* selected in the *Settings* section at the Print backstage area, click the Print button.

Check Your Work

Quick Steps

Create a Task in the Task Window
1. Click New Task button in New group on Home tab.
2. Type subject text.
3. Change other options as required.
4. Click Save & Close.

 New Task

Creating Tasks in the Task Window

You can also create tasks in the Task window, shown in Figure 5.2 on page 152. Open the Task window by clicking the New Task button in the New group on the Home tab. In the Task window, type a description of the task in the *Subject* text box, change other fields as required, and then click the Save & Close button in the Actions group on the Task tab.

Create a task using the Task window to assign a start date and/or a due date to the task, or to attach other information, such as a status, priority, or instructional notes. The default status for a new task is *Not Started*. Enter a different status by clicking the *Status* list box arrow and choosing from *In Progress, Completed, Waiting*

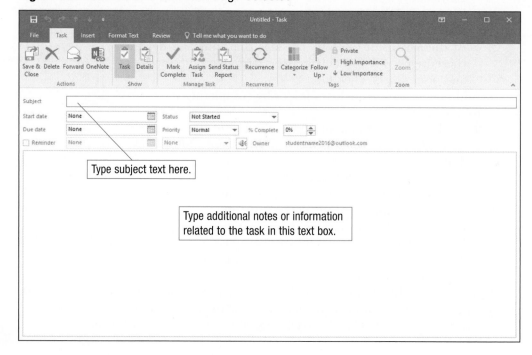

Categorize

on someone else, and *Deferred* at the drop-down list. The default priority for a task is *Normal*, and it can be changed to *Low* or *High*. Outlook inserts the name of the current user as the owner of the task. Use the Categorize button in the Tags group on the Home tab to assign a color category to the task, just as you would assign a color category to other Outlook items. Use the white text box at the bottom of the window to type additional notes, instructions, or other information that you want to store with the task details.

Details

Click the Details button in the Show group on the Task tab to display the Details page. At this page, you can store the date the task was completed, the number of hours estimated to complete the task, and the actual number of hours worked on the task. If the work you are doing is to be billed out, enter information in the *Company, Mileage,* and *Billing information* text boxes. Use the *Update list* option to save the names of individuals who have assigned the task to others. Doing so allows you to send an update message when the task is modified or completed by the task recipient or to send a status report back to the task originator.

Figure 5.2 Task Window with Task Page Selected

Exercise 2 Creating a Task Using the Task Window

1. With Outlook open and the Tasks module active, add a new task using the Task window by completing the following steps:
   a. Click the New Task button in the New group on the Home tab.

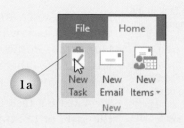

b. With the insertion point positioned in the *Subject* text box, type Start budget estimates for next year.

c. Click the *Status* list box arrow and then click *In Progress* at the drop-down list.

d. Click the Save & Close button in the Actions group on the Task tab. Outlook adds the task below a flag with the heading *No Date*.

2. Click to select the task *Start budget estimates for next year* in the To-Do list and then read the task information that displays in the Reading pane. **Note:** *If necessary, click the View tab, click the Reading Pane button in the Layout group, and then click* Right *at the drop-down list to turn on the Reading pane.*

3. Print only the task added in Step 1 by clicking the File tab and then clicking *Print*. With *Memo Style* selected in the *Settings* section at the Print backstage area, click the Print button.

Check Your Work

Creating Tasks Using Outlook on the web

Click the Microsoft Apps button (waffle icon) and then click the Tasks tile to display the Tasks module. Click the New button on the Menu bar and then type a description of the task in the *Subject* text box on the Task page. Add a due date and/or add and format text in the text box. Click the Save button on the Menu bar when finished.

Click here to add more fields to the Task page, such as *Status* and *% complete*.

Creating Tasks at Outlook.com

Click the Microsoft Apps button (waffle icon) and then click the Tasks tile to display the Tasks module. Click the New button on the Menu bar to open a new Task page in the right pane. Type a subject, add a due date, and type more information about the task in the text box below the toolbar if desired. Click the Save button on the Menu bar when finished.

Click here to add more fields to the Task page, such as *Status* and *% complete*.

Updating Tasks

TIP In Simple List or Detailed view, mark a task as completed by clicking to insert a check mark in the check box at the left of the task subject.

Mark Complete

Updating tasks can include activities such as changing the due date, start date, status, priority, or percentage (%) complete. When a task is finished, you can either delete the task from the task list or change the task status to *Completed*. To change the task status, open the Task window and change the *Status* field to *Completed*, or click the Mark Complete button in the Manage Task group on the Task tab. Marking a task as completed automatically changes the *% Complete* option to *100%*. A task that is marked as completed is removed from the To-Do List view; however, the task is not deleted from the Tasks folder. In a view other than To-Do List view, a completed task is displayed with a line drawn through dimmed text.

Double-click a task in the task list to open the Task window and make changes to the task details as required. To edit only the subject text, click to select the task entry in the task list. With the task highlighted, click the task text box a second time to open the task text box for editing and display an insertion point. Insert or delete text as required and then click outside the task text box to finish editing.

Exercise 3 Updating Tasks

1. With Outlook open and the Tasks module active, change the status for the task entry *Assemble research on social media* by completing the following steps:
   a. Double-click the task entry *Assemble research on social media* to open the Task window.
   b. Click the *Status* list box arrow and then click *In Progress* at the drop-down list.
   c. Select *0%* in the *% Complete* measurement box and then type 60. **Note: *The up- and down-pointing arrows at the right of the* % Complete *measurement box incrementally increase or decrease the value by 25%.***
   d. Click the Save & Close button in the Actions group on the Task tab.

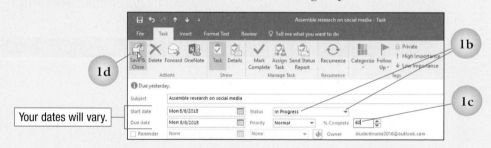

Your dates will vary.

2. Change the status for a task to *Completed* by completing the following steps:
   a. Double-click the task entry *Upload pictures to Flickr.com*.
   b. Click the Mark Complete button in the Manage Task group on the Task tab. A task marked as completed is removed from the To-Do List view; however, the task information is retained in the Tasks folder and can be accessed in a view other than To-Do List view.

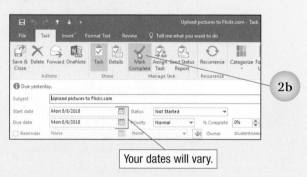

Your dates will vary.

3. Change the current view and expand column widths by completing the following steps:

a. Click the Detailed button in the Current View group on the Home tab. In Detailed view, the columns *STATUS, DUE DATE, MODIFIED, DATE COMPLETED, IN FOLDER,* and *CATEGORIES* are added to the task list. Notice that tasks marked as completed are displayed with a line drawn through dimmed text.

b. If necessary, double-click the right column boundaries for the *TASK SUBJECT* column and the *STATUS* column to expand the column widths to fit the longest entries.

c. Double-click the right column boundary for the *MODIFIED* column.

	TASK SUBJECT	STATUS	DUE DATE ▲	MODIFIED	DATE COMPLETED
	Click here to add a new Task				
	Start budget estimates for next year	In Progress	None	Mon 8/6/2018 5:37 PM	None
	Assemble research on social media	In Progress	Mon 8/6/2018	Tue 8/7/2018 11:29 AM	None
	Upload pictures to Flickr.com	Completed	Mon 8/6/2018	Tue 8/7/2018 11:31 AM	Tue 8/7/2018

4. Click the File tab and then click *Print*. If necessary, click *Table Style* to select it in the *Settings* section at the Print backstage area. Click the Print button.

Check Your Work

o⃞ Updating Tasks at Outlook.com

Click the Edit button in the Reading pane for the active task to open the Task page for editing. Make the required changes and then click the Save button on the Menu bar. Click the Edit button arrow and then click *Delete* to remove a task from the To-Do list.

Start budget estimates for next year

Due None

✏ Edit

Status	In progress	Owner:	studentname2016@outlook.com
% complete	0	Total work	0 hours
Start date	None	Actual work	0 hours
Priority	Normal	Mileage	None
Date complete	None	Billing	None
Companies	None		

☐ Reminder

None ▼   ▼

☐ Mark private

Repetition   Never

Click the Edit button open the Task page for editing, or click the down-pointing arrow for the options *Delete, Categorize, Charm,* or *Open in a separate window.*

Quick Steps

Create a Recurring Task
1. Click New Task button in New group on Home tab.
2. Type subject text.
3. Click Recurrence button in Recurrence group on Task tab.
4. Choose recurrence options.
5. Click OK.
6. Click Save & Close.

Recurrence

Creating a Recurring Task

A task that you perform on a regular basis can be set up in a manner similar to a recurring appointment. A recurring task appears only once in the task list. When you change the status for that occurrence of the task to *Completed*, Outlook automatically generates the next occurrence in the task list.

To create a recurring task, open the Task window, type a description of the task in the *Subject* text box, and then click the Recurrence button in the Recurrence group on the Task tab. Select the options as required in the *Recurrence pattern* and *Range of recurrence* sections in the Task Recurrence dialog box, shown in Figure 5.3 on page 156, and then click OK.

Figure 5.3 Task Recurrence Dialog Box

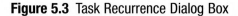

Enter the number of recurrences or an end date for a recurring task with a set duration.

Exercise 4 Creating a Recurring Task

1. With Outlook open and the Tasks module active in Detailed view, add a recurring task to the task list by completing the following steps:

   a. Click the New Task button in the New group on the Home tab.

   b. With the insertion point positioned in the *Subject* text box, type Compile month end reports.

   c. Click the Recurrence button in the Recurrence group on the Task tab.

   d. At the Task Recurrence dialog box, click *Monthly* in the *Recurrence pattern* section.

   e. Click *The* in the *Recurrence pattern* section. Depending on the current date, the options next to *The* display the occurrence as *first*, *second*, *third*, *fourth*, or *last* and the current day of the week. If necessary, click the occurrence list box arrow and then click *first*. Click the day-of-the-week list box arrow and then click *Thursday* so that the Recurrence pattern becomes *The [first] [Thursday] of every [1] month(s)*.

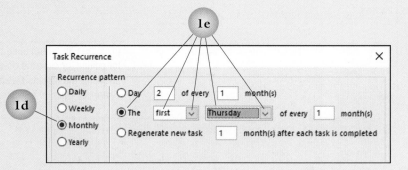

   f. Click OK to close the Task Recurrence dialog box. The information bar in the Task window above the subject text displays the recurrence pattern details.

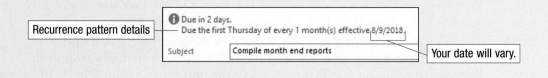

Recurrence pattern details

Your date will vary.

g. Click the Save & Close button in the Actions group on the Task tab. The first recurring task appears in the list. Notice the recurring icon for the task next to the task subject.

2. Click the Simple List button in the Current View group on the Home tab.
3. Print the tasks in Table style.

Check Your Work

⬛ Updating Tasks and Creating Recurring Tasks Using Outlook on the web

Click the Edit button to open the active task for editing on the Task page in the Reading pane. Mark a task completed by selecting the task in the To-Do list and then clicking the Complete button on the Menu bar.

Click the Show more details button on the Task page to expand the task options. Select a recurrence option from the *Repetition* drop-down list to create a recurring task.

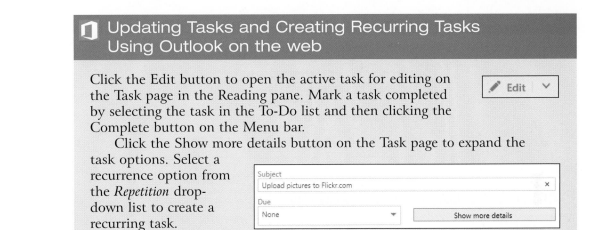

Assigning a Task to Someone Else

Quick Steps

Assign a Task Using the New Items Button
1. Click New Items button in New group on Home tab.
2. Click *Task Request*.
3. Enter recipient in *To* text box.
4. Type subject text.
5. Change options as required.
6. Click Send.

New Items

Assign Task

You can assign a task to someone else by emailing the individual a task request. The recipient of the task request can choose to accept the task, decline the task, or assign the task to someone else. When the recipient accepts the task, the task is automatically added to his or her task list. If you receive a task request and accept the task, you become the owner of the task. The owner is the only person who can make changes to the task details. If you decline the task, you can provide a reason for declining and the task is returned to the originator of the task request so that he or she can assign it to someone else.

To create a task request, perform one of the following actions:
- Click the New Items button in the New group on the Home tab, and then click *Task Request* at the drop-down list.
- Display the shortcut menu in an unused area within the Content pane, and then click *New Task Request* at the shortcut menu.
- Click the Assign Task button in the Manage Task group on the Task tab in a Task window.

A Task Request window opens similar to the one shown in Figure 5.4 on page 158. At the *To* text box above the *Subject* text box, type the email address of the person to whom you are assigning the task. The two check boxes located below the *Due date* are checked by default. These options instruct Outlook to keep an updated copy of the task in the originator's task list and to send a completed status report back to the originator when the task is completed. When you are finished entering the task parameters to send a task request to the person via email, click the Send button.

Figure 5.4 Task Request Window

Add the email address for the task recipient here.

Consider using this area to type additional instructions or explanations to the task recipient so that he or she knows exactly what you want him or her to do.

Exercise 5 Assigning a Task to Someone Else

Note: In this exercise, you will send a task request by email to the student with whom you have been exchanging messages in earlier chapters. If you are not able to exchange emails with another student, check with your instructor for alternative instructions or send the task request to yourself at a secondary email address.

1. With Outlook open and the Tasks module active in Simple List view, send a task request by completing the following steps:

   a. Click the New Items button in the New group on the Home tab and then click *Task Request*.

   b. Type the email address of the recipient for the task request in the *To* text box.

   c. Click in the *Subject* text box and then type Research three social media trends for our presentation.

   d. Click the *Priority* list box arrow and then click *High* at the drop-down list.

   e. Select *None* in the *Due date* text box and then type one week from today.

   f. Click Send. The task is added to your task list and an email message is sent to the task recipient.

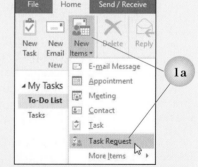

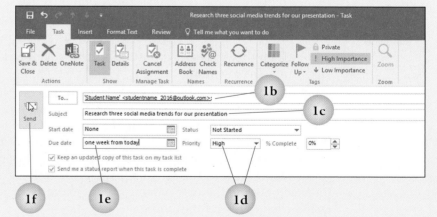

2. Double-click the entry in your task list for the task that you assigned to someone else in Step 1. Review the message in the information bar that indicates the status of the task request and the name next to *Owner* in the Task window.

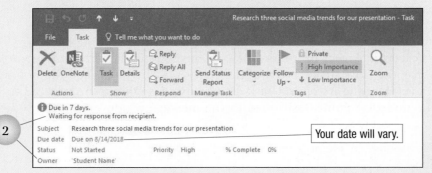

3. Click the File tab in the Task window and then click *Print*. With *Memo Style* selected in the *Settings* section at the Print backstage area, click the Print button.
4. Close the Task window.

Check Your Work

Responding to a Task Request

TIP Once a task recipient has accepted or declined the task, Outlook automatically deletes the task request message from his or her Inbox.

Exchange Server

Outlook automatically tracks the status of an assigned task for the task originator. When the task owner changes any of the task details, Outlook generates an update and sends it to the name(s) stored in the *Update* list on the Details page.

The process for responding to a task request message is similar to the process for responding to a meeting request message. If you are the task recipient, you will receive a message in your Inbox. Select the message header in the Content pane and then click the Accept or Decline button in the Reading pane. Alternatively, double-click the message header to open the task request message in a separate window and then click the Accept or Decline button in the Respond group on the Task tab.

If you have received a task request message and want to reassign the task to someone else, open the Task window and then click the Assign Task button in the Manage Task group on the Task tab. Then identify the person to whom the request should be sent.

When you click *Accept* or *Decline*, a message window appears with the information that the task will be accepted and moved into the Tasks folder for *Accept* or moved to the Deleted Items folder for *Decline*. You can select the option *Edit the response before sending*, which allows adding a few words of explanation, or you can select *Send the response now*, which sends the task originator the default response message of *User name has accepted*.

A task request sent to someone connected to an Internet mail server that is not compatible with Outlook's tracking features displays the standard Reply and Forward buttons in the Reading pane or message window.

Exercise 6 Accepting a Task Request

Note: To complete this exercise, another student must have sent you a task request from Exercise 5. Depending on the type of server to which you are connected, the task request message looks and functions differently. The following instructions include all likely scenarios; however, if your screen does not match what appears in the instructions, check with your instructor for assistance.

1. With Outlook open and the Tasks module active, accept the task assignment sent to you by a classmate by completing the following steps:

   a. Display the Mail module with the Inbox folder active in the Content pane. If necessary, click to select the message header for the message with the subject *Task Request: Research three social media trends for our presentation*.

   b. Click the Accept button or click the Reply button in the Reading pane.

   c. If you clicked the Accept button in the previous step, click *Edit the response before sending* in the Accepting Task dialog box and then click OK. If you clicked the Reply button in the previous step, the Accepting Task dialog box does not appear; proceed to Step 1d.

   d. With the insertion point positioned in the message window, type the following text:

   > I will send you my research and presentation notes within a week.

   e. Print the message in Memo style.

   f. Click Send.

   g. If necessary, close the Task Request Message window.

2. Display the Tasks module in the Content pane.

3. If you clicked the Accept button in Step 1b, Outlook automatically added the task to your task list. Note that two tasks are shown with the subject *Research three social media trends for our presentation*. One is the task you assigned to someone else when you completed Exercise 5 and the other is the task request you accepted in Step 1b of this exercise. If you clicked the Reply button in Step 1b, the accepted task was not added to your task list. You see only the task request you assigned to another student when you completed Exercise 5.

> **Check Your Work**

Sending Task Information to Other Users

Quick Steps

Send a Task Status Report
1. Open Task window.
2. Click Send Status Report button in Manage Task group on Task tab.
3. Enter recipient address(es) in *To* and/or *Cc* text box(es).
4. Type message text.
5. Click Send.

Send Status Report

If you want to email comments about a task to other users or report the status of a task to the task originator, open the Task window and then click the Send Status Report button in the Manage Task group on the Task tab. A message window opens similar to the one shown in Figure 5.5.

Figure 5.5 Task Status Report Message Window

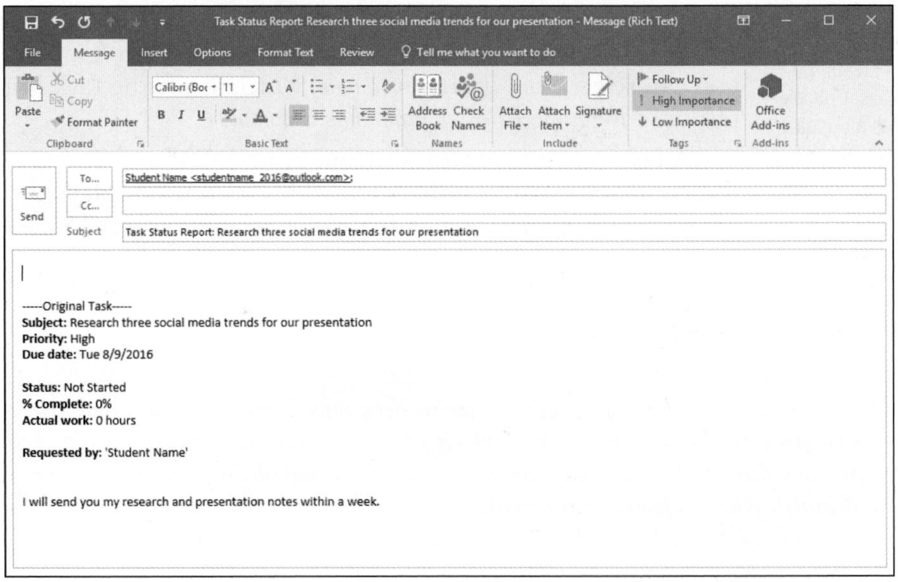

If the active task is one that was assigned to you by someone else, the name(s) of the task originator(s) in the *Update* list from the Details page will automatically be inserted in the *To* text box. If the task was not assigned or you need to add status report recipients, type the required email addresses in the *To* and/or *Cc* text box(es), type the text for your report in the message text window, and then click the Send button.

To send a copy of the task to another user, begin by opening the Task window. For a task request, click the Forward button in the Respond group on the Task tab, and for a normal task, click the Forward button in the Actions group on the Task tab. A message window similar to the one shown in Figure 5.6 opens with the task subject automatically inserted in the *Subject* text box after *FW:*. A copy of the Task window is automatically inserted in the message as a file attachment. Type the email address of the person to whom you want to send the task information in the *To* text box, type an explanatory message in the message text window, and then click the Send button. The recipient of the email message can view the task details by double-clicking the attached task file.

Quick Steps

Send Task Details
1. Open Task window.
2. Click Forward button in Respond or Actions group on Task tab.
3. Type address in *To* text box.
4. Type message text.
5. Click Send.

 Forward

Figure 5.6 Forwarded Task Message Window

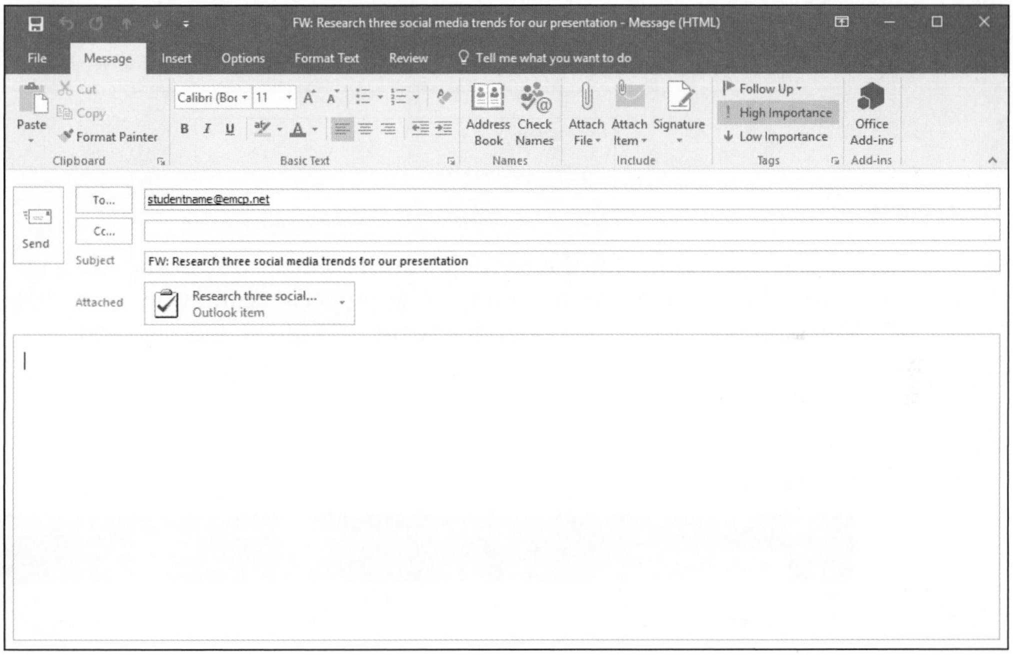

Exercise 7 Updating and Forwarding Task Information to Another User

Note: In this exercise, you will send task details by email to the student with whom you have been exchanging messages in earlier chapters. Check with your instructor for alternative instructions if you are unable to send task information to that person for this exercise.

1. With Outlook open and the Tasks module active in Simple List view, update the *Start budget estimates for next year* task by completing the following steps:
   a. Double-click the task entry with the subject *Start budget estimates for next year* to open the Task window.

    b. Change the *Priority* option to *High*.

    c. Click in the text window below the *Reminder* check box and then type the following text:

> Create an Excel worksheet with last year's budget and calculate this year's values as 1.8% higher than last year's values.

2. With the *Start budget estimates for next year* Task window still open, send the task information to another user by completing the following steps:

    a. Click the Forward button in the Actions group on the Task tab.

    b. Click OK at the Microsoft Outlook message box stating that the original item must be saved before completing the operation.

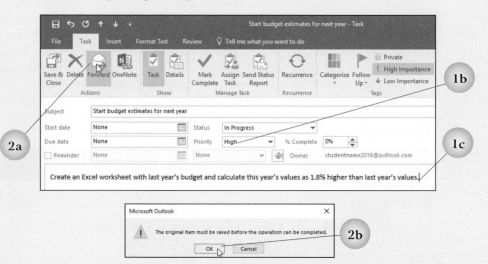

c. Type the email address for the recipient in the *To* text box in the Message window.

d. Type the following message including an appropriate salutation at the beginning of the message and your name as the sender at the end of the message text:

> I need your help to prepare the budget estimates for next year. The task details with instructions are attached to this message. Can we meet next week about this?

e. Print the message in Memo style.

f. Click Send.

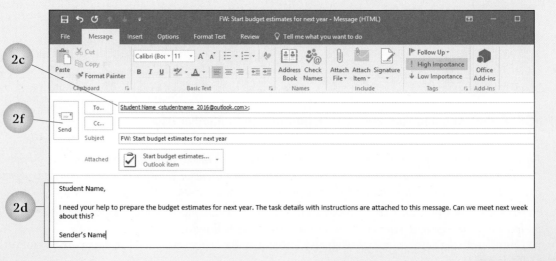

3. Close the Task window.

Check Your Work

Changing the Task View to Create Task Lists

TIP Find a task quickly in a long task list by typing a keyword from the task subject in the *Search To-Do List* text box located at the top of the Content pane.

In the exercises in this chapter, you have seen the To-Do List view, the Detailed view, and the Simple List view. The Current View group on the Home tab provides the following other view options to create task lists:

- **Prioritized.** A list of all tasks grouped by the *Priority* option.
- **Active.** A filtered list of all tasks not marked as completed.
- **Completed.** A filtered list of tasks that have been marked as completed.
- **Today.** A filtered list of tasks due today plus overdue tasks.
- **Next 7 Days.** A filtered list of all tasks with due dates within the next seven days and sorted in ascending order by due date.
- **Overdue.** A filtered list of all tasks that are not marked as completed and are past their due dates.
- **Assigned.** A filtered list of tasks that have been assigned to other individuals, grouped by name.

You can also change the view to one of the options described above from the Change View button drop-down list in the Current View group on the View tab. Additional sort and group options for viewing tasks are included in the Arrangement group option box on the View tab. For example, you can use the *Categories* option in the Arrangement group option box to group tasks by assigned color category.

View Settings

Customize the current view by clicking the View Settings button in the Current View group on the View tab to open the Advanced View Settings dialog box. (This dialog box can also be accessed by clicking the *View Settings* option in the Arrangement group expanded option box.) Change the sort and filter options and add and remove columns by following steps similar to those learned in Chapter 4, Exercises 7, 8, and 14. In the next exercise, you will create a customized task list by removing and adding columns in a view.

Exercise 8 Creating a Customized Task List and Editing Tasks

1. With Outlook open and the Tasks module active in Simple List view, create a customized task list by completing the following steps:

   a. Click the Active button in the Current View group on the Home tab.
   Note: *Click the More button in the Current View group to expand the options and then click* Active *if you cannot see the Active button in the Current View group.*

   b. Right-click the *CATEGORIES* column heading and then click *Remove This Column* at the shortcut menu.

   c. Right-click the *TASK SUBJECT* column heading and then click *Field Chooser* at the shortcut menu.

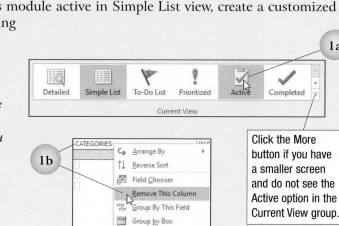

Click the More button if you have a smaller screen and do not see the Active option in the Current View group.

d. Scroll down to the bottom of the *Field Chooser* list box and then drag the field button for the *Total Work* field from the list box to the column headings row between *TASK SUBJECT* and *STATUS*. A red arrow appears above and below the field button in the column headings row, indicating where the new field will be placed.

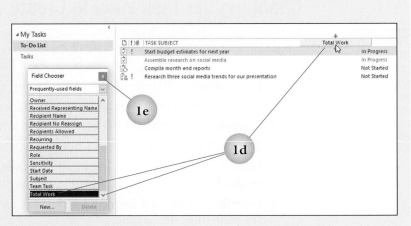

e. Click the Close button on the Field Chooser dialog box.

f. Adjust the column width of the *TOTAL WORK* column so that the entire column heading is visible.

g. If necessary, adjust the column widths for the other columns so the column headings and data in all the columns are visible.

2. Edit the details for the tasks using the columns in the task list by completing the following steps:

a. Click in the *TOTAL WORK* column in the task row for the task with the subject *Start budget estimates for next year*. Click in this field a second time to open the field for editing and place an insertion point in the field.

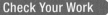

b. Move the insertion point as needed, delete *0*, and then type *2* so that the field reads *2 hours*.

c. Click in an unused area within the Content pane to end task editing.

3. Print the tasks in Table style.

4. Change the view to Simple List view.

Check Your Work

⬛ Changing the Task View Using Outlook on the web

By default, Outlook on the web displays tasks in Active view, sorted by the due date, and with the oldest task at the top of the list. Click the Active option box arrow at the top right of the To-Do list to change the view to *All, Overdue,* or *Completed*.

Use the options in the *Sort by* section of the drop-down list to change the field by which the tasks are grouped and arranged and/or change the order tasks are shown in the list to *Newest on top* by clicking the last option in the drop-down list.

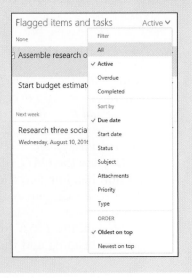

Tasks are displayed in Active view, sorted by the due date, and with the oldest task at the top of the list by default. Click the Active option box arrow at the top right of the To-Do list to change the view to *All, Overdue,* or *Completed.*

Use the options in the *Sort by* section of the drop-down list to change the field by which the tasks are grouped and arranged and/or change the order of tasks to *Newest on top* by clicking the last option in the drop-down list.

Using the To-Do Bar

To-Do Bar

Turn the To-Do bar on and off at the right side of the Tasks window using the To-Do Bar button in the Layout group on the View tab. Click the View tab, click the To-Do Bar button, and then click *Calendar, People, Tasks,* or *Off* in the drop-down list as appropriate. You can add a calendar to the To-Do bar and contacts that have been added to your favorites list.

Turning on the To-Do bar in the Mail, Calendar, or People modules is useful so that you can view the items in the To-Do list from other Outlook modules. Note that you can also add new items to the task list by typing a description of the task in the *Type a new task* text box at the top of the To-Do bar and then pressing Enter.

Exercise 9 Turning the To-Do Bar On and Off in the Tasks and Inbox Folders

1. With Outlook open and the Tasks module active in Simple List view, turn on and customize the To-Do Bar by completing the following steps:
   a. Click the View tab.
   b. Click the To-Do bar button in the Layout group.
   c. Click *Calendar* at the drop-down list to select this option. (A check mark displays before the option when it is selected.) Outlook displays the To-Do bar at the right side of the Task window with the current month displayed at the top. If the To-Do bar was already visible with the Calendar option shown, this step turned the Calendar off in the To-Do bar.
   d. Click the To-Do Bar button in the Layout group and then click *People* at the drop-down list. Outlook adds a *Contacts* section to the bottom of the To-Do bar with a *Search People* box and *FAVORITES* section. If Contacts was already active in the To-Do bar, this step removed the Contacts section from the To-Do bar.

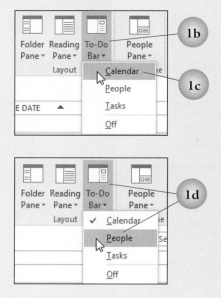

2. Display the Mail module with the Inbox active in the Content pane. Notice that the To-Do bar is not turned on for the Inbox folder.
3. Turn on the To-Do bar to show the current task list in the Inbox by completing the following steps:
   a. Click the View tab.
   b. Click the To-Do Bar button in the Layout group.
   c. Click *Tasks* at the drop-down list. Outlook adds the To-Do list to the top of the To-Do bar at the right side of the window.
4. Click the To-Do Bar button and then click *Off* at the drop-down list to remove the To-Do bar from the Mail module.
5. Display the Tasks module, click the View tab, click the To-Do Bar button, and then click *Off*.

Changing Task Options

To view or modify task options, click the File tab, click *Options*, and then click *Tasks* in the left pane of the Outlook Options dialog box. At the Outlook Options dialog box with the Tasks pane active, shown in Figure 5.7, you can set reminders for tasks with due dates, deselect the default options for tracking assigned tasks, change the colors in which overdue and completed tasks are displayed, and set the default flag applied in the *Quick Click* column (right column in To-Do List view with flag icons). In the *Work hours* section, you can set the default task hours for a working day and working week.

Figure 5.7 Outlook Options Dialog Box with *Tasks* Selected

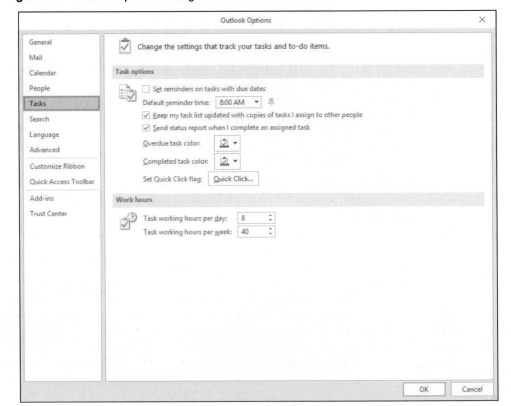

Creating and Managing Notes

In Outlook, a *note* contains a small amount of text that is not structured in any way but is meant to act as a reminder or placeholder to store thoughts, ideas, and other information that you do not want to forget. Important notes can be placed on the desktop in a location that can be easily seen. To activate the Notes module, click the Navigation Options button (three dots) on the Navigation bar and then click *Notes* at the pop-up list.

Creating Notes and Changing the Notes View

Quick Steps

Create a Note Using the New Note Button
1. Make Notes folder active.
2. Click New Note button in New group on Home tab.
3. Type note text.
4. Click Note window Close button.

New Note

To create a new note, display the Notes module and then perform one of the following actions:

- Click the New Note button in the New group on the Home tab.
- Right-click in an unused area within the Content pane and then click *New Note* at the shortcut menu.
- Double-click in any unused space within the Content pane.

A yellow Note window, similar to the one shown in Figure 5.8, opens in which you can type the text you would like to store. The Note window is small, because notes are meant to store brief reminders and ideas. The text up to the first hard return (or press of the Enter key) is used as the note title and is displayed below the note icon in Icon view or as the subject text in Notes List view. Double-click a note icon to view the remaining text inside the note, if additional text is included and not visible in the current view. Click the Note window Close button to close the note.

TIP Notes are stored only on the local device. In other words, Outlook.com users will not see their notes when signed in with the browser version at another computer.

Outlook stores the date and time that the note was created and displays this information at the bottom of the Note window. Drag the three diagonal lines at the bottom right of the Note window to make the viewing area wider and taller. Doing this will be necessary if you need to type more text than can fit in the current note size and want to view all the text at once. Double-click the bar at the top of the Note window to maximize the window so that it fills your computer screen, or to return a maximized window to its default size.

Buttons in the Current View group on the Home tab are used to display notes in Icon view, Notes List view, or Last 7 Days view.

Figure 5.8 Note Window

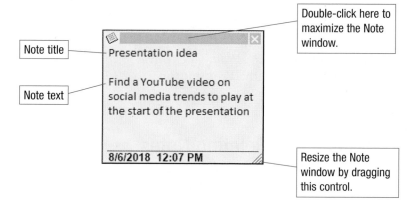

Exercise 10 Creating Notes and Changing the Notes View

1. With Outlook open, click the Navigation Options button (three dots) on the Navigation bar and then click *Notes* at the pop-up list.

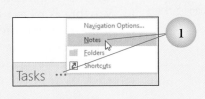

2. Create a new note by completing the following steps:
   a. Click the New Note button in the New group on the Home tab.
   b. With the insertion point positioned in a Note window, type Research pros and cons of refilling ink cartridges for printer.
   c. Click the Note window Close button. A note icon appears in the Content pane with the note title displayed below the icon.

3. Create another new note by completing the following steps:
   a. Double-click in any unused area within the Content pane.
   b. With the insertion point positioned in a Note window, type Presentation idea and then press Enter two times.
   c. Type Find a YouTube video on social media trends to play at the start of the presentation.
   d. Click the Note window Close button. Notice that only the first line of text that you typed in the second note is shown in the Note window.

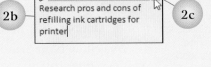

4. Click the Notes List button in the Current View group on the Home tab. Notes List view displays note text in table format with columns for the date and time the note was created and the assigned category.

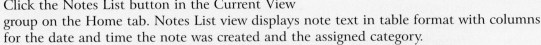

5. Click the File tab and then click *Print*. Click *Table Style* in the *Settings* section at the Print backstage area and then click the Print button.

Check Your Work

Editing and Deleting Notes

You can edit the content of a note by double-clicking the note icon to open the Note window. Insert and delete text as required and then click the Close button. A selected note can be deleted by pressing Delete or by clicking the Delete button in the Delete group on the Home tab.

Exercise 11 Changing the Notes View and Creating, Editing, and Deleting Notes

1. With Outlook open and the Notes module active, change the Notes view and then create, edit, and delete notes by completing the following steps:
   a. Click the Icon button in the Current View group on the Home tab.
   b. Right-click in an unused area within the Content pane and then click *New Note* at the shortcut menu.
   c. With the insertion point positioned in a Note window, type Renew license before end of next month and then click the Close button.
2. Edit the *Presentation idea* note by completing the following steps:
   a. Double-click the *Presentation idea* note icon.
   b. With the insertion point positioned at the beginning of the note text, select and delete *Presentation idea* and the space below the note title so that the note now includes only the text *Find a YouTube video on social media trends to play at the start of the presentation.*
   c. Click the Close button.
3. Delete a note by completing the following steps:
   a. Click to select the *Research pros and cons of refilling ink cartridges for printer* note icon.
   b. Click the Delete button in the Delete group on the Home tab.
4. Click the Last 7 Days button in the Current View group on the Home tab. In this view, only notes created in the last seven days are shown, arranged in table format.
5. Print the notes in Table style.

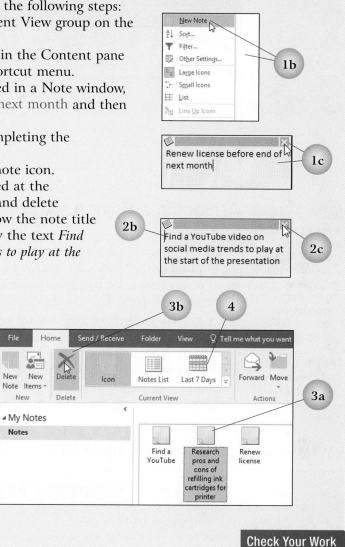

Check Your Work

Placing a Note on the Desktop

TIP Use Notes for those quick reminders for which you are tempted to put a sticky note on your monitor!

Since notes are useful for storing reminders, you might find it helpful to place a note on your desktop to remind you of something that is time sensitive. To do this, copy a note created in the Notes folder by resizing the Outlook window until you can see a portion of the desktop, and then dragging the desired note icon from the Content pane to the desktop. The note is copied to the desktop as a separate file with the extension *.msg.* The new note on your desktop and the original note in Outlook are not linked; changes made to one of the copies will not be reflected in the other. Figure 5.9 on page 170 shows the *Renew license before end of next month* note copied from the Outlook window to the desktop.

Figure 5.9 Note Placed on Desktop

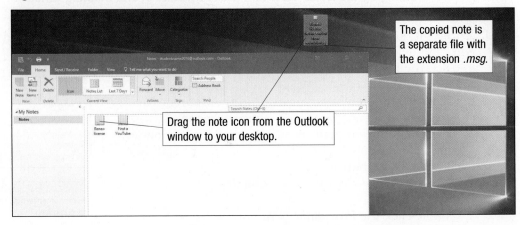

The copied note is a separate file with the extension *.msg*.

Drag the note icon from the Outlook window to your desktop.

Quick Steps

Assign a Color Category While Creating a Note
1. Click New Note button in New group on Home tab.
2. Type note text.
3. Click note icon at top left of Note window.
4. Point to *Categorize*.
5. Click desired color category.
6. Close Note window.

Assigning a Color Category to a Note

Applying a color category to a note is one way of organizing the Notes folder. Notes are typically used for unstructured text, and if you create notes for many items, the Content pane can quickly become filled with notes that are not related in an obvious manner. By default, notes are not listed by title when viewed as icons in the Content pane. Instead they are listed in descending order by date created.

The color categories available for notes are the same as those available for other Outlook items. Click to select a note icon in the Content pane, click the Categorize button in the Tags group on the Home tab, and then click the desired color category at the drop-down list. You can also assign a category while creating a note by clicking the note icon at the top left of the Note window, pointing to *Categorize* in the drop-down list, and then clicking the desired color category.

Exercise 12 Applying Color Categories to Notes

1. With Outlook open and the Notes module active, create a new note and apply a color category by completing the following steps:
   a. Change the Notes view to Icon view.
   b. Click the New Note button in the New group on the Home tab.
   c. Type Ask Kelly to help with the graphics for the Social Media presentation in the Note window.
   d. Click the note icon at the top left of the Note window.
   e. Point to *Categorize* and then click *Social Media Essay* or *Blue Category*. Outlook changes the color of the note to blue.
   f. Click the Close button.
2. Right-click the *Renew license before end of next month* note icon, point to *Categorize*, and then click *Personal* or *Orange Category* at the shortcut menu. Outlook changes the color of the note to orange.

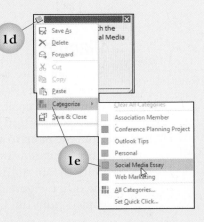

3. Click to select the *Find a YouTube video on social media trends to play at the start of our presentation* note icon, click the Categorize button in the Tags group on the Home tab, and then click *Social Media Essay* or *Blue Category* at the drop-down list.

4. Change the current view to Notes List view.

5. Print the notes in Table style.

6. Change the current view to Icon view.

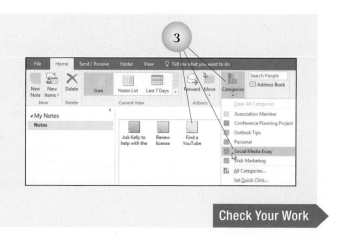

Check Your Work

Customizing Notes Views

As you have learned in Exercises 10, 11, and 12, the Current View group on the Home tab contains buttons to show notes in Icon view, Notes List view, and Last 7 Days view. In all three views, the notes are arranged in the order they were created, with the most recent note at the top of the list.

Click the View tab to further customize the way in which notes are displayed or organized in the Content pane. In Icon view, the Arrangement group on the View tab contains buttons to change the size of the notes from large icons to small icons or to show notes in a list format. When the notes are displayed in Notes List view or Last 7 Days view, the Arrangement group option box on the View tab provides options to group the notes by color categories or creation dates.

Exercise 13 Customizing a Notes View

1. With Outlook open and the Notes module active in Icon view, create a new note by completing the following steps:
   a. Click the New Note button in the New group on the Home tab.
   b. Type Book Alaska flights in the Note window.
   c. Assign the note to the Personal or orange color category.
   d. Close the Note window.
2. Change the view to Notes List view.
3. Click the View tab and then click the *Categories* option in the Arrangement group option box. The notes are now arranged in the Content pane grouped by color category.
4. Print the notes in Table style.
5. Click the Change View button in the Current View group and then click *Icon* at the drop-down list.
6. Click the List button in the Arrangement group on the View tab.

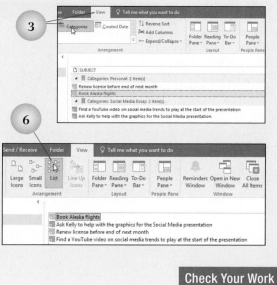

Check Your Work

Forwarding a Note

Select a note in the Content pane and then click the Forward button in the Actions group on the Home tab to open an email message window with the note attached as a file, which you can then forward to one or more recipients. You can also click the note icon at the top left of a Note window and then click *Forward* at the drop-down list to open an email message window.

Type the email address of the person to whom you want to send the note, type the message text, and then click the Send button. The note is automatically attached to the message. The recipient of a forwarded note can click the file name in the Reading pane to view the note text or double-click the file name to open the Note window.

Creating and Managing Journal Entries

Quick Steps

Create a Journal Entry Using the Journal Entry Button
1. Make Journal folder active.
2. Click Journal Entry button in New group on Home tab.
3. Type subject text.
4. If necessary, change entry type and start time.
5. Enter duration value.
6. Type additional notes if required.
7. Click Save & Close.

 Journal Entry

TIP In the workplace, some people use journal entries to keep track of their time for reporting or billing purposes.

The Journal module is a place in which you can keep track of events or items that you want to remember, such as what was said during a telephone conversation or how much time was spent working on a project. Create a journal entry in the Journal to record an activity such as a telephone call. To display the Journal, click *Folders* from the Navigation Options button pop-up list and then click *Journal* in the Folder pane. The Journal window opens in Timeline view by default, as shown in Figure 5.10. A journal entry displays below the date in the timeline for which the entry was created.

Creating a Journal Entry

To create a new journal entry in the Journal module, perform one of the following actions:

- Click the Journal Entry button in the New group on the Home tab.
- Right-click in an unused area within the Content pane and then click *Journal Entry* at the shortcut menu.

Figure 5.10 The Journal Module in Timeline View

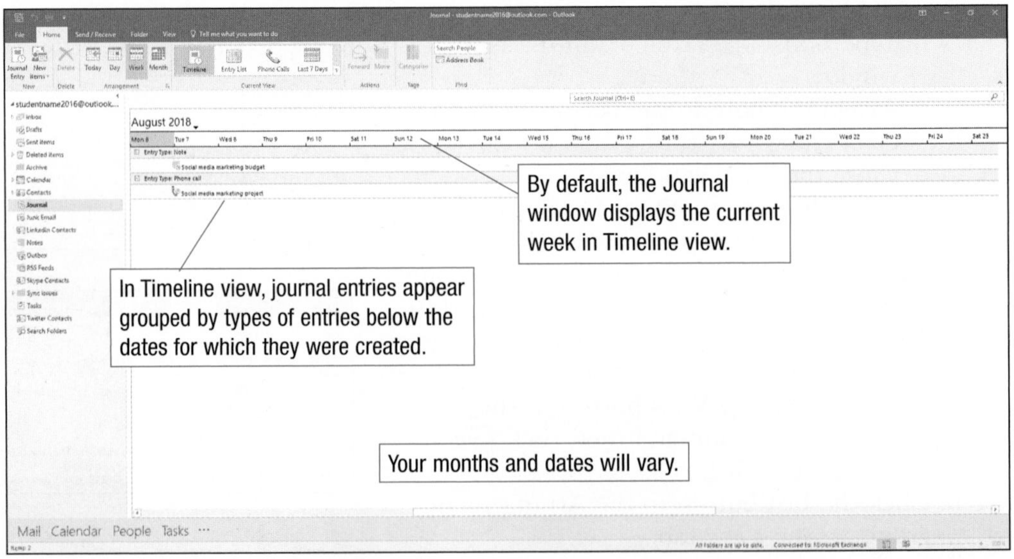

By default, the Journal window displays the current week in Timeline view.

In Timeline view, journal entries appear grouped by types of entries below the dates for which they were created.

Your months and dates will vary.

At the Journal Entry window, shown in Figure 5.11, type a description of the activity in the *Subject* text box. Use the *Entry type* list box arrow to change the activity from *Phone call* to *Note*, *Remote session*, *Task*, *Task request*, or *Task response* if necessary. Enter other details about the activity that you want to store, such as the start day and time and duration of the activity. When finished, click the Save & Close button in the Actions group on the Journal Entry tab.

Figure 5.11 Journal Entry Window

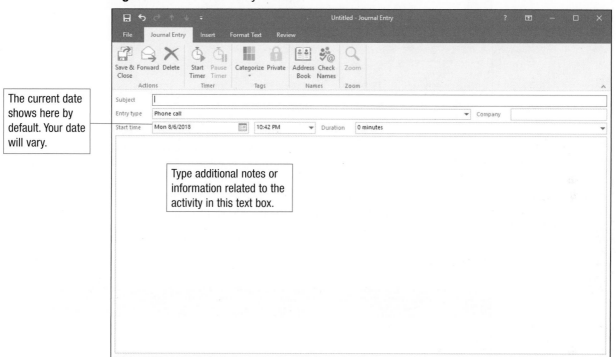

The current date shows here by default. Your date will vary.

Type additional notes or information related to the activity in this text box.

Exercise 14 Creating Journal Entries

1. With Outlook open, display the Journal module by completing the following steps:
   a. Click the Navigation Options button (three dots) on the Navigation bar and then click *Folders* at the pop-up list.
   b. Click *Journal* in the Folder pane.
2. Create a journal entry to record a telephone call by completing the following steps:
   a. Click the Journal Entry button in the New group on the Home tab.

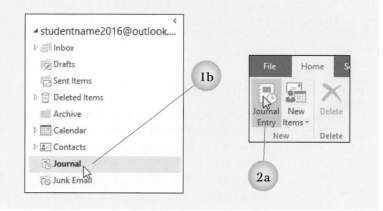

b. Type Social media marketing project in the *Subject* text box.

c. Click the *Duration* list box arrow and then click *30 minutes* at the drop-down list.

d. Click in the text box below *Start time* and then type the following text: Spoke with Tory O'Shea from O'Shea Market Research. She can provide consulting services for us on the European project at an hourly rate of $150, billed monthly.

e. Click Save & Close.

3. Create another journal entry to record a discussion by completing the following steps:

a. Click the Journal Entry button in the New group on the Home tab.

b. Type Social media marketing budget in the *Subject* text box.

c. Click the *Entry type* list box arrow and then click *Note* at the drop-down list.

d. Click in the text box below *Start time* and then type the following text: Spoke with Cal about the budget for the social media marketing project. He said $5,000 is available. Cal mentioned that head office approval is required for any payments over $1,000.

e. Click Save & Close.

4. Click the Entry List button in the Current View group on the Home tab.

5. Print the journal entries in Table style.

6. Click the Timeline button in the Current View group on the Home tab.

Check Your Work

TIP Use the Start Timer button in the Timer group on the Journal Entry tab to start a timer while you make a phone call, conduct a meeting, or work on a project. Click the Pause Timer button when finished and the time is automatically recorded in the *Duration* list box.

Editing and Deleting a Journal Entry

Double-click a journal entry in the Content pane to open the Journal Entry window and then make changes to the journal entry details. You can attach a file to a journal entry using the Attach File button in the Include group on the Insert tab. Outlook adds a shortcut icon for the file in the text box below *Start time*. Launch the file by double-clicking the file icon in the Journal Entry window. For example, you can attach a report for a project on which you are working to the journal entry in which you are keeping track of your time. Delete a selected journal entry by clicking the Delete button in the Delete group on the Home tab.

Chapter Summary

- Add jobs to your To-Do list as tasks in the Task window.
- Add new tasks in the *Type a new task* text box at the top of the task list in To-Do List view.
- Tasks can also be created in a Task window in which you type a description of the task and change other options, such as the task status and priority.
- When you have finished a task, you can either delete it from the task list or mark it as completed.
- Update or edit a task by double-clicking the task entry to open the Task window and then making changes to the task details.
- A task that you perform on a regular basis can be set up as a recurring task. A recurring task appears only once in the task list.
- You can assign a task to someone else by emailing him or her a task request. The task recipient can choose to accept the task, decline the task, or reassign the task to another person.
- When you accept a task request, you become the owner of the task. The owner is the only person who can make changes to the task details.
- Email comments about a task by clicking the Send Status Report button in the Manage Task group on the Task tab.
- A copy of a task can be sent via email by clicking the Forward button in the Respond group or in the Actions group on the Task tab.
- A variety of task lists that sort, filter, and group tasks are available with options in the Current View group on the Home tab or the Change View button in the Current View group on the View tab.
- Turn on and customize the To-Do bar for each Outlook folder to display at the right side of the window a calendar, contacts control, and To-Do list.
- Open the Outlook Options dialog box with *Tasks* selected in the left pane to change the colors in which overdue and completed tasks are displayed or to change options for tracking assigned tasks, reminders, and work hours.
- Create a note in the Notes module as a reminder or placeholder to store a thought or idea.
- Double-click a note to edit the note text. Delete a selected note by clicking the Delete button in the Delete group on the Home tab.
- Copy to the desktop a note that contains a time sensitive reminder.
- Applying color categories to notes is one way of organizing the folder.
- Show notes in Icon view, Notes List view, or Last 7 Days view. Use options in the Arrangement group on the View tab to customize the current view.
- A selected note can be forwarded as a file attachment in an email message.
- Create a journal entry in the Journal folder to keep track of an activity such as a telephone call, meeting, or other job. You can also store details about the activity, including the start date and time as well as the time spent.

Commands Review

FEATURE	BUTTON	RIBBON TAB AND GROUP, OR OTHER METHOD	SHORTCUT
Apply color category to task or note		Home, Tags OR Task, Tags OR click note icon at top left of Note window	
Assign task to someone else	OR	Home, New OR Task, Manage Task	
Create journal entry		Home, New	Ctrl + N
Create note		Home, New	Ctrl + N
Create task		Home, New	Ctrl + N
Customize current task view		View, Current View OR click *View Settings* option in Arrangement group expanded option box	
Delete task, note, or journal entry		Home, Delete	Ctrl + D
Display task details		Task, Show	
Display task options		File, *Options*, *Tasks*	
Mark task as completed		Task, Manage Task	
Send task information by email		Home, Respond OR Task, Actions	Ctrl + F
Send task status report		Task, Manage Task	
Set recurring task		Task, Recurrence	Ctrl + G
Turn on or off To-Do bar		View, Layout	

CHAPTER 6

Customizing and Integrating Outlook Components

Performance Objectives

Precheck

Check your current skills to help focus your study.

Upon successful completion of Chapter 6, you will be able to:

1 Specify the module that displays when Outlook is started

2 Customize the Folder pane and Navigation bar

3 Specify email options, change the message font, and change the mail format

4 Mark an Outlook item as private

5 Forward a calendar item and create an appointment or task from a message

6 Create and use a Quick Part in a message

7 Perform an email merge using contact data

8 Create and use a new Outlook data file

9 Compact an Outlook data file and back up your personal information store

10 Add another email account to Outlook

A multitude of options are available for customizing Outlook to operate in the way that best suits your preferences and work habits. Outlook provides tools with which you can integrate information in Outlook modules with information in other Outlook modules or in other Microsoft Office suite applications, such as Microsoft Word. You can create an additional data file in which to store Outlook items and/ or add multiple accounts to manage information. You should compact and back up your Outlook data file routinely to safeguard the information and keep the file a manageable size.

In this chapter, you will learn about options for customizing Outlook and integrating data; for managing your personal information store, which contains all your Outlook data; and for adding a second data file and email account to your Outlook profile.

SNAP

If you are a SNAP user, launch the Precheck and the Tutorial from your Assignments page.

Specifying the Starting Module

Quick Steps

Specify the Starting Module
1. Click File tab.
2. Click *Options*.
3. Click *Advanced* in left pane.
4. Click Browse button in *Outlook start and exit* section.
5. Click desired folder name.
6. Click OK two times.

When Outlook is started, Mail is the active module and Inbox is the active folder within that module. Open the Outlook Options dialog box and display the *Advanced* options, shown in Figure 6.1, to change the module that appears when Outlook opens. For example, you may prefer to see your Calendar first whenever Outlook is started so that you can immediately see the day's appointments, meetings, and events.

Figure 6.1 Outlook Options Dialog Box with *Advanced* Selected

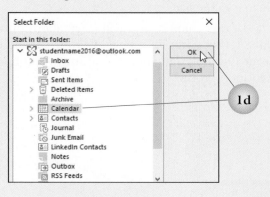

Click the Browse button and choose another folder to change the module that displays on startup.

Exercise 1 Setting Calendar as the Starting Module when Outlook Is Opened

1. With Outlook open, change the starting module to the Calendar by completing the following steps:
   a. Click the File tab and then click *Options* at the backstage area.
   b. At the Outlook Options dialog box, click *Advanced* in the left pane.
   c. Click the Browse button next to *Start Outlook in this folder* in the *Outlook start and exit* section.
   d. At the Select Folder dialog box, click *Calendar* in the *Start in this folder* list box and then click OK.
   e. Click OK to close the Outlook Options dialog box.
2. Exit Outlook.

3. Start Outlook. If necessary, sign in with your user name and password. The Calendar module displays when Outlook opens.

4. Change the starting module back to Mail with Inbox the active folder by completing the following steps:

    a. Click the File tab and then click *Options*.

    b. Click *Advanced* in the left pane in the Outlook Options dialog box.

    c. Click the Browse button in the *Outlook start and exit* section.

    d. Click *Inbox* and then click OK two times.

Customizing the Navigation Bar and Folder Pane

Quick Steps

Hide the Folder Pane
1. Click View tab.
2. Click Folder Pane button in Layout group.
3. Click *Off*.

Show the Folder Pane in the Normal State
1. Click View tab.
2. Click Folder Pane button in Layout group.
3. Click *Normal*.

Minimize the Folder Pane
1. Click View tab.
2. Click Folder Pane button in Layout group.
3. Click *Minimized*.

▭ Folder Pane

◁ Minimize the Folder Pane

▷ Expand button

📌 Pin the Folder Pane

TIP Increase or decrease the width of the Folder pane by dragging the right border to the right or left, respectively, when the pointer changes to a vertical double line with a right-and-left-pointing arrow.

The Navigation bar displays text labels or icons for the four most used modules in Outlook: Mail, Calendar, People, and Tasks. You can show more or fewer modules and/or change the order of the modules to suit your preferences. Click the Navigation Options button (three dots) on the Navigation bar and then click *Navigation Options* at the pop-up list to open the Navigation Options dialog box, shown in Figure 6.2. Here you can change the number of modules shown in the Navigation bar and/or change the order of the modules.

To free up space in the Content pane, you can minimize or hide the Folder pane while viewing a module with a large amount of information. Minimize the Folder pane by clicking the Minimize the Folder Pane button (left-pointing arrow) at the top right of the Folder pane. Performing this action reduces the Folder pane to a bar along the left edge of the Outlook window. Hide the Folder pane by clicking the View tab, clicking the Folder Pane button in the Layout group, and then clicking *Off* at the drop-down list.

Expand the Folder pane after it has been minimized by clicking the Expand button at the top of the Folder bar and then clicking the pushpin icon at the top right of the expanded pane. Redisplay a hidden Folder pane by clicking the View tab, clicking the Folder Pane button in the Layout group, and then clicking *Normal*.

Use the keyboard shortcut Alt + F1 to cycle through minimizing the Folder pane, turning off the Folder pane, and showing the Folder pane in its Normal state. You can also change modules using the keyboard shortcuts Ctrl + 1 for Mail, Ctrl + 2 for Calendar, Ctrl + 3 for People, and Ctrl + 4 for Tasks.

Figure 6.2 Navigation Options Dialog Box

When the check box for *Compact Navigation* contains a check mark, the Navigation bar displays icons instead of text labels.

Navigation Options

Maximum number of visible items: 4

☐ Compact Navigation

Display in this order
Mail
Calendar
People
Tasks
Notes
Folders
Shortcuts

Move Up
Move Down

Reset   OK   Cancel

Exercise 2 Changing the Folder Pane and Customizing the Navigation Bar

1. With Outlook open and the Calendar module active, hide the Folder pane, change modules and views, and minimize the Folder pane by completing the following steps:

   a. Click the View tab, click the Folder Pane button in the Layout group, and then click *Off* at the drop-down list.

   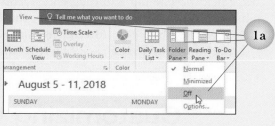

   b. Press Ctrl + 3 to display the People module.

   c. Change the view to Business Card view. *Note: Skip this step if your Contacts are already displayed in Business Card view.* Notice that hiding the Folder pane allows the Content pane to show more contacts in the window.

   d. Use the keyboard shortcut Alt + F1 to redisplay the Folder pane, or click the View tab, click the Folder Pane button, and then click *Normal.*

   e. Click the Minimize the Folder Pane button at the top right of the Folder pane.

2. Pin the Folder pane and customize the appearance of the Navigation bar by completing the following steps:

   a. Click the Expand button at the top of the minimized Folder pane.

   b. Click the pushpin icon at the top right of the expanded Folder pane.

   c. Click the Navigation Options button (three dots) on the Navigation bar, and then click *Navigation Options* at the pop-up list.

   d. Click the *Maximum number of visible items* decrement (down) arrow to change *4* to *3* and then press Enter or click OK. The Navigation bar now shows text labels or icons for only the first three modules: Mail, Calendar, and People.

3. Change the order of the text labels or icons on the Navigation bar by completing the following steps:

   a. Open the Navigation Options dialog box.

   b. Click *Tasks* in the *Display in this order* list box and then click the Move Up button two times.

   c. Click OK to close the Navigation Options dialog box. Tasks is now the second text label or icon on the Navigation bar, positioned next to the Mail text label or icon.

   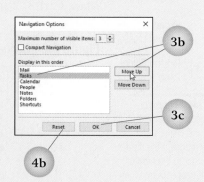

4. Restore the Navigation bar to the default number of items and order by completing the following steps:

   a. Open the Navigation Options dialog box.

   b. Click the Reset button.

   c. Click OK.

Setting Email Options

Quick Steps
Set Email Options
1. Click File tab.
2. Click *Options*.
3. Click *Mail*.
4. Change desired options.
5. Click OK.

To change email options, click the File tab, click *Options* to open the Outlook Options dialog box, and then click *Mail* in the left pane. The *Message arrival* section in the Outlook Options dialog box with the Mail pane selected, shown in Figure 6.3, allows you to control the actions that occur when messages are received in the Inbox. The *Conversation Clean Up* section provides options for handling messages that are deleted when duplicated messages in a thread are automatically removed. The *Replies and forwards* section provides options for how the original message text is threaded within messages that are replied to or forwarded to someone else.

The *Save messages* and *Send messages* sections at the Outlook Options dialog box with the Mail pane selected display the options shown in Figure 6.4 on page 182. You can use these options to control the actions that occur when messages are saved and sent.

The *Tracking* section, shown in Figure 6.5 on page 182, provides options for controlling how read receipts, meeting requests, and polls are processed. For example, you can specify that you want a delivery receipt and/or a read receipt for each message sent, or you can specify how you want Outlook to handle read receipts attached to messages that you receive.

In the next three exercises, you will examine the available mail options, experiment with changing advanced mail options, and practice restoring default email option settings.

Figure 6.3 *Message arrival, Conversation Clean Up*, and *Replies and forwards* Sections at Outlook Options Dialog Box with *Mail* Selected

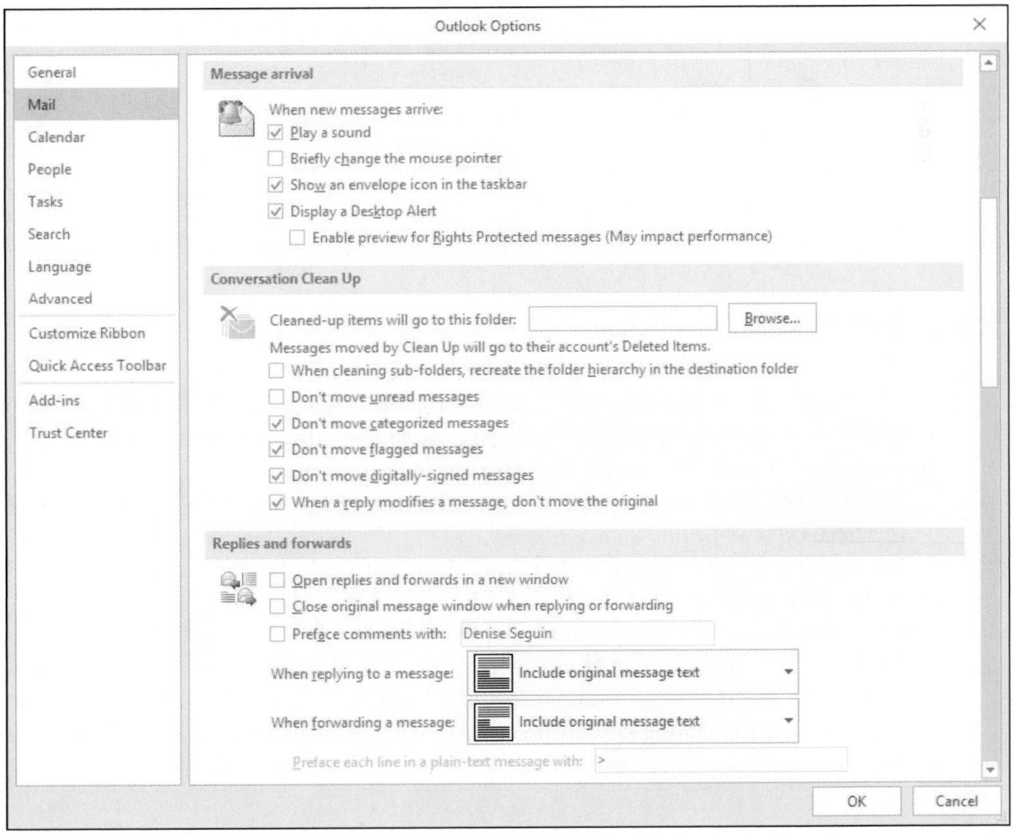

Figure 6.4 *Save messages* and *Send messages* Sections at Outlook Options Dialog Box with *Mail* Selected

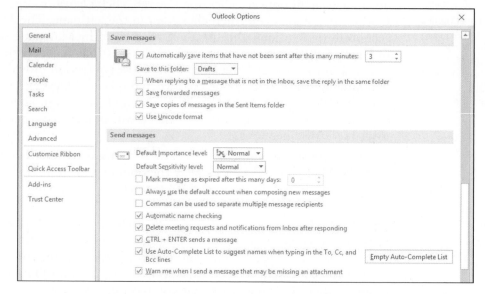

Figure 6.5 *Tracking* Section at Outlook Options Dialog Box with *Mail* Selected

Exercise 3 Changing Mail Options

1. With People the active module, instruct Outlook to turn off desktop alerts, indent the original message text when replying to a message, and lengthen the time period before draft messages are saved by completing the following steps:

   a. Display the Mail module with Inbox the active folder in the Content pane.

   b. Click the File tab, click *Options*, and then click *Mail* in the left pane at the Outlook Options dialog box.

   c. Click to remove the check mark from the *Display a Desktop Alert* check box in the *Message arrival* section. **Note:** *Skip this step if the check box is already empty.*

   d. Scroll down the dialog box to the *Replies and forwards* section and then read each option included within the section.

e. Click the *When replying to a message* option box arrow and then click *Include and indent original message text* at the drop-down list.

f. If necessary, scroll down the dialog box to the *Save messages* section.

g. Select the current entry in the *Automatically save items that have not been sent after this many minutes* measurement box and then type 5. ***Note:*** *If this box is currently empty, click the* Automatically save items that have not been sent after this many minutes *check box to turn on the feature.*

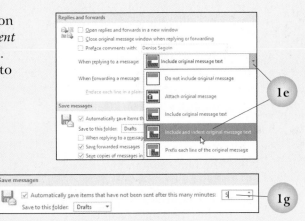

2. Leave the Outlook Options dialog box open for the next exercise.

Exercise 4 Changing Advanced Mail Options

Note: In this exercise, you will send a message to the student with whom you have been exchanging messages in earlier chapters. If that person is not available, check with your instructor.

1. With the Mail pane selected in the Outlook Options dialog box, instruct Outlook not to delete meeting requests after you have responded, to turn off attachment reminders, and to always send a read receipt by completing the following steps:

a. If necessary, scroll down the dialog box to the *Send messages* section.

b. Click to remove the check mark from the *Delete meeting requests and notifications from Inbox after responding* check box.

c. Click to remove the check mark from the *Warn me when I send a message that may be missing an attachment* check box.

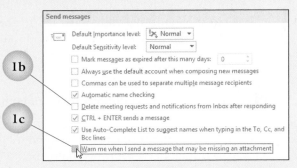

d. If necessary, scroll down the dialog box to the *Tracking* section.

e. Within the *Tracking* section, locate the item *For any message received that includes a read receipt request* and then click to select *Always send a read receipt*, if the option is not already selected.

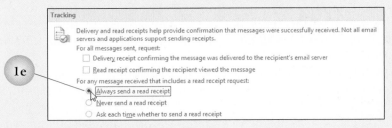

f. Click OK to close the Outlook Options dialog box.

2. Create and send a message to test the new options by completing the following steps:

a. Open a new message window.

b. Type the email address of the student with whom you are exchanging messages in the *To* text box.

c. Type Email Options in the *Subject* text box.

d. Type the following message text, double space, and then add your name as the sender:

> Student Name, [Substitute first name of message recipient for *Student Name*.]
>
> I've attached a picture taken during my recent vacation.

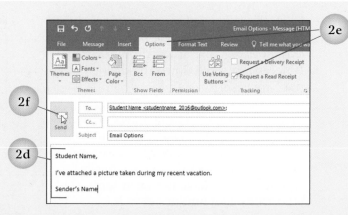

e. Click the Options tab and then click to insert a check mark in the *Request a Read Receipt* check box in the Tracking group.

f. Click Send. Notice that no attachment reminder message appeared before the message was sent because you turned off the reminder option in Step 1c.

g. Click the Send/Receive All Folders button on the Quick Access Toolbar to update the Inbox. When new messages arrive in your Inbox, notice that each message appears without a desktop alert notifying you that new mail has arrived. There is no alert because of the change you made to the mail options in Exercise 3, Step 1c.

h. Open the message window for the message received from Step 2f and then click the Reply button. Notice the original message included below the insertion point is indented because of the change you made to the option in Exercise 3, Step 1e.

i. Type the following reply message text:

> The picture was not attached to the message.

j. Print the message, send the message, and then close the message window. A read receipt will also be automatically returned to the sender even though you were not prompted to send one, because of the change you made in Step 1e of this exercise.

> **Check Your Work**

Exercise 5 Restoring Mail Options to the Default Settings

1. Restore the mail options to the original default settings by completing the following steps:
   a. Open the Outlook Options dialog box with the Mail pane active.
   b. Click to insert a check mark in the *Display a Desktop Alert* check box in the *Message arrival* section.
   c. Scroll down the dialog box to the *Replies and forwards* section, click the *When replying to a message* option box arrow, and then click *Include original message text* at the drop-down list.
   d. If necessary, scroll down the dialog box to the *Save messages* section.
   e. Change the value in the *Automatically save items that have not been sent after this many minutes* measurement box to *3*.
   f. If necessary, scroll down the dialog box to the *Send messages* section.
   g. Click to insert a check mark in the *Delete meeting requests and notifications from Inbox after responding* check box.
   h. Click to insert a check mark in the *Warn me when I send a message that may be missing an attachment* check box.
   i. If necessary, scroll down the dialog box to the *Tracking* section.
   j. Find the item *For any message received that includes a read receipt request* and then below it, click to select the *Ask each time whether to send a read receipt* option, unless you are instructed to choose another option.
2. Click OK to close the Outlook Options dialog box.

Click the Settings button (gear icon) on the Menu bar, and then click *Options* to open the Options pane. **Note:** *For some releases of Outlook on the web, you will need to click the Settings button, and then click* Mail *on the Your app settings tab to open the Options pane.* Email options are grouped by these sections: *Automatic processing, Accounts, Attachment options,* and *Layout.* Click a section to view the available options in the right pane. Make the desired changes, click the Save button, and then click the Back button to close the Options pane.

Click the Settings button (gear icon) on the Menu bar and then click *Options* to open the Options pane. Mail options are grouped by these sections: *Automatic processing, Accounts, Attachment options, Junk email,* and *Layout.* Click a section in the left pane to view options in the right pane. Click the Save button, then click the Back button to close the Options pane when finished.

Changing the Font for Messages

Quick Steps

Change Font for New Messages or Replies or Forwards
1. Click File tab.
2. Click *Options*.
3. Click *Mail*.
4. Click Stationery and Fonts button.
5. Click Font button in *New mail messages* section or in *Replying or forwarding messages* section.
6. Change font as desired in Font dialog box.
7. Click OK three times.

TIP Calibri is an easy-to-read font. If you change fonts for new messages, replies, or forwards, choose a font that is pleasing to read. Decorative fonts are not suitable for email.

New messages use 11-point Calibri font, which is the same font used in Microsoft Word documents and Excel worksheets. Change the font in an individual message using the font and font size options in the Basic Text group on the Message tab. To change the font for all new messages, open the Signatures and Stationery dialog box with the Personal Stationery tab active (see Figure 6.6). To do this, click the File tab, click *Options*, click *Mail* in the left pane, and then click the Stationery and Fonts button in the *Compose messages* section. Click the Font button in the *New mail messages* section or in the *Reply or forwarding messages* section to open the Font dialog box, choose a new font, and then click OK three times.

Figure 6.6 Signatures and Stationery Dialog Box with Personal Stationery Tab Active

Use the Theme button to choose a message theme, which is a set of fonts, colors, and graphics.

Click the Font button to customize the font in all new messages or in all replies and forwards.

Changing the Mail Format

Quick Steps

Change the Mail Format for a Message
1. Open message window.
2. Click Format Text tab.
3. Click HTML button, Plain Text button, or Rich Text button in Format group.

Aa Plain Text

Aa Rich Text

By default, messages are composed and sent using *hypertext markup language (HTML)*. Other mail format options are plain text and rich text. *Plain text* does not include any formatting of the text. *Rich text* includes formatting options such as font changes, alignment, and bullets. HTML displays features in addition to those provided in rich text, such as backgrounds, horizontal lines, and pictures. You should use HTML format in most cases, unless you are sending a message to someone that you know has an email program that does not support formatting options.

To change the mail format in a message window, click the Format Text tab and then click the HTML button, Plain Text button, or Rich Text button in the Format group. To change the mail format for all new messages, open the Outlook Options dialog box with the Mail pane selected, click the *Compose messages in this format* option box arrow in the *Compose messages* section, click *HTML*, *Rich Text*, or *Plain Text* at the drop-down list, and then click OK.

Exercise 6 Changing the Mail Format for an Individual Message

1. With Outlook open and the Mail module with the Inbox folder active, create a new message using the plain text format by completing the following steps:
   a. Open a new message window.
   b. Type your own email address in the *To* text box.
   c. Type Mail Format in the *Subject* text box and then press Enter.
   d. Click the Format Text tab.
   e. Click the Plain Text button in the Format group. Notice that all the buttons relating to changing the appearance of the text are now dimmed on the Format Text tab.
   f. Type the following message text:

   > In a plain text message all formatting options, including bold and italics, become unavailable. Most people type an asterisk before and after a word to *emphasize* it in a plain text message.

2. Print the message.
3. Click the Send button to send the message.

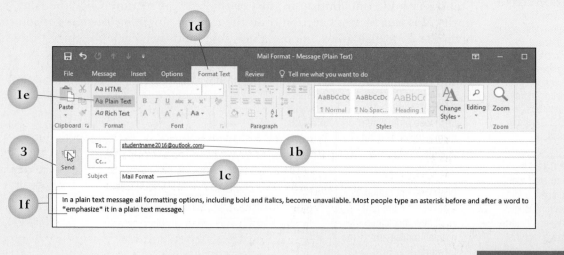

Check Your Work

Changing the Mail Format in Outlook on the web

Change the mail format for the current message by clicking the More commands button (three dots), and then clicking *Switch to plain text* at the drop-down list.

To change the mail format from HTML to plain text for all new messages, display the Options pane and then change the option for *Compose messages in this format* to *Plain text* in the *Message format* category of the *Layout* section. Click the Back button to close the Options pane when finished.

Your option list might vary.

•••
Save draft
Insert signature
Show Bcc
Show From
Check names
Set importance >
Switch to plain text
Show message options...

Marking Outlook Items as Private

You can grant another user permission to view your appointments, meetings, contacts, and tasks by granting delegate access, or by adding the person to the Permissions list at the folder's Properties dialog box. Doing this allows you to let others see your information, which is helpful in the workplace for an assistant or for team members with whom you work. If you are creating an appointment, contact, or task and do not want someone with access to your data to see the item, click the Private button in the Tags group on the Appointment tab, Contact tab, or Task tab. You will see the item and details when you view your Outlook data, but others will see only a placeholder for the item, not the details.

Users connected to an Outlook account that accesses an Internet mail server do not have the ability to grant others access to their Outlook items. In those cases, the Private tag is not necessary.

Exercise 7 Creating a Private Appointment

1. With Outlook open and the Mail module with the Inbox folder active, display the Calendar module and then display the date *October 19, 2018* in Day view in the Content pane. Display the current date if you did not use October 2018 dates in Chapter 3.
2. Create a new appointment and mark it as private by completing the following steps:
   a. Double-click next to *12 PM* in the Appointment area to open an Appointment window.
   b. Type Lunch with Denny in the *Subject* text box.
   c. Type The Waterfront Bistro in the *Location* text box.
   d. Change the end time to *1:30 PM*.
   e. Click the Private button in the Tags group on the Appointment tab.

f. Click Save & Close. The appointment appears in the Appointment area with an icon of a padlock at the bottom right in the appointment box, indicating that the appointment is private.

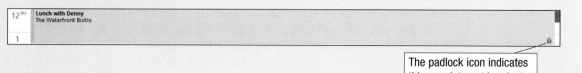

The padlock icon indicates this appointment is private.

3. Print the calendar in Daily style.
4. Make Inbox the active folder.

Check Your Work

Forwarding a Calendar Item by Email

Quick Steps

Forward a Calendar Item by Email
1. Select calendar entry in Appointment area.
2. Click Forward button in Actions group on Calendar Tools Appointment tab.
3. Enter message recipient, subject, and message text.
4. Click Send.

You can send appointment, event, or meeting details to someone via email as a file attachment. The recipient opens the file attachment to view the details. He or she can add the item to his or her calendar using the Copy to My Calendar button in the Actions group on the Meeting tab. Consider this option to send a calendar entry to someone with whom you do not share your calendar.

Select the calendar item in the Appointment area and then click the Forward button in the Actions group on the Calendar Tools Appointment tab. At the message window that opens, enter the recipient, subject text, an explanatory note, and then click Send.

Marking Appointments and Tasks as Private in Outlook on the web

To mark an appointment, meeting, or event as private, click to insert a check mark in the *Private* check box below the *All day* check box on a new Event page.

Mark a task as private by clicking the Show more details button on the Task page, and then clicking to insert a check mark in the *Mark private* check box below the *% complete* text box.

12:00 PM ▼	☐ All day
1:30 PM ▼	☐ Private

% complete	Priority
0	Normal ▼
☐ Mark private	

Marking an Appointment as Private at Outlook.com

To mark a calendar item as private, click to insert a check mark in the *Private* check box located in the start and end time section on the Details page for a new Calendar event.

Start			
Fri 10/19/2018 ▼	12:00 PM ▼	☐ All day	
End			
Fri 10/19/2018 ▼	1:30 PM ▼	☐ Private	

Creating an Appointment or Task from a Message

Quick Steps

Create an Appointment or Task from an Email Message
1. Drag message header to Calendar or Tasks text label or icon on Navigation bar.
2. Add details as required in Appointment or Task window.
3. Click Save & Close.

An email message often contains information that is needed to create an appointment, meeting, event, or task entry in the Calendar module or Tasks module. To create this kind of entry, you do not need to switch to the other Outlook module, open a new window, and then enter the details. Instead, drag the message header to the Calendar or Tasks text label or icon on the Navigation bar and Outlook automatically opens an Appointment or Task window, respectively. The subject of the email message is automatically entered as the subject of the appointment or task. Outlook also copies the email message—including the *From, Sent, To,* and *Subject* details—from the message header into the white text box in the Appointment or Task window. Change the date and time, assign tags, and add other options as needed to complete the item and then click the Save & Close button.

To create a meeting request from an email message, drag the message to the Calendar text label or icon on the Navigation bar, and then use the Invite Attendees button in the Attendees group on the Appointment tab to add the *To* text box and the Send button to the Appointment window. You can also generate a meeting request from a message by opening the message window from the Inbox and then clicking the Meeting button in the Respond group on the Message tab. Outlook opens a Meeting window and automatically adds to the *To* text box both your email address and the email address of the message sender.

Meeting

Exercise 8 Creating a Task from an Email Message

1. With Outlook open and the Mail module with the Inbox folder active, select the message header for the message received in Exercise 6 with the subject *Mail Format*.
2. Create a task from the email message by completing the following steps:
   a. Drag the message header with the subject *Mail Format* from the Content pane to the Tasks text label or icon on the Navigation bar.

   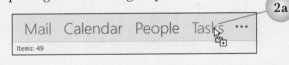

   2a

   b. Click after the text *Mail Format* in the *Subject* text box, press the spacebar, and then type - find out which email client programs do not support HTML.
   c. Click Save & Close.

3. Make Tasks the active module. Double-click to open the task created in Step 2. Print the task in Memo style and then close the Task window.

Check Your Work

Creating and Using a Quick Part

A Quick Part is preformatted text, referred to as a **building block**, that is saved in the *AutoText* gallery and can be reused in any Outlook item. Create a Quick Part for any text that you will repeat in messages, appointments, contacts, or tasks. For example, you can create a Quick Part to insert a standard paragraph that is added frequently when composing or replying to email messages. Consider creating Quick Part building blocks for these types of reusable content in email messages:

- Answers to frequently asked questions
- Directions to your business location
- Holiday messages with different hours for operations or business closings

To create a new Quick Part for the *AutoText* gallery, open a message window and then type and format the text you want to save to the gallery. Next, select the formatted text, click the Insert tab, click the Quick Parts button in the Text group, point to *AutoText* at the drop-down list, and then click *Save Selection to AutoText Gallery*. Type a name to identify the saved text at the Create New Building Block dialog box and then click OK.

When you want to reuse the text, click the Insert tab, click the Quick Parts button, point to *AutoText*, and then click the entry in the *AutoText* gallery. Once you have inserted the text, you can edit and format it as needed for an individual message.

Quick Steps

Create a Quick Part
1. Open message window and type, format, and select Quick Part text.
2. Click Insert tab.
3. Click Quick Parts button in Text group.
4. Point to *AutoText*.
5. Click *Save Selection to AutoText Gallery*.
6. Type name for Quick Part.
7. Click OK.

 Quick Parts

Exercise 9 Creating and Using a Quick Part

1. With Outlook open, make the Mail module with the Inbox folder active and then open a new message window.
2. Create a new Quick Part that inserts text by completing the following steps:
   a. Click in the message text box and then type the following text:

   Thank you for your order. You will receive another email with tracking information once your items have been shipped.

   Please email me or call me at 800-555-6233 if you need to make changes to your order. I will be happy to assist you with any questions or concerns.
   [Press Enter two times.]

   b. Select the text (including the two blank lines), change the font and font size to 12-point Cambria, and apply the Dark Red font color (first option in the *Standard Colors* section).
   c. Select the telephone number, apply bold formatting, and apply the Black font color.
   d. Select the text and blank lines.
   e. Click the Insert tab, click the Quick Parts button in the Text group, point to *AutoText*, and then click *Save Selection to AutoText Gallery*.

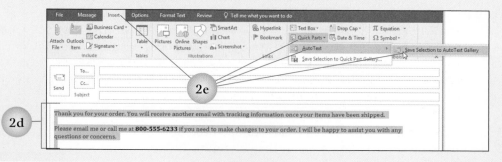

f. Type Orders in the *Name* text box at the Create New Building Block dialog box and then click OK.

3. Close the message window. Click No when prompted to save changes.

4. Create a new message that reuses the Quick Part by completing the following steps:
   a. Open a new message window.
   b. Type your email address in the *To* text box.
   c. Type Orders Quick Part in the *Subject* text box.
   d. Click to place the insertion point in the message text box.
   e. Click the Insert tab.
   f. Click the Quick Parts button, point to *AutoText*, and then click the *Orders* option in the *AutoText* gallery.

The *AutoText* gallery displays previews of the saved text with the building block names.

5. Print and then send the message.

The Orders Quick Part is added to the message in Step 4f.

Check Your Work

TIP Save a message that you send often (such as a status report) as a message template to be reused as needed. Use *Save As* from the File tab of an open message and change the *Save as type* option to *Outlook Template.* A template is an Outlook form.

You can also improve your efficiency by saving frequently sent messages as Outlook templates. The advantage to creating a template is that the message recipients and subject text can be saved in addition to the standard message text. See the Tip on this page for information on how to save a message as a template. To reuse a message template, make the Mail module with the Inbox folder active, click the New Items button in the New group on the Home tab, point to *More Items* at the drop-down list, click *Choose Form* at the side menu, and then change the *Look In* option box to display *User Templates in File System.* Double-click the template name in the list box to open the saved message template. Make changes as needed and then send the message.

Performing an Email Merge to Multiple Contacts

Quick Steps

Create an Email Merge from Contacts
1. Display People module.
2. Display desired view.
3. Add/remove columns as needed.
4. If necessary, select contact records.
5. Click Mail Merge button in Actions group on Home tab.
6. Change required merge options in Mail Merge Contacts dialog box.
7. Click OK.
8. Create main document in Microsoft Word.
9. Click Finish & Merge button in Finish group on Mailings tab in Word.
10. Click desired merge option at drop-down list.
11. Exit Word.

Mail Merge

You can filter or sort contact data in the People module and then use this data as the data source with the mail merge feature in Microsoft Word to produce printed letters or generate email messages. A *mail merge* involves using a list of names and addresses from one file, called the *data source*, to create form letters, mailing labels, or envelopes. A second file, called the *main document*, contains the standard text for each letter, label, envelope, catalog, or email. Formatting instructions and field codes that instruct Word as to the placement of the *Name* and *Address* fields are also included in the main document. The contact information for the exported contacts is sent to a temporary mail merge file while the main document is being created in Word.

To perform a mail merge using Outlook and Word, complete the following three steps:

1. Export the contact data from the People module as a data source from Outlook to Word.

2. Create the main document in Word by typing standard text and inserting the merge fields as required where contact information is to be added.

3. Merge the data source with the main document to create a new Word document that can be saved separately, sent directly to the printer, or exported as an email message.

Exporting Contacts Data to Create a Data Source

Complete the following steps to create a data source from the People module:

1. Change to the view that contains the fields you want to merge, and sort or filter the contact data to the order you want the letters or messages generated. Add and remove fields to and from the current view as required for the merge. If you do not want a letter, label, email, or envelope generated for each record, select the contacts to include in the merge. Use the keyboard shortcut Ctrl + click to select individual records, or click the first record and then Shift + click the last record to select contacts that are next to each other.

2. Click the Mail Merge button in the Actions group on the Home tab to open the Mail Merge Contacts dialog box, shown in Figure 6.7 on page 193. *All contacts in current view* is selected in the *Contacts* section unless you selected contact records prior to opening the dialog box. In that case, the *Only selected contacts* option is active instead.

3. In the *Fields to merge* section, click *Contact fields in current view*. With the default option *All contact fields* selected, all contact data is sent to the data source file. In most cases, it is unnecessary to include all the fields in contact records.

4. In the *Document file* section, accept the default option *New document* or click *Existing document* and then use the Browse button to navigate to the folder and file name of the document that you want to merge with the contact records.

5. If you want to save the exported contact information for future mail merges, click the *Permanent file* check box in the *Contact data file* section to insert a check mark and then use the Browse button to navigate to the folder and file name in which to store the data source.

6. In the *Merge options* section, select the type of main document that you will create in Word in the *Document type* drop-down list. The options include *Form Letters, Mailing Labels, Envelopes,* and *Catalog.*

7. Select where to send the merged records in the *Merge to* list box. The data can be sent to *New Document, Printer,* or *Email.* When you select *Email,* a text box is added to the dialog box, in which you type the subject text for the email message.

8. Click OK.

Figure 6.7 Mail Merge Contacts Dialog Box

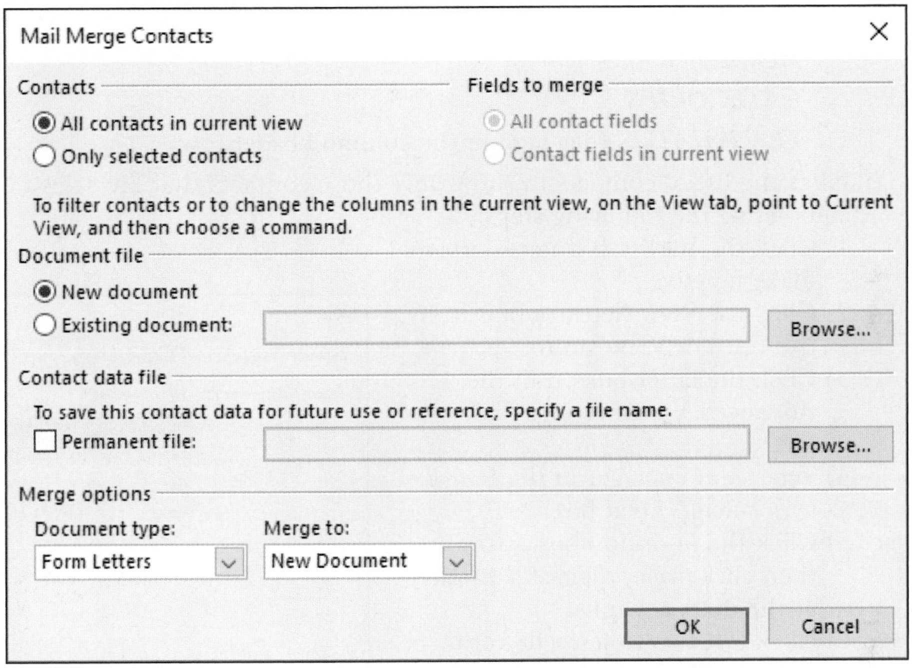

Completing the Merge in Word

When the contact data has finished exporting, you will be at a Microsoft Word document window with the Mailings tab active. To create the main document, type the text in the document to the point at which you need to insert the recipient's name and/or address from your contacts list. Click the Insert Merge Field button in the Write & Insert Fields group to select a field from the contact record. Insert spaces and other punctuation as required between the merge fields. Continue inserting merge fields and typing text until the main document is complete.

Click the Preview Results button in the Preview Results group to ensure the fields will merge with the text as desired. When you are satisfied with the results, click the Finish & Merge button in the Finish group and then click *Edit Individual Documents, Print Documents,* or *Send Email Messages* at the drop-down list. Microsoft Word generates an individual letter or email message to each contact in the data source.

 Insert Merge Field

Finish & Merge

TIP If you want to use the same letter or email for future merges, save the main document with the text and merge codes.

Exercise 10 Creating an Email Merge Using Contacts Data

1. With Outlook open and the Mail module with the Inbox folder active, display the People module and then change the current view to List.
2. Start a mail merge to create an email to a list of filtered contacts by completing the following steps:
   a. Remove the following columns from the current view:

   > FILE AS
   >
   > COUNTRY/REGION
   >
   > DEPARTMENT
   >
   > BUSINESS FAX
   >
   > HOME PHONE
   >
   > CATEGORIES
   >
   > FLAG STATUS (flag icon in the column header row)

   b. Filter the list of contacts to show only those contacts that are sales managers by completing the following steps:
      1) Click the View tab if necessary to make it active.
      2) Click the View Settings button in the Current View group.
      3) Click the Filter button in the Advanced View Settings dialog box.
      4) Type sales manager in the *Search for the word(s)* text box.
      5) Click the *In* option box arrow and then click *frequently-used text fields* at the drop-down list.
      6) Click OK two times. The contacts are now filtered to include only those individuals that have *sales manager* in their job title.

   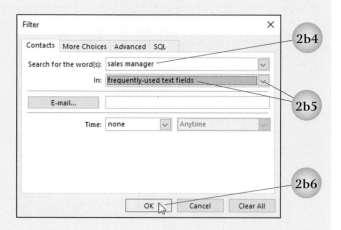

   c. Click the Home tab and then click the Mail Merge button in the Actions group.
   d. At the Mail Merge Contacts dialog box, click *Contact fields in current view* in the *Fields to merge* section.
   e. In the *Merge options* section, click the *Merge to* option box arrow and then click *Email* at the drop-down list.
   f. Click in the *Message subject line* text box and then type Confirmation for online order access.
   g. Click OK. ***Note:*** *Click OK if a Mail Merge dialog box appears informing you that your selection contains contact groups that will not be merged.*

   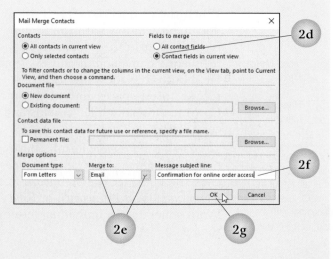

3. Outlook exports the selected records as a data source in Microsoft Word. Word is started with a blank document open and the Mailings tab active. Create the main document by completing the following steps:

a. Type We are in the process of setting up your account on our secure website for processing orders. Your company,

b. Press the spacebar and then click the Insert Merge Field button arrow in the Write & Insert Fields group on the Mailings tab.

c. Click *Company* at the drop-down list. Word inserts a merge field code in the document that will cause Word to retrieve the contact's company name and insert it at that location in the document when the email message is generated. A merge field is inserted in the document with pairs of left- and right-pointing chevrons («, ») at the ends of the field name.

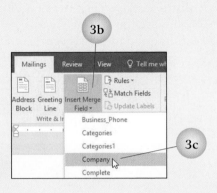

d. Type , indicated an interest in using our web-based ordering system. and then press Enter.

e. Type Please confirm the following information is accurate before we set up your account on our server: and then press Enter.

f. Click the Insert Merge Field button arrow and then click the field *Full_Name* at the drop-down list.

g. Press Enter.

h. Repeat Steps 2f through 2g to add the *Job_Title* and *Business_Phone* fields below *Full_Name*.

i. Type the email closing below the last merge field, substituting your name for *Student Name*. Press Shift + Enter to insert a line break after typing your name and before typing the title.

Regards,

Student Name

Web Administrator

3f **3h**

We are in the process of setting up your account on our secure website for processing orders. Your company, «Company», indicated an interest in using our web-based ordering system.

Please confirm the following information is accurate before we set up your account on our server:

«Full_Name»

«Job_Title»

«Business_Phone»

Regards,

Student Name
Web Administrator

3a-3e **3i**

---

4. Merge and send the email messages by completing the following steps:

a. Click the Finish & Merge button in the Finish group on the Mailings tab and then click *Send Email Messages* at the drop-down list.

b. At the Merge to E-mail dialog box, with *All* already selected in the *Send records* section, click OK. The main document is merged with the selected contact records and a message is sent to each contact's email address.

Merge to E-mail ? ×

Message options

To: Email

Subject line: Confirmation for online order access

Mail format: HTML

Send records

○ All
○ Current record
○ From: ___ To: ___

OK   Cancel

4b

5. Exit Microsoft Word. Click *Don't Save* when prompted to save the changes.
6. In Outlook with the People module active, change the view to Business Card view.
7. Make Mail active and display the Sent Items folder in the Content pane.
8. If necessary, click the Send/Receive All Folders button on the Quick Access Toolbar to update the message list.
9. Note the messages sent to the individuals in the filtered contacts list you created in Step 2. (Since the email addresses for the contacts are fictitious, you will receive messages from the mail server saying that your message is undeliverable for these contacts.)
10. Open one of the messages sent from the email merge at Step 4. Notice the data placed in the message where you inserted merge fields in the main document for *Company, Full_Name, Job_Title,* and *Business_Phone*.

11. Print the message and then close it.
12. Display the Inbox folder.

Check Your Work

Creating an Outlook Data File

All messages, appointments, contacts, and tasks in Outlook modules are stored in a single data file that is referred to as a ***personal information store*** and has the file name extension *.pst*. Outlook users who are connected using Microsoft Exchange server have all their data stored on the organization's Exchange server in a file referred to as a ***private store***. On the computer used to connect to the Microsoft Exchange server, a data file that contains a copy of the Outlook items stored on the server is saved in a file with the extension *.ost* for ***offline information store***.

One of many methods available for organizing Outlook data is to create multiple data files (information stores). For example, suppose you are working on a project in which you send and receive numerous email messages and need to ensure that you have quick access to the messages. You can create a folder within the current data file or create a separate data file. One advantage of creating a separate data file is that the file can be used as the project archive. Once the project is completed, you can close the data file and move it to a backup storage location.

If you are using Outlook connected to an Exchange server, you may want to create a data file on your local computing device and use it to store a copy of messages you want to archive separately, or to store messages that you receive at work that are personal in nature.

Complete the following steps to create a new Outlook data file:

1. Click the File tab, click the Account Settings button at the Account Information backstage area, and then click *Account Settings* at the drop-down list.

2. At the Account Settings dialog box, shown in Figure 6.8, click the Data Files tab.

3. Click the Add button.

4. At the Create or Open Outlook Data File dialog box, browse to the drive and/or folder in which to store the data file, type a name in the *File name* text box, and then click OK. Outlook adds the file to the list in the Data Files tab in the Account Settings dialog box and displays the file name in the Folder pane at the bottom of the current folder list. Data files that you create have the file extension *.pst*.

5. Click the Close button to close the Account Settings dialog box.

Once the new data file is created, you can move or copy Outlook items to it by creating new folders within the information store and dragging items to the new folders. For example, you can create folders within the new .pst file for mail, appointments, contacts, and tasks and then move or copy messages, calendar entries, contacts, and to-do items to the new folders.

Figure 6.8 Account Settings Dialog Box with Data Files Tab Active

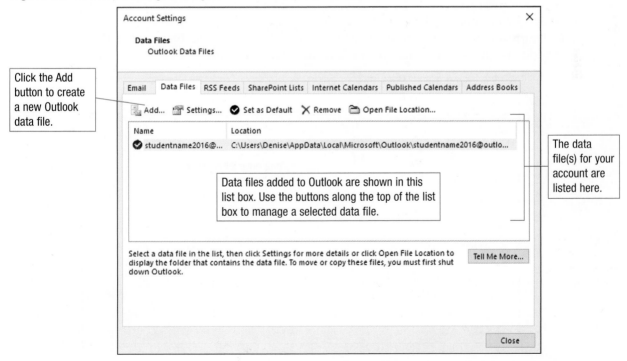

Exercise 11 Creating and Using a New Data File

Note: Make sure you have access to your USB flash drive or other storage medium before starting this exercise.

1. With Outlook open and the Mail module with the Inbox folder active, create a new data file by completing the following steps:
   a. Click the File tab.
   b. Click the Account Settings button and then click *Account Settings* at the drop-down list.
   c. At the Account Settings dialog box, click the Data Files tab.
   d. Click the Add button.

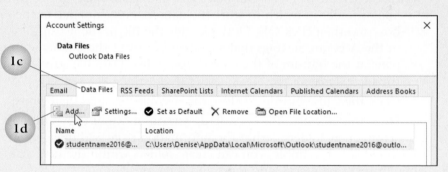

   e. At the Create or Open Outlook Data File dialog box, click *This PC* in the Navigation pane (left pane), and then double-click the drive for your storage medium in the *Devices and drives* section in the Content pane. *Note: You may need to scroll down the Navigation pane or Content pane.*
   f. Select the current name in the *File name* text box, type PersonalFolder-StudentName (substituting your name for *StudentName*), and then click OK. Notice that the new entry is added to the data files list in the Account Settings dialog box.

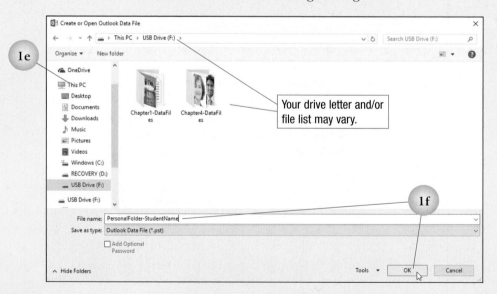

   g. Click the Close button to close the Account Settings dialog box.

2. Create a folder for storing email messages and move a message to the folder in your new data file by completing the following steps:

a. Right-click *personalfolder-studentname* (where your name is substituted for *studentname*) in the Folder pane.

b. Click *New Folder* at the shortcut menu.

c. Type Training in the folder name text box and then press Enter. Notice that Outlook automatically adds *Deleted Items* and *Search Folders* to the folder list.

d. If necessary, click *Inbox* in the Folder pane below the name of your email account.

e. Drag the message with the subject *Mail Format* to the folder named *Training* in the Folder pane.

f. Click the *Training* folder name in the Folder pane to view the moved message.

3. Make Inbox the active folder.

Quick Steps
Compact a Data File
1. Click File tab.
2. Click Account Settings button.
3. Click *Account Settings.*
4. Click Data Files tab.
5. Click to select data file name.
6. Click Settings button.
7. Click Compact Now button at Outlook Data File dialog box; or, click Advanced tab at Microsoft Exchange dialog box, click Outlook Data File Settings button, and then click Compact Now button.
8. Click OK (click two times if Microsoft Exchange account).
9. Click Close button.

Compacting an Outlook Data File

Your data files become very large after you have worked in Outlook for a while. When you delete an item in Outlook, the file is automatically compacted as a background application when you are not using your computer and Outlook has been left open. You can also manually start a compact operation. Complete the following steps to compact a .pst file, as shown in Figure 6.9 on page 200:

1. Click the File tab, click the Account Settings button in the Account Information backstage area, and then click *Account Settings* at the drop-down list.

2. Click the Data Files tab in the Account Settings dialog box and then click the data file name in the list box that you want to compact.

3. Click the Settings button.

4. At the Outlook Data File dialog box, click the Compact Now button. For Microsoft Exchange accounts, click the Advanced tab, click the Outlook Data File Settings button, and then click the Compact Now button.

5. Click OK to close the Outlook Data File dialog box, or click OK to close the Outlook Data File Settings dialog box and then click OK to close the Microsoft Exchange dialog box.

6. Click the Close button to close the Account Settings dialog box.

Figure 6.9 Compacting an Outlook Data File

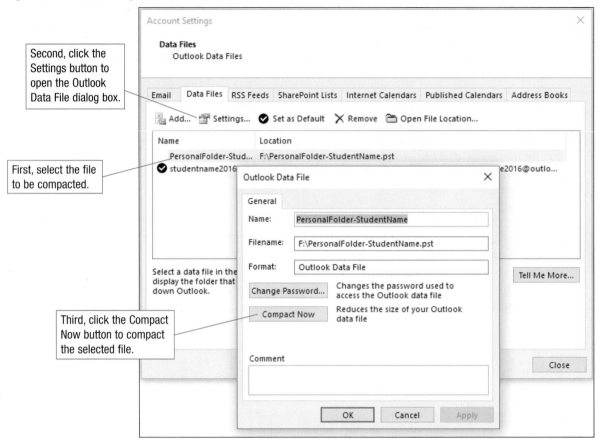

Second, click the Settings button to open the Outlook Data File dialog box.

First, select the file to be compacted.

Third, click the Compact Now button to compact the selected file.

Backing Up the .PST File

Exchange Server

Users connected to Outlook with an account on a Microsoft Exchange server need not be concerned with backing up the information stored on the server, because the system administrator for the server runs daily backups. However, a data file created on the user's local hard drive should be copied periodically for backup purposes.

Use Windows Copy and Paste commands to copy a .pst file to a removable device or to cloud storage for backup purposes. To select and copy a file from within Outlook, open the Account Settings dialog box with the Data Files tab active. Select the file to be backed up and then click the Open File Location button. Outlook opens a File Explorer window in which the data file's drive and folder are already active and the file is automatically selected in the Content pane. Use the Copy and Paste buttons on the Home tab to make a copy of the data file at another location.

Adding Another Email Account to Outlook

Many people have more than one email account. Consider adding your other email accounts—such as Gmail and Yahoo! accounts—to Outlook so that you can manage all your messages in one place. To add an account to Outlook, complete the following steps:

1. Click the File tab and then click the Add Account button at the Account Information backstage area. This opens the Add Account dialog box, shown in Figure 6.10 on page 201.

Quick Steps

Add Another Email Account
1. Click File tab.
2. Click Add Account button at Account Information backstage area.
3. Type your name, email address, and password (two times) in appropriate text boxes.
4. Click Next.
5. Click Finish.

➕ Add Account

TIP For each email account, Outlook adds a set of mail folders to the Folder pane. When you initially add a new email account, the new email address is added to the bottom of the Folder pane and the mail folders are collapsed below the email address. Expand the mail folders below the email address to view the messages in the Inbox for the new account.

2. Type your name, email address, and password (two times) in the text boxes, as shown in Figure 6.10, and then click the Next button. Outlook attempts to automatically configure the account by auto detecting the mail server settings.

3. Click the Finish button when the account setup is complete. A message will display that Outlook needs to be restarted.

Messages similar to those shown in Figure 6.11 display as Outlook completes each step in the account setup process. If the account cannot be set up automatically by Outlook, a message appears with information about a problem Outlook has encountered. Try again after retyping your email address and password in case you typed these entries incorrectly. If the setup still fails, use the *Manual setup or additional server types* option at the Add Account dialog box to enter the server settings on your own. You will need to know the type of service (POP, IMAP, or Exchange Server), the incoming mail server name, the outgoing mail server name, and other server settings required by your email provider. Contact your email provider for help if necessary.

Figure 6.10 Add Account Dialog Box

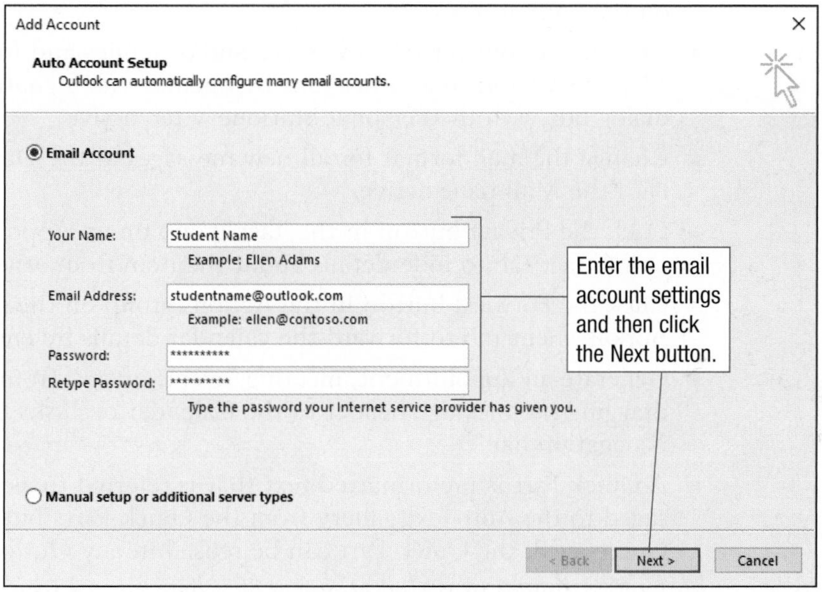

Figure 6.11 Add Account Dialog Box with Messages for Successful Email Account Setup

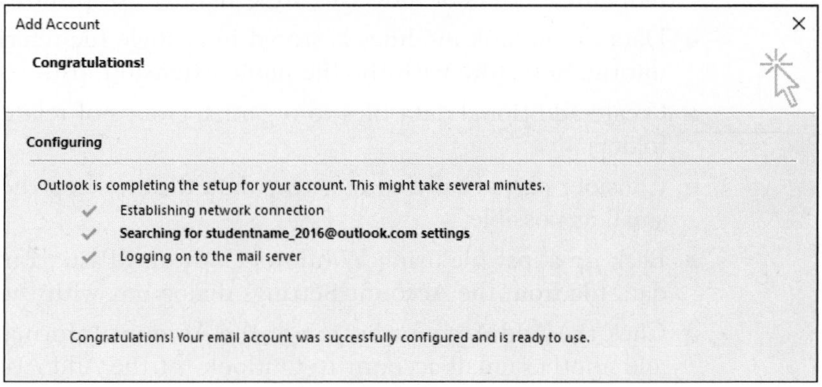

Chapter Summary

- Any Outlook module can be set as the starting module that displays when Outlook is launched. To set a different module, change the folder name in the Outlook Options dialog box with the Advanced pane active.

- Customize the Navigation bar by showing more or fewer options or by changing the order in which options are shown.

- Use the Folder Pane button in the Layout group on the View tab to minimize, turn off, or restore the pane to its normal view.

- Use keyboard shortcut Alt + F1 to cycle through the three Folder pane states: Normal, Minimized, and Off.

- To modify email options, open the Outlook Options dialog box and click *Mail* in the left pane.

- Mail formats available for creating and sending email are plain text, rich text, and HTML.

- The mail format for the current message can be changed from HTML, which is the default, to plain text or rich text at a message window in the Format group on the Format Text tab.

- Change the font for new messages and/or replies and forwarded messages from 11-point Calibri to another font by opening the Signatures and Stationery dialog box with the Personal Stationery tab active.

- Change the mail format for all new messages at the Outlook Options dialog box with the Mail pane active.

- Click the Private button in the Tags group on an Appointment tab, Task tab, or Contact tab to hide details about the item from other users of your folder.

- Click the Forward button in the Actions group on the Calendar Tools Appointment tab to forward the calendar details by email as a file attachment.

- Generate an appointment, meeting, event, or task from an email message by dragging the message header to the Calendar or Tasks text label or icon on the Navigation bar.

- A Quick Part is preformatted text that is referred to as a building block and saved to the AutoText gallery from the Quick Parts button on the Insert tab. Once saved, the Quick Part can be reused in any Outlook item.

- Export filtered or sorted contacts as a data source to perform a mail merge. Create the main document with the merge fields in a Word document. The contact data from Outlook is then merged with the main document and individual letters or messages are generated for printing or emailing.

- Data in Outlook modules is stored in a single file referred to as a personal information store with the file name extension .pst.

- Create additional data files to organize groups of related data in different folders.

- Consider periodically compacting data files to keep the size of the .pst file as small as possible.

- Back up a .pst file using Windows Copy and Paste commands after locating the data file from the Account Settings dialog box with the Data Files tab active.

- Click the Add Account button at the Account Information backstage area to add another email account to Outlook. At the Add Account dialog box, add your name, email address, and password.

Commands Review

FEATURE	BUTTON	RIBBON TAB AND GROUP, OR OTHER METHOD	SHORTCUT
Access email options		File, *Options*, *Mail*	
Add another email account	+ Add Account	File	
Change mail format to plain text	Aa Plain Text	Format Text, Format	
Change mail format to rich text	Aa Rich Text	Format Text, Format	
Compact .pst file		File, Account Settings, *Account Settings*	
Create appointment or task from message		Drag message header to Calendar or Tasks on Navigation bar	
Create mail merge to contacts		Home, Actions	
Create meeting from message		Message, Respond	
Create Outlook data file		File, Account Settings, *Account Settings*	
Create Quick Part		Insert, Text	
Customize Navigation bar	•••	Navigation bar, *Navigation Options*	
Expand Folder pane	OR > ,	View, Layout OR top of minimized Folder pane	Alt + F1
Hide Folder pane		View, Layout	Alt + F1
Minimize Folder pane	OR <	View, Layout OR top right of expanded Folder pane	Alt + F1
Set private appointment, contact, or task		Appointment, Contact, or Task, Tags	
Set startup module		File, *Options*, *Advanced*	

Index

journal entries, 174
meeting request response, 95
notes, 168
signatures, 37, 38
updating meetings, 97
electronic mail, 11. *see also* messages
email accounts
adding another, 200–201
mail folders in Folder pane, 201
setting up, 12
email, forwarding a calendar item by, 188
email merges, 192–193
email messages. *See* messages
email options, setting, 181–182
email profile, 12
created using Internet mail server, 15–16
Enable Editing button, 24
events
examples, 81
scheduling at Outlook.com, 82
scheduling in Outlook on the web, 82
scheduling new, 81
Exchange ActiveSync, 103
contact groups and, 141
Exchange Server. *See* Microsoft Exchange Server
Expand button, 48, 50, 115
Expand folder pane, 179
expanding folders, 56
extensions
.ics, 96
.msg, 169
.ost, 13, 196
.pst, 13, 196

F

fields, 110, 118
sorting contacts, 123
fields, in Contacts folder, 110, 111, 114, 115, 118, 123
about, 110
adding contacts, 111, 114
Advanced Find Dialog box, 134
All Fields page, 118
customizing in Current View, 135–136

editing and deleting contacts, 115
File As field, 123
file attachment tools, 26–27
files
attaching to messages, 24
at Outlook.com, 27
in Outlook on the web, 27
File tab, 13
backstage area, 13
Mailbox Cleanup Tool using, 70
used for printing messages, 19
used to create new rules with Rules Wizard, 64
using Mailbox Cleanup tool, 70
using to add another email account, 200, 201
using to archive folders, 66
using to archive items, 66, 67
using to change calendar options, 99
using to change contact options, 137
using to change message font, 185
using to change task options, 166
using to check account type, 103
using to compact data files, 199
using to create data files, 197
using to create new rule using Rules Wizard, 64
using to create templates, 191
using to restore archived items, 70
using to set email options, 181
using to specify starting module, 178
filing cabinet, 13
Filter button, 126
Filter dialog box with Contacts Tab selected, 126
filters
contacts, 126, 127

junk email and phishing, 65
modifying junk email, 65
finding contacts. *See* searching contacts
finding messages. *See* searching messages
Find Now button, 134
Finish & Merge button, 192, 193
First Time Setup dialog box, 57
flagging messages, 34–35
flags
clearing, 35
follow-up, 121, 123
Folder pane, 12
customizing, 179
Date Navigator section, 74
deleting calendars, 105
email account mail folders added to, 201
expanding archives, 70
expanding folders, 56, 57
expanding the, 179
hiding, 179
increasing or decreasing width of, 179
Journal in, 172
Junk Email folder in, 64
minimizing, 179
My Calendars section, 103
redisplaying a hidden, 179
searching folder name in, 47
searching messages, 46
Folder pane button, 179
folders. *see also specific folders*
all Outlook, 13
archiving, 66–70
backup copy, 70
default settings, 66
manually, 67, 68–69
retrieving archived items from, 70
using AutoArchive, 66, 68
creating a new, 56–57, 61
expanding, 56
maintenance using Mailbox Cleanup, 70
moving messages to, 57–59
creating a rule for, 60–64
at Outlook.com, 60
in Outlook on the web, 59
organizing messages in, 60

Follow Up button, 34, 121, 123
Follow-Up flags, 121
follow-up flags, 121
font
    Calibri, 185
    changing for messages, 185
Format text tab, 28
formatting
    applying options at
        Outlook.com, 31
    applying options in Outlook
        on the web, 30
    applying to text in a
        message, 28–30
    creating conditional rule
        with color, 90–91
forms. *See* templates
Forward button, 161, 172
Forwarded Task message
    window, 161
forwarding
    Calendar item by email, 188
    calendar items, 96
    copy of task to another user,
        161
    messages, 19, 20, 21–22
        at Outlook.com, 22
        in Outlook on the web,
            22
        to several people, 20
    notes, 172

G

global address list (GAL), 5
Global AutoArchive Settings, 66
Gmail accounts, 200
Go To Date
    scheduling appointments
        using, 76–77

H

Help task pane, 38
Help, using, 38
hiding search folders, 47
High Importance button, 31, 32
Home tab, 13
    Archive button in Delete
        group on, 67
    changing calendar options,
        99
    changing calendar view, 85
    Delete button in Delete
        group on, 23

Follow Up button in Tags
    group on, 34
Junk button in Delete group
    on, 65
moving messages using, 57
New Contact button, 110
New Email button in New
    group on, 15, 16
New Meeting button in
    New group on, 92
Rules button in Move group
    on, 60
scheduling appointments,
    74, 75
scheduling events, 81
using to add new contacts,
    117
using to archive items, 67
using to change calendar
    view, 85
using to delete and ignore
    conversations, 52
using to schedule meetings,
    92
using to work with notes,
    167, 168, 170, 171, 172
using to work with tasks,
    151, 152, 157, 163
working with conversations,
    52
HTML (hypertext markup
    language), 28, 186
Hyperlink button, 27
hyperlinks, embedding in
    messages, 27, 28, 29

I

iCalendar text file (*.ics* file), 96
.ics file, 96
Ignore button, 52
ignoring messages in a
    conversation, 52
images. *see also* pictures
    adding to profile, 5, 6
    embedded in a message, 27,
        28, 30
IMAP (Internet Message Access
    Protocol), 15–16
Inbox folder, 13
    archiving contents of, 66
    contents, 13
    creating subfolder within,
        56, 57
    deleting messages from, 23

    Do not archive items in this
        folder default, 66
    managing, 56
    moving messages from, 60,
        62
    searching using Instant
        Search, 44
    task request message in, 159
    unread messages in, 19
Inbox Properties dialog box, 67
Insert Merge Field button, 193
Instant Search box, 44
Instant Search feature, finding
    messages with, 44
Instructor eResources, 7
international addresses, 114
Internet Service Provider (ISP),
    12
Invite Attendees button, 189

J

journal entries
    creating, 172–173
    deleting, 174
    editing, 174
    storage of, 173
    uses, 172
Journal Entry button, 172
Journal Entry window, 173, 174
Journal folder, 149
    about, 172
    in Timeline View, 172
Junk button, 65
Junk Email folder, 65
  archiving contents of, 66
    checking contents of, 64
    Do not archive items in this
        folder default, 66
    managing mishandled
        messages, 65
    modifying filter settings, 65
Junk Email Options dialog box,
    65

K

keyboard shortcuts, 179, 192
keyword(s)
    finding appointments using,
        83
    finding messages using, 44

L

labels, from contact records, 111
LinkedIn, 127

List button, 128
live.com, 15
local area network, 15
Low Importance button, 31

M

Mailbox Cleanup dialog box, 70
Mailbox Cleanup tools, 43, 70
mail clients, 15
mailing labels, contact records
    and, 111
Mail Merge button, 192
Mail Merge Contacts dialog
    box, 193
mail merges, 191–192
Mail module, 13, 14. *see also*
    messages
    as default starting module,
      178
    saving messages as
      templates, 191
mail protocols, 15–16
mail server, 15
main document, 192
Mark Complete button, 154
Mark Complete option, 123
Meeting button, 139
meetings
    automatically scheduling
      needed resources, 98
    canceling, 97
    requested from an email
      message, 189
    rescheduling, 97
    responding to requests
      accepting, 95–96
      promptness in, 95
      suggesting new time, 95
      tracking, 98–99
    scheduling, 92–94
      automatically, 94
      from Contacts folder,
        139, 140
      from Contacts folder in
        Outlook.com, 140
      meeting room, 92
      at Outlook.com, 94
      in Outlook on the web,
        94
    updating, 97
Meeting window, 92
memos. *See* messages; notes

Message arrival section, in
    Outlook Options dialog box,
    181
messages
    applying color categories to,
      53–55
      at Outlook.com, 56
      in Outlook on the web,
        55
    applying formatting options
      in, 28
      at Outlook.com, 31
      in Outlook on the web,
        30
    archiving, 66–67, 70
    arranged by conversations,
      50–51
    arrangement of, 19
    assigning importance to, 31
      at Outlook.com, 33
      in Outlook on the web,
        33
    assigning options, 31
      at Outlook.com, 33
      in Outlook on the web,
        33
    attaching files to, 24, 25
      at Outlook.com, 27
      in Outlook on the web,
        27
    attachment tools for, 26–27
    blocking senders, 65
    business etiquette for, 15
    changing email options,
      181–182
      at Outlook.com, 185
      in Outlook on the web,
        185
    changing font for, 185
    changing formatting
      options, 186
      in Outlook on the web,
        187
    changing read status, 34
    comments about or status of
      a task, 160
    company policy for saving,
      67
    composing new, 16
      at Outlook.com, 18
      in Outlook on the web,
        18
    contact group for sending,
      141
    creating, 15

    creating appointments
      using, 189
    creating tasks using, 189
    deleting, 23
      in a conversation, 52–53
      in Outlook on the web,
        24
    delivery options, 31
    desktop alert for new, 19
    embedding images in, 27
    emptying Deleted Items
      folder, 23
    finding using Instant
      Search, 44
    finding using search
      techniques, 44–46
    flagging, 34–35
    formatting text in, 27, 28
    forwarding, 20, 21
      at Outlook.com, 22
      in Outlook on the web,
        22
    grouped by conversations,
      50
    grouping in Content pane,
      48–49
    ignoring in a conversation,
      52–53
    inserting hyperlinks in, 27
    junk email, managing, 65
    managing mishandled by
      junk email filters, 65
    managing using
      Conversations view,
      50–51
    meeting request responses
      received via, 95
    moving, 57
      automatically, 60, 62
      creating a rule for, 60,
        61–62
      at Outlook.com, 60
      in Outlook on the web,
        59
    opening, 19
    organized by thread, 50
    performing merges to
      multiple contacts,
      192–193
    printing, 19
    Quick Parts created for, 190
    reading, 19
    read receipt, 31, 32
    read status, changing, 35,
      36

Propose New Time button, 95
Propose New Time dialog box, 95
Propose Time button, 95
Protected view, 24
.pst extension, 13, 196
.pst files, backing up, 200

Q

Quick Access Toolbar, 12, 13
    Print button added to, 19
Quick Part, creating a, 190
Quick Parts button, 190

R

Reading pane, 12
    attached messages, 24
    displaying in Calendar, 85, 87
    Forward button in, 20
    Message Tags Information Bar in, 33
    reading, replying, forwarding messages from, 19, 20
    read status, 34
    Replay All button in, 20
    respond buttons, 95
    responding to task requests, 159
    sending messages to contacts, 138
    viewing messages in, 19, 24
    View Source, 115
Reading pane button, 85
read receipts, 31, 32, 33
read report message sent to sender, 32, 33
read status of message, changing, 34, 35, 36
    at Outlook.com, 36
    in Outlook on the web, 36
reassigning tasks, 159
Recent Items section, 24
Recent Searches button, 45, 132
recent search request, 45
record, in Contacts folder, 110
Recurrence button, 79, 155
recurring appointments, scheduling, 79–81
recurring tasks, creating, 155–156
    using Outlook on the web, 157

reminders
    for events, appointments, and meetings, 73, 75
    flagging contacts for follow-up, 121
    by flagging messages, 34, 41
    notes as small unstructured, 149
    scheduling events, 82
    scheduling events and appointments in Calendar, 73, 75, 82
    for tasks, 166
renaming color categories, 53
renaming folders, 60
replies
    Automatic Replies feature, 64
    in conversations, 50, 52
    directed to someone else, 31
    meeting requests, 95–96
    to messages, 19, 20
        at Outlook.com, 22
        in Outlook on the web, 22
    to task requests, 159
Replies and forwards section, in Outlook Options dialog box, 181
Reply All button, 20
Reply button, 20
Respond buttons in meeting request message, 95
ribbon, 12, 13
Ribbon Display Options button, 12
Rich text button, 186
rich text format, 186
Room Finder pane, 92
Rules button, 60
rules, creating, 60, 61–62
    at Outlook.com, 63
    in Outlook on the web, 63
    using Rules Wizard, 63–64
Rules Wizard, 63–64

S

Save & Close button, 111, 189
Save messages section, in Outlook Options dialog box, 181, 182
saving email message, company policy and, 67

saving folders. *See* archiving folders
scheduling
    appointments
        at Outlook.com, 78, 81
        in Outlook on the web, 77, 80
        recurring, 79–80
        recurring at Outlook.com, 81
        recurring in Outlook on the web, 80
        using Appointment window, 74–75
        using click and type, 74
        using Go To Date, 76–77
    events, 81
        at Outlook.com, 82
        in Outlook on the web, 82
    meetings, 92–94
        automatically, 94
        with a contact, 139
        with a contact at Outlook.com, 140
        from Contacts folder, 139
        from Contacts folder in Outlook.com, 140
        at Outlook.com, 94
        rescheduling, 97
Scheduling Assistant button, 98
Search Contacts box, 131, 134
Search Contacts box, 132, 134
search folders
    creating, 47, 48
    showing and hiding, 47
searching contacts, 131
    with Advanced Find dialog box, 134
    at Outlook.com, 135
    in Outlook on the web, 134
    using Advanced Find dialog box, 134–135
    using *Search Contacts* box, 132
    using *Search People* box, 131
searching messages
    modifying using Search Tools, 46
    at Outlook.com, 46
    in Outlook on the web, 46
    refining a search, 45
    refining with Search Tools, 45

search folders for, 47–48
Search Tools used for modifying, 46
using Instant Search, 44
Search People box, 131, 134
Search Tools
modifying a search using, 46
refining a search using, 45
Search Tools button, 132, 134
Search Tools Search Tab, 45, 132, 134
Search Tools Search tab, 132
Send Cancellation button, 97
Send messages, in Outlook Options dialog box, 181, 182
Send/Receive All Folders button, 13
Send/Receive tab, 13
Send Status Report button, 160
Send Update button, 97
Sent Items folder
archive items options in, 66
contents, 56
Settings button, 199
Share Contacts button, 145
sharing a calendar, 105
sharing Contacts folder, 145
shortcut menu
New Task Request, 157
Show Columns dialog box, 136, 137
showing search folders, 47
Signature button, 36, 38
signatures
creating, 36–38, 39
at Outlook.com, 39
in Outlook on the web, 39
deleting, 38
editing, 37, 38
Signatures and Stationary dialog box, 185
Simple List view in Tasks folder, 154
Smart Lookup option, 38
social media accounts
contacts from added to people list on Outlook.com, 127
Sort dialog box, 123
sorting
contacts, 123
contacts at Outlook.com, 125

contacts in Outlook on the web, 125
sound, new email message chime, 19
spam, 64, 65
Status bar, 12
Stay Organized templates, 63
Stay Up to Date templates, 63–64
storage
of journal entries, 173
of notes, 167
store, 13
subject text box, 16
Subject text box, 189
system requirements, 7–8

T

table format, displaying Calendar in, 85
Tags group, 31, 34
Task Recurrence dialog box, 155, 156
Task Request window, 157, 158
tasks
creating from email message, 189
marking as private, 187
Quick Parts created for, 190
Tasks folder
about, 149
archive items options in, 66
assigning tasks to someone else, 157
changing task options, 166
changing task view, 163
at Outlook.com, 165
using Outlook on the web, 164
contents, 13
creating tasks
new at Outlook.com, 153
new in the Task window, 151–152
new in *Type a new task* text box, 150
recurring, 155–156
recurring tasks on Outlook on the web, 157
using Outlook on the web, 153
customized task list, creating, 163–164

deleting tasks, 150
forwarding information to other users, 161
marking tasks as completed, 154
quickly finding tasks, 163
reassigning tasks, 159
responding to task requests, 159
sending copy of task to another user, 161
sending task status report, 160–161
To-Do bar, 165
To-Do List view, 150, 154
updating tasks, 155
at Outlook.com, 155
on Outlook on the web, 157
viewing tasks, options for, 163
Task Status Report message window, 160
Tasks Window with Task Page selected, 152
Task window, 151–152, 189
Tell Me Feature, 38, 39–40
Tell Me text box, 38, 39, 40
templates
saving frequently sent messages as, 191
Stay Organized, 63
Stay Up to Date, 63–64
threads, 20, 50, 51, 52
Timer button, 174
timing, for journal entries, 174
title bar, 12
To-Do bar button, 165
To-Do Bar in Tasks folder, using, 149
To-Do List view, Tasks folder in, 150, 154
Tracking button, 98
Tracking group, 31
Tracking Response Options on the Tracking Page, 99
Tracking section, in Outlook Options dialog box, 181, 182
Twitter, 127

U

Undo button, 13
unread email messages, 19

Unread/Read button, 34
updating
 tasks, 154
  at Outlook.com, 155
updating meetings, 97, 98
user name, 15

V

View Settings button, 90, 123,
 126, 163
View tab, 13
 using the To-Do Bar, 165

using to create conditional
 formatting rule, 90
using to customize
 Navigation bar, 179
using to display calendar in
 table format, 85
using to filter contacts, 126
using to organize messages
 by conversations, 50, 51
using to read messages, 19
using to sort contacts, 123
View Settings button, 123
Voting buttons, 31, 32

W

waffle button, 78
Welcome to Outlook screen, 12
Windows 10 operating system,
 7, 8
Word, mail merges in, 192, 193

Y

Yahoo! accounts, 200
yellow Note window, 167